The Christian Hope

The Christian Hope

REVISED EDITION

Brian Hebblethwaite

OXFORD
UNIVERSITY PRESS

OXFORD
UNIVERSITY PRESS

Great Clarendon Street, Oxford OX2 6DP

Oxford University Press is a department of the University of Oxford.
It furthers the University's objective of excellence in research, scholarship,
and education by publishing worldwide in

Oxford New York

Auckland Cape Town Dar es Salaam Hong Kong Karachi
Kuala Lumpur Madrid Melbourne Mexico City Nairobi
New Delhi Shanghai Taipei Toronto

With offices in

Argentina Austria Brazil Chile Czech Republic France Greece
Guatemala Hungary Italy Japan Poland Portugal Singapore
South Korea Switzerland Thailand Turkey Ukraine Vietnam

Oxford is a registered trade mark of Oxford University Press
in the UK and in certain other countries

Published in the United States
by Oxford University Press Inc., New York

British Library Cataloguing in Publication Data

Data available

Library of Congress Cataloging in Publication Data

Library of Congress Control Number: 2010925660

Typeset by SPI Publisher Services, Pondicherry, India
Printed in Great Britain
on acid-free paper by
MPG Books Group, Bodmin & King's Lynn

ISBN 978–0–19–958946–3 (Pbk.)
      978–0–19–958947–0 (Hbk.)

1 3 5 7 9 10 8 6 4 2

BV
4638
.H38
2010

For David Galilee

Preface

Hope may not be the greatest of the theological virtues. St Paul was convinced that, of faith, hope, and love, love has the primacy. But hope is an essential element in Christianity nonetheless. Christian faith in the love of God carries with it, necessarily, hope for the future of humankind, both as individuals and as the human community, and hope for the future of creation as a whole. Christianity is one of the chief exponents in the history of religions of the view that human beings and the universe, as God's good creation, have an eternal destiny, that history has a transcendent goal in the divine intention, and that in the end God's creative purpose will be finally realized. As we shall see in the course of this study, Christianity does not teach that this goal will be achieved automatically through the outworking of processes built into the created order from the beginning. Rather the basis for Christian hope for the consummation of all things in God lies firmly in God's own re-creative, transforming, resurrecting power and action.

In this study we shall trace the background to this Christian hope in the faith of Israel, examine its primary basis in the acts of God in the story of Jesus Christ, and follow the history of Christian attitudes to the future of humanity and of creation throughout the Christian centuries. The treatment, in Part One, of the background and basis of Christian hope in the Old and New Testaments will be relatively brief. This is a well-trodden path and references to further literature will be found in the Bibliography. It seemed preferable to devote the bulk of the book to telling the story of the different strands, emphases, and problems that have developed between biblical times and our own. Moreover, attention will be concentrated on the modern period, the last four chapters being devoted solely to the period since 1900. For modern Christian theology has witnessed a remarkable recovery of interest in hope and the future as dominant motifs in its reflections. As we come to this more recent period, we shall, of course, have to pay particular attention to the way in which the discoveries of modern science have affected Christian hope and Christian understanding of creation and its ultimate destiny.

Every subject has its own technical terminology, and Christian theology is no exception. We must not be afraid of technical terms, but set ourselves to discover what words like 'eschatology' and 'apocalyptic' mean. These concepts are no more and no less difficult to grasp than the more familiar notions of resurrection and eternity, which are standard elements in Christian discourse, firmly embedded in the creeds. Students of the Christian hope need to learn how to explore the meaning of such religious and theological ideas.

We shall discover that, at different stages in the history of the church, very different stress has been laid on the present or on the future, on hope for the individual or on hope for society, on this-worldly hope or on other-worldly hope. One of the chief aims of this book is, through a study of the basis of Christian hope and of the history of its interpretation, to achieve a balanced view of these different elements in the Christian tradition.

The first edition of this book came out in 1984. In revising it for a new edition I have made a number of stylistic alterations, but chiefly I have tried to bring the book up to date by taking note of the more important contributions to have appeared over the last twenty-five years. In the nature of the case, the additional material is mainly to be found in Chapters 9 and 10 and in the Bibliography.

Brian Hebblethwaite
Easter 2010

Contents

Part One

The Hope of Israel and the First Christians

1

The Old Testament Background

Introduction

The basis for the Christian hope is undoubtedly to be found in the events concerning Jesus Christ. But it is only against the background of what Christians call the Old Testament that those events can be understood. It is this rootedness of the Christian message in the faith of Israel that Jesus is presumably referring to when, in the fourth Gospel, he says, 'Salvation is of the Jews' (John 4: 22). This does not mean that an understanding of the Old Testament background is sufficient to explain the Christian hope. On the contrary, with Jesus and the Church, something quite new and revolutionary appeared within the history of religions. But to appreciate this new faith and this new hope it is certainly necessary to acquire some picture of Israel's faith and hope; for these provided the context for the coming of Jesus and the ideas in terms of which he understood his own mission and his followers understood his significance.

If we are to acquire a historically accurate picture of the hope of Israel, we need to divest our minds of two later Christian presuppositions. Christians are used to seeing Israel's hope as having been fulfilled in the coming of Jesus Christ. They are also used to a developed theology of future resurrection. The ultimate Christian hope is hope of heaven. Both these presuppositions are central and important for Christianity and will be examined in their own right later in this book. But they can only mislead us if we allow them to colour our historical reconstruction of the Old Testament background, especially in its early stages. Certainly Israel's hope was based on trust in God and in the promises of God. But for most of the period covered by the Old Testament it was rarely focused on a single individual, and it remained a concrete political hope for God's action in the historical rather than the heavenly future.

The People of God and the Significance of History

What was it that differentiated the faith of Israel from other religions in the ancient world? Historians of religion and Old Testament scholars alike have suggested that its special features were a unique sense of election—of having been chosen for a purpose by God—and a unique conviction of the significance of history as the sphere of divine promise, action, and fulfilment. Such a broad generalization is a hazardous enterprise in the history of religions and cries out for qualification. For one thing, we are speaking of a faith and a tradition that developed over many centuries. The books of the Old Testament alone stem from nearly a thousand years, and we can trace in them a many-sided growing and changing tradition. But it is noteworthy that the historian of religion Mircea Eliade, in many of his books (for example, *Patterns in Comparative Religion* (1958)), contrasts this sense of history as a forward-moving, meaningful process under the providence of a God who acts in history, with a recurrent, cyclical sense of the world and human life as re-enacting certain basic, archetypal patterns, established for ever by the gods in primordial time. Eliade finds this latter view characteristic of most of the more archaic religions in the world, with their sense of timeless present and eternal return. All the more noteworthy is his recognition of Israel's sense of the significance of history, despite his own lack of sympathy for it.

Other historians qualify this basic contrast. On the one hand, they point to some sense of history and the significance of history in other religions, such as those of ancient Babylon or Egypt. On the other hand, they point to more cyclical, recurrent motifs in the faith of Israel itself—its wisdom literature, its regular festivals, and its sense of God's blessing in the reliable seasons and fruits of the earth. But it is hard to believe that these qualifications, necessary though they may be, undermine the fundamental importance of ancient Israel's conviction that God had called it to a special place in history and given it a special promise for the future. At any rate, we are not concerned with a complete picture of the faith of Israel here. Our interest is in hope, and in Israel's faith only as background to the Christian hope. We can afford to be selective. We can ignore the cultic life of Israel and its remarkable wisdom literature and concentrate attention on the element of promise for the future.

In the oldest texts of the Hebrew Bible we find God's promise taking a very definite, this-worldly, form. It is the promise of a land flowing with milk and honey (cf. Exod. 3: 8). God brings the people out of bondage in Egypt. He will give them victory over their enemies (Num. 23: 24–5) and they will multiply. At this early stage and for a long time after the establishment of the monarchy under Saul and David, Israel's hope is for its own identity and prosperity as a peculiar people under God. There is as yet no sense of responsibility for humankind at large, no sense of the individual's destiny, no hope for an ultimate transcendent future. It is as though this conviction of its own history and its own future had first to grow and mature before the significance of universal history and an ultimate future could be brought within the horizon of Israel's hope.

It seems that at first there was some doubt whether this chosen people of God, with their special relationship to the God of history, ought to be given a monarchic form of government such as the surrounding people had; for God alone was their king (1 Sam. 8). But it was not long before the Davidic monarchy itself came to be regarded as the sign of God's blessing and the focus of the divine promise. David himself is promised a son to succeed him, whose royal throne will be established for all time (2 Sam. 7).

It looks as though, in their earliest form, these fundamental ideas of election and promise were thought of as unconditional. In God's covenant with Abram, for example (Gen. 15: 18–21), there were no conditions at all attached to God's intended gift of the promised land. But in the course of time and in the light of a very chequered history, including the division of the monarchy after Solomon's death and the series of disasters leading to the destruction of the northern kingdom and the removal of the remnant of the southern kingdom into exile, the recognition grew that the promise was not one-sided and unconditional but that the blessing of God depended on the people's religious and ethical response. God's covenant now came to be thought of as binding the people to keep God's commandments if they were to enjoy the promised blessing, though the blessing was still thought of in terms of national and political prosperity. We see this conditional promise expressed in the telling of the story of the exodus. At Mount Sinai, God says to the people through Moses, 'If you will obey my voice and keep my covenant, you shall be my own possession among all peoples' (Ex. 19: 5). Psalm 89 is particularly instructive in this connection. It looks as if an original celebration of an unconditional covenant with David (vv. 3–29) has been supplemented by a later recognition of the covenant's dependence on the people not forsaking God's law (vv. 30–45).

The notion of a covenant between God and Israel whereby God's promise is conditional upon the people's obedience became a very powerful tool in enabling Israel to make sense of its chequered history. We shall see shortly how the prophets used this notion in warning of divine judgement as well as confirming the divine promise. But it also provided the so-called deuteronomic historian with his key for telling the story of the kings of Israel and Judah. (After the division of the monarchy, 'Israel' in the narrower sense refers to the northern kingdom. The southern kingdom centred on Jerusalem is referred to as 'Judah'.) For the story of the chosen people in the promised land was a story of disaster more than of success. Certainly the settlement in Canaan was a considerable achievement for a group of relatively small nomadic tribes and could well be seen as the fulfilment of God's promise. But the settlement was achieved only by repeated struggles against the indigenous population, and, when success came, it was short lived. If the reigns of David and Solomon gave further substance to the idea of the fulfilment of God's promise, the division of the kingdom after Solomon's death and the subsequent history of Israel and Judah could be reconciled with that idea only by stressing the way in which the covenant had been broken on the chosen people's side. Thus we find the prosperity or disasters of the reigns of the kings of Israel and Judah correlated by the deuteronomic historian with their obedience or disobedience to God's commands. Moreover, as the tiny kingdoms came within the reach of the major empires of the ancient Middle East, first Assyria, then Babylon, the possibility of complete destruction had to be faced, first in the northern kingdom, then in the south. What could be made of God's promise and of hope for the future then?

The Prophets: Judgement and Hope

The theme of impending judgement on God's people for their failure to keep their part of the covenant dominates the preaching of the great prophets from Amos to Ezekiel, whose words were collected (and probably embellished) into the books we now find in the latter part of the Hebrew Bible. The eighth-century prophets of the northern kingdom, Amos and Hosea, inveigh against the injustice and apostasy of Israel, as do Isaiah and Micah in the later eighth century against the southern kingdom. These prophets insist that the chosen people cannot rely on their election if they disobey God's laws. At this stage it was Assyria that was the agent of doom for the northern kingdom and that reduced Judah to a fragment of what it had been. This fragment itself was threatened with similar destruction by the sixth-century prophets Jeremiah and Ezekiel at the hands of Babylon. Jerusalem was indeed finally sacked by the Babylonians in 587 BC and the majority of its inhabitants deported into exile.

Two interesting features may be singled out, as we consider these prophecies of doom. In the first place, prophetic denunciation was not restricted to Israel and Judah. The surrounding nations too are denounced for their corruption and pride and threatened with a similar fate. Even the great power of Assyria is threatened with divine judgement by Isaiah and, after him, by Nahum and Habakkuk. Israel's God, we learn, is God of all the nations. It has even been argued that there is an implicit natural law ethic in this conviction of all people's responsibility before God. We shall note a corresponding concern with all the nations when we return to the positive motif of hope in the prophets' writings.

Then, secondly, we notice that the predictions of doom take on an increasingly cosmic nature and the coming judgement is portrayed in increasingly extravagant language. At first God's judgement will be mediated through defeat at the hands of foreign powers, but, as the predictions of doom are broadened to include the foreign powers themselves, so the agents of destruction are pictured in terms of the heavenly host, their visitation accompanied by the darkening of the sun, moon and stars (Isa. 13). This tendency reaches a climax in the words of the post-exilic prophet Joel, who prophesies a day of judgement for all the earth, when the Lord will 'roar from Zion... and the heavens and the earth shall shake' (Joel 3: 16).

The theme of 'the day of the Lord' appears as early as the eighth century with Amos in the north (Amos 8: 9) and with Isaiah of Jerusalem in the south (Isa. 2: 12). Its negative side—the emphasis on doom and judgement—is typified by the prophecy of Zephaniah in seventh-century Jerusalem: 'That day will be a day of wrath, a day of distress and anguish, a day of ruin and devastation, a day of darkness and gloom...' (Zeph. 1: 15). But the message of judgement is only one side of the picture. The prophetic books, as we have them in the Hebrew Bible, also contain a message of hope. It is not necessary to decide here whether oracles of hope have been added later on to the writings of the earlier prophets of doom or whether they were always included as a reminder of the underlying promise of God in the original covenant. But certainly after the fall of Jerusalem the exilic and post-exilic prophets speak of a time when God will restore Israel (or at least a remnant of Israel), establish a new coven- ant written on their hearts, and bring about a time when they will again be his people and he their God. Such prophecies of hope occur frequently in Jeremiah, Deutero-Isaiah, and Ezekiel, and they repre- sent the highest point in the development of Israel's faith, despite unmitigated disaster. These prophets, writing during the Babylonian exile, still think of the divine promise in historical and political terms—a return to Jerusalem, the rebuilding of the temple, a time of peace and prosperity. But, just as the prophecies of doom took on an increasingly cosmic dimension and the language of judgement grew more and more extravagant, so the language of hope grows more idealistic, portraying the promised blessing in the imagery of paradise—'The wolf shall dwell with the lamb...' (Isa. 11: 6–8, assuming this chapter to be a later addition)—and portraying the rebuilt temple in the most extravagant terms (Ezek. 40–2.). Moreover, just as the prophecies of judgement came to include all nations, so the renewed promise of blessing takes on a universal scope. Israel is to be a light to the nations (Isa. 42: 6). God is God of the whole earth, to whom every knee shall bow (Isa. 45: 22–3). The day of the Lord, therefore, as well as being a day of universal judgement, will also be a day of salvation and healing: 'On that day living waters shall flow out from Jerusalem, half of them to the eastern sea and half of them to the western sea; it shall continue in summer as in winter. And the Lord will become king over all the earth; on that day the Lord will be one and his name one' (Zech. 14: 8–9).

This universal and cosmic language may already represent a further dimension to the hope of Israel after the return from exile, when disappointment with the actual achievements in building a new temple and a new community led to renewed hope for a more transcendent, elemental act of God. This is certainly the case with Joel, whose threats of universal judgement are accompanied by promises of blessing: 'In that day the mountains shall drip sweet wine and the hills shall flow with milk ... and a fountain shall come forth from the house of the Lord ...' (Joel 3: 18). But it has to be acknowledged that Joel has lost something of the universal vision of Deutero-Isaiah and the later chapters of Zechariah. The spirit to be poured out on all flesh (Joel 2: 28) means restoration of the fortunes of Judah and Jerusalem, but judgement on the nations.

Old Testament Eschatology

The question has been much debated in Old Testament theology, whether these themes of promise and fulfilment and these prophecies of judgement and hope can be thought of as constituting an 'eschatology'. This dispute provides us with our first opportunity to consider this important term. Strictly speaking, 'eschatology' means talk about the last things, and if we take 'last' to mean last in time, it seems that 'eschatology' ought to be restricted to the subject of the end of the world, to the final acts of God in bringing history to a close. Thus Sigmund Mowinckel defines 'eschatology' as

a more or less developed doctrine, or complex of ideas, about the 'last things' which includes a dualistic conception of the course of history, the conflict of divine and demonic powers, and which looks for the end of this present world order through a cosmic catastrophe, and for the ushering in of a new, entirely different and supra-historical world order by the power of God.[1]

---

[1] Sigmund Mowinckel, *He that Cometh*, Eng. trans. (Oxford: Basil Blackwell, 1956), 125–6.

This definition hardly seems to apply to the material that we have surveyed so far. From the promise of a land through to the promise of an idealized future when God will be king of all the earth, the hope of Israel seems to have been a this-worldly hope, just as the threats of judgement were threats of military defeat and the overthrow of empires within history. Only the later tendencies in the direction of the language of cosmic disaster and cosmic restoration approach anything like Mowinckel's definition of 'eschatology', and even then there is little hint of dualism. God's universal sovereignty may be portrayed as to be realized through supernatural, trans-historical, means, but it is still the future of this world and of Jerusalem that is envisaged, however transformed. Mowinckel's definition in fact seems much more applicable to apocalyptic, as we shall see. But so far no mention of 'apocalyptic' has been made; and indeed apocalyptic is a late and marginal phenomenon as far as the whole Old Testament is concerned.

Other scholars give very different definitions of 'eschatology'. Gerhard von Rad, for example, points out that the idea of an end to time and history did not arise at all in the bulk of the Old Testament period, including that of pre-exilic, exilic, and post-exilic prophecy. The keynote of Old Testament prophecy, for Rad, is expectation of something soon to happen through some act of God within the course of history. This suggests a much broader definition of 'eschatology' in terms of talk of God's decisive future acts in judgement and vindication. This is in fact the kind of definition that the majority of Old Testament scholars have in mind when they write of the eschatology of the Old Testament. The possibility of such a wider definition depends on taking 'last things' to mean, not last in time, but ultimate in significance. Admittedly, for the Old Testament prophets, these ultimately significant acts of God are still future and the subject of expectation and hope. Later on, we shall discover yet another sense of eschatology (at certain stages in the history of Christian thought) where time drops out of the picture altogether in the religious perception of what is ultimately significant. But this is to anticipate. As far as the Old Testament is concerned, the hope of Israel was certainly for God's acts in the future, although we have seen reason to emphasize that it was the historical future that the prophets had in mind.

The Messianic Hope

One feature of Israel's hope, which later came to have predominant significance in Christian thought, has been omitted in this sketch of the development of prophetic eschatology. This is the 'messianic' element in Old Testament prophecy. It is instructive to omit this element in an initial presentation of the hope of Israel, since the later Christian interpretation and use of this theme distort a purely historical picture of the prophets' message.

The expectation of a particular individual saviour-figure to be God's agent in the restoration and vindication of Israel goes back to the promise, already quoted, that God would establish the throne of David's kingdom for ever (2 Sam. 7). Many of the prophets, though by no means all, speak of a king of David's line as the symbol and agent of God's action in restoring Israel to its former glory, reuniting the divided kingdoms, re-establishing Jerusalem as the centre of a prosperous nation, and exercising sovereignty over the other nations. 'In that day I will raise up the booth of David that is fallen and repair its breaches, and raise up its ruins, and rebuild it as in the days of old' (Amos 8: 11). Our familiarity with Handel's *Messiah* may prevent us from recognizing that the child to be born and called 'wonderful, counsellor, mighty god, everlasting father, prince of peace' (Isa. 9: 6) is none other than a Davidic king, of whom it is said, 'of the increase of his government and peace there will be no end, upon the throne of David and over his kingdom to establish it, and to uphold it with justice and with righteousness from this time forth and for evermore'. Jeremiah reassures the exiles that God has not broken his covenant nor withdrawn his promise that the descendants of David will rule over the descendants of Abraham, Isaac, and Jacob (Jer. 33: 20–6), and Ezekiel proclaims God's word that his servant David shall be king over the restored people, and that they shall all have one shepherd (Ezek. 37: 24). This hope of an anointed Davidic king (the word 'messiah' means 'anointed one') is the origin of the messianic hope of Israel.

There is no hint as yet that the expected saviour-figure will be a supernatural quasi-divine individual. Even the epithets in Isaiah 9: 6 are such as could be used of the king himself, as we can gather from the royal psalms, although these too, in the course of time, were to be taken by Christians to refer to the divine Saviour. In the next section we shall trace the emergence of more supernatural figures in the later 'apocalyptic' writings, but for the prophetic period it was the human figure of a Davidic king that featured most prominently in the messianic prophecies of hope.

Many Old Testament scholars now take the 'servant' of the 'servant songs' in Deutero-Isaiah (Isa. 42: 1–4, 49: 1–6, 50: 4–9, 52: 13–53: 12) to be not a royal messianic figure but rather a symbol for Israel or the remnant of Israel itself.[2] Others suppose the servant to be an anticipated prophet entrusted with a special mission not only to Israel but also to the world. At all events these poems represent the climax of Old Testament prophecy in their universal scope and their recognition of the possibility of salvation through redemptive suffering. Even here, it should be noted, the content of the hope is this-worldly; it is hope for a world of justice and truth, established not now by victory through battle or monarchic power but specifically through suffering.

This figure of the 'suffering servant' was to become one of the chief interpretative keys for the New Testament understanding of Jesus Christ. In their own time and context, these prophecies constitute a meditative, poetic, summary of prophetic experience in face of disaster and suffering, reaching rare heights of spiritual perception.

The Rise of Apocalyptic

It is a commonplace that, as we come towards the end of the Old Testament period, prophecy dies out and comes to be replaced by apocalyptic. The word 'apocalyptic' means 'uncovering' or 'revelation', and apocalyptic writings are writings in which the details of God's future action are revealed (albeit symbolically) and portrayed in vivid, dramatic, and pictorial form. Moreover, just because a more decisive and climactic 'end' to present history and its replacement by God's everlasting dominion are apparently envisaged than was the

---

[2] See Horst Dietrich Preuss, *Old Testament Theology*, ii (Edinburgh: T. & T. Clark, 1996), 37.

case with earlier prophecy, the majority of scholars hold that apocalyptic introduced a heightened eschatology into the faith of Israel.

This view was challenged by Christopher Rowland in his book *The Open Heaven.*[3] Rowland saw little evidence of a *transcendent* future for creation in Jewish apocalyptic. Rather he interpreted it simply as the revelation of God's hidden control of and future purpose for human history on earth. This interpretation requires considerable playing down of the ideas of 'the end' and of God's 'everlasting dominion'. It remains a minority view in Old Testament scholarship.

In the Old Testament itself, the book of Daniel provides us with the main example of apocalyptic, although apocalyptic passages have been included in older prophetic books in the form in which we have them today (e.g. Isa. 24–7, the so-called Isaiah apocalypse). Apocalyptic came to dominate the literature and thought-forms of at least some main strands in the Judaism of the inter-testamental period and of the time of Jesus. But, for the moment, we shall take the book of Daniel in the Hebrew Bible to illustrate the genre. Most scholars regard the book of Daniel, despite the inclusion of some older material, as stemming from the second century BC, at the time of the Maccabean wars, when the Jews rose in revolt against Antiochus Epiphanes, the Seleucid monarch who attempted to impose Hellenistic religion and culture throughout his empire, including Palestine. (The Seleucids were one of the main dynasties that took over the dismembered empire of Alexander the Great.) In these troubled times Jewish faith in God was inspired and sustained by a book such as Daniel, which portrays world history as being wholly in God's hands and about to culminate in God's decisive intervention to judge the world and give the kingdom to 'the saints of the Most High'. The technique of such writing was to attribute the apocalyptic visions to a much earlier figure, in this case the Jewish captive, Daniel, at the court of the Babylonian king in the sixth century BC, whose dreams then portray in symbolic form the successive empires down to the present (that is, the second century BC), as though the whole historical span was exactly predetermined in God's intention, and then to crown the revelation with a vivid picture of the imminent day of judgement and vindication. We find all this in Daniel 7–8.

[3] Christopher C. Rowland, *The Open Heaven: A Study of Apocalyptic in Judaism and Early Christianity* (London: SPCK, 1982).

An interesting feature of this relatively early example of apocalyptic writing is the absence of any specifically messianic hope. Admittedly, the figure of 'one like a son of man', who comes with the clouds of heaven to the Ancient of Days and 'is given dominion and glory and kingdom' (Dan. 7: 13) was taken to refer to Jesus and was combined with other genuinely messianic prophecies to form New Testament interpretations of the Christ. But it seems more likely that in Daniel the 'one like a son of man' is a symbolic figure for the saints of the Most High to whom the kingdom is to be given (see Dan. 7: 22). He comes *to* God in the sky, not from him. It seems that for a time, with the continued suppression of the Jewish people, messianic hope was in abeyance, until, in later apocalyptic, it revived, as we shall see, in much more supernatural forms.

It has been held by some Old Testament scholars that apocalyptic was the natural development of prophetic eschatology, growing out of it perhaps under the influence of more dualistic, Persian, modes of thought, as the Jews came under the sway of the Persian empire and its successors. The problem of influence apart, it might indeed appear that apocalyptic visions such as Daniel's take the prophetic tradition only one stage further; for we have already noted the tendency of prophecy to become more universal in scope and more cosmic in imagery. This feature of apocalyptic—its vision of history moving towards a universal culmination and of God as Lord of the totality of history—is the feature of Jewish apocalyptic that modern Christian theologians have singled out as being of decisive importance for a theological interpretation of history as a whole and of the place of Jesus Christ within universal history. We shall be examining these views in later chapters of this book. But one main feature of apocalyptic stands in marked contrast to the earlier prophetic tradition, including its eschatology, and constitutes the main reason why most Old Testament scholars now reject the idea that apocalyptic continues the prophetic tradition. That feature is the striking determinism of the apocalyptic view. For the prophets, the future is not wholly predetermined by God. God's initiative, whether in judgement or in grace, is not fixed irretrievably in advance. For the larger part of the Old Testament period, it was believed that God responds freely to his people's obedience or disobedience. For the apocalyptic writers, by contrast, the course of history is fixed in advance and simply unfolds according to a predetermined plan, disclosed in symbolic visions to the apocalyptic seer. It is this difference between prophecy and apocalyptic that led scholars such as Gerhard von Rad to attribute the rise of apocalyptic to the wisdom tradition in Israel rather than to the prophetic tradition.[4]

The Emergence of Belief in Life after Death

Before we pursue the story of the development of Israel's hope in the inter-testamental period, we must retrace our steps a little and take note of another remarkable fact about the religion of the Old Testament—namely, how late belief in life after death arose to become an essential element in Jewish hope. For the larger part of the Old Testament period, both promise and hope were for the future of Israel as a people and as a nation. The individual as such had no future beyond the grave. As Psalm 115 puts it: 'The dead do not praise the Lord, nor do any that go down into silence' (v. 17). Ancient Israel certainly possessed the concept of a place of the dead, which they called 'Sheol', but this is comparable to the Greek 'Hades' or to certain notions of shadowy insubstantial survival to be found in the religions of non-literate tribes in Africa, and its religious significance is minimal. A mark of its religious inadequacy is the rare presence in the Hebrew Bible of the strange idea that certain very holy men, such as Enoch and Elijah, escaped this fate and were taken directly away from earth to be with God. But there is no trace as yet of any generalization of this idea. For the most part, in ancient Israel's belief, the breath of life is God's own spirit animating a human being, and when that human being dies this spirit 'returns to God who gave it' (Eccles. 12: 7). It is quite mistaken to take this as referring to the immortality of the soul. Rather, it is God's spirit that returns to God. When the conviction of life after death does eventually arise in the development of Israel's religion, it is much more a question of the resurrection of the dead than of the immortality of the soul.

The reason why belief in resurrection was a late phenomenon in the faith of Israel is the aforementioned fact that, for most of the Old

---

[4] See Gerhard von Rad, *Wisdom in Israel*, Eng. trans. (London: SCM Press, 1972).

Testament period, that faith and the hope it engendered were concerned with the nation rather than the individual. Even in as late a case as that of the prophet Ezekiel, when the idea of individual responsibility has indeed come to be stressed, it is a mistake to take the well-known story of the valley of dry bones (Ezek. 37) to be about the resurrection of individuals. It is God's power to reanimate and revive the nation that is pictured so vividly there.

Another passage mistakenly supposed to refer to belief in resurrection is Job 19: 25–7 Job's conviction—'I know that my redeemer liveth . . .' and 'though worms destroy this body, yet in my flesh shall I see God'—is often taken to indicate just such a belief. But, sadly, this is a misinterpretation of the Hebrew words, which most probably refer to no more than a strong conviction that, despite everything, Job will be vindicated before he dies. Indeed the prose conclusion to the book of Job spells out just such a vindication in terms of renewed earthly prosperity.

All the same, there is some plausibility in the suggestion that the seeds of belief in a future life with God beyond death are there in the Hebrew Bible in such episodes as those of Enoch and Elijah and in God's repeated promise of life (e.g. Deut. 30: 19).[5] But it is not until we come to the later, apocalyptic, literature that belief in the resurrection of the dead appears as a common aspect of Jewish faith and hope, and becomes integrated into the message of both judgement and salvation. We find this both in the 'Isaiah Apocalypse' (Isa. 26: 19) and, most explicitly, in Daniel 12: 2: 'And many of those who sleep in the dust of the earth shall awake, some to everlasting life, and some to shame and contempt.' It seems that three factors in particular contributed to the emergence of this belief: the growing sense of the significance and responsibility of the individual, the conviction of the permanence of people's relationship with God (we see this already in some of the later psalms), and the belief, in the face of martyrdom and innocent suffering, that a just God is bound by his own nature to raise the dead.

Nevertheless it was a long time before belief in resurrection came to prevail in Judaism. Even in the time of Jesus, as we know from his

---

[5] See Kevin J Madigan and Jon D. Levenson, *Resurrection: The Power of God for Christians and Jews* (New Haven: Yale University Press, 2008), chs. 7–9.

disputes with the Sadducees (Matt. 22: 23–33), conservative groups retained the older faith, in which resurrection had no place.

The Inter-Testamental Period

The importance of the Old Testament background for an understanding of the Christian hope cannot be denied. But the Judaism in which Jesus grew up and that formed the immediate context of his teaching and the framework within which both his teaching and the events of his life, death, and resurrection were first received, was Judaism as it was some two hundred years after the close of the Old Testament period. The literature that has survived from the time between the Testaments, including Jewish literature contemporary with Jesus and the early Church, must also be considered if we are to appreciate the basis of the specifically Christian hope in its full context. It is true that the books of what Christians call the Old Testament already constituted the canonical Scriptures of the Hebrew Bible, read in the synagogues and authoritative for Jewish faith and morals in a way no other literature could be, but a large body of secondary literature grew up that coloured the interpretations of the Scriptures and contributed to the various developments in Judaism at the time of Jesus.

First among these writings to be mentioned are the Apocryphal and Deuterocanonical books that appear in many of our Bibles under the loose heading of the 'Apocrypha'. Most of these appeared in the Greek versions of the Jewish Bible itself; for, while the list of the books of the Law and the Prophets were fixed at a relatively early stage (second century BC), those contained in the third main section of the Jewish Bible—the Writings—were still undetermined at the time the Greek translations were made. What we call the Apocrypha includes a notable and somewhat later apocalyptic text in 2 Esdras, very much in the same genre as Daniel 7–8. It is interesting to learn that another apocalyptic text, Ethiopian Enoch, from among the so-called inter-testamental Pseudepigrapha, is given scriptural status in the Ethiopic Church, which regards it as part of the Old Testament canon. Other apocalyptic writings from before the time of Jesus include the twelfth book of the Jewish Sibylline Oracles (modelled on the Roman ones) and, from among the Dead Sea Scrolls of the Qumran community, the Damascus Document and especially the War Scroll. Later examples are the two Apocalypses of Baruch and, perhaps most striking of all, IV Ezra.

Great variety and remarkable freedom of speculation are to be found in these writings. This contrasts with the controlled exegesis of the Torah, the Jewish Law, given in the Pentateuch. Such exegesis (later called Halakah) came to be carefully codified by the rabbis in writings known as the Mishna. But eschatological speculation tended to develop without strict control and in association with particular groups within Judaism such as the Qumran community, each going its own way, without interrelation or systematization.

It seems that in the second century BC there emerged within Judaism a group or party of pious Jews (the Hasidim) determined to resist the Hellenization of Judaism that reached its climax in the reign of Antiochus Epiphanes. Their support was enlisted by the Maccabees in the revolt against the Seleucid king. We have already noted that the book of Daniel took its present from within this period. Two movements in particular evolved out of the Hasidim: the Pharisees, who come to take a leading role in the Jewish religious parliament (Sanhedrin) in Jerusalem, and the Essenes, who retreated into quasi-monastic isolation as enclosed communities such as that of Qumran by the Dead Sea. Among the Essenes apocalyptic flourished, sometimes including messianic expectation, sometimes developing the more supernatural expectations that we have already seen in Daniel 7–8. The Qumran community illustrate the extraordinary variety of messianic hope that developed in such circles. They expected three figures, who would usher in the end-time: 'the prophet and the messiahs of Aaron and Israel'. The idea of a prophet who would announce the messianic age is familiar to us from the New Testament. It was probably based on Deuteronomy 18: 15. And the idea of two messiahs, a priestly messiah and a royal messiah, goes back to Zechariah 4, where two olive trees are seen as symbolizing the anointed ones.

Despite this variety, the basic pattern of apocalyptic follows that of Daniel. The visions are attributed to a prophet or patriarch of old, such as Enoch, Baruch, or Ezra; the intervening history is symbolically portrayed in terms of a succession of periods about to culminate in the end of 'the present age' and the ushering-in of 'the age to come'.

The tribulations of the end-time are described in the terrifying language of the 'messianic woes' and the final defeat of the forces of evil spelled out in much greater detail. In some later apocalypses, attempts are made both to combine the earthly and the supernatural saviour figures and to reconcile the historical and transcendent forms of eschatology. This produces the notion of a two-stage eschatology: a messianic age in which the messiah reigns on earth over a restored Israel for a fixed time—sometimes for 400 years (IV Ezra 7: 28–9), sometimes for 1,000 years (as in the New Testament book of Revelation, to be considered in Chapter 2)—followed by the end of history, the final resurrection, and the last judgement. Belief in resurrection is by now firmly established in apocalyptic circles, although the Qumran texts are surprisingly silent on this theme.

The details of apocalyptic hope need not be described here. For our purposes it is enough if we gain some idea of the main lines of its development—its universal scope, its concept of judgement on every human being as well as on the nations, its pronounced dualism between the present age and the age to come, and its highly deterministic view of the future. The older hope for a restored Israel and an earthly messianic rule is still incorporated within this wider framework, but the emphasis becomes much more cosmic and transcendent. We have noted the great variety of detailed speculation permitted within this broad horizon, a variety to which the New Testament itself bears witness in its incidental references to messianic groups, more or less political, which had appeared on the contemporary scene (cf., e.g., Acts 5: 36–7 and 21: 38). For, in addition to the groups already mentioned, there were political movements, most notably the Zealots, who believed that armed resistance to the Roman occupation would usher in the messianic age.

One final historical point may be mentioned here. By the end of the second century AD apocalyptic hope had ceased to play a role in mainstream Judaism. Two factors can account for this. One was the final and complete destruction of Jerusalem by Hadrian in 135 AD. From that time on, Judaism became to all intents and purposes the religion of the Torah, a tendency that only completed the shift of emphasis that had begun after the first exile. The other factor was the increasing use of apocalyptic writings by the early Christian Church. Many of the later Jewish apocalypses were themselves turned to Christian use and embellished with Christian additions and interpretations. In these circumstances mainstream Judaism renounced apocalyptic, retaining only the bare outline of messianic hope. The story of much later revivals of purely Jewish Messianism lies outside the scope of this book.

Conclusion

This brief sketch of the Old Testament and inter-testamental background to the Christian hope will have indicated something of the varied and changing nature of Israel's eschatology. We have pointed out the developments, within prophecy itself, from hope for a this-worldly, national prosperity, presided over by a Davidic king, through expectation of a day of general judgement and vindication, to hope for the universal rule of God over a just and peaceful world, centred on Jerusalem. But it will have become clear that the story of the further development from prophecy to apocalyptic is a rather ambiguous story. It is difficult, religiously and theologically speaking, to believe that we are dealing here simply with the history of unfolding revelation. No doubt the Christian mind will see in the extension of hope from the nation to the world, in the growth of confidence in God as the Lord of universal history, in the recognition of an ultimate, transcendent dimension to human destiny under God (including the conviction that God will raise the dead), new insights into the purposes of God that can indeed be held to possess lasting revelatory significance. Moreover, the messianic hope of Israel, for all its variety and speculative extravagance, did provide the materials out of which a way of interpreting the saving events of Christ's life, death, and resurrection could be fashioned. But it is widely felt that the story is also a story of decline. The prophets' insight into God's moral government of human history, his sovereign freedom in both judgement and grace, seems to have faded away. One has only to compare Deutero-Isaiah with Daniel 7–8 to realize that the profound insights into the meaning of redemptive suffering and into Israel's vocation as a light to the nations have not fully been maintained. Instead, under the pressure of repeated disaster and tyranny, and perhaps under the influence of Iranian religious speculation, the Jewish mind—in part, at least—was beginning to feel the attractions of a deterministic world view in which the details of history, including its imminent end, were fixed in advance by the inscrutable will of God.[6] The careful student of these texts, aware of the history of apocalyptic literature from Daniel to IV Ezra and of the nature of this genre of religious writing, will try to reach a just assessment of both the gains and the losses involved in these developments. Moreover, Christian scholars, despite their recognition of the importance of apocalyptic for New Testament faith and hope, will also be concerned to show how many of these developments were repudiated by Jesus and the early Church, as they recovered the spirit of genuine prophecy and, for the most part, rejected deterministic views of history. What they did not reject, of course, were the concerns of apocalyptic for universal history and for the resurrection of the dead.

[6] In the history of Judaism and of Christianity, apocalyptic texts have often been interpreted, quite out of context, as referring to the course of human history hundreds or even thousands of years later. There can be no doubt that such interpretations are mistaken.

2

The New Testament

Introduction

The New Testament is alive with a strong sense of hope for the future of creation. It is evident that Jesus himself, by his deeds, his preaching, and his personality, inspired not only his followers but also many poor, sick, and outcast people with a new and immediate hope. But it was, above all, the resurrection of Jesus and the outpouring of the Spirit at Pentecost that created the transcendent hope that finds expression alike in Paul's letters and in the book of Revelation. It was a hope anchored in present experience of salvation, but its other focus was the ultimate future of humanity opened up by this experience of being 'in Christ': 'since we are justified by faith, we have peace with God through our Lord Jesus Christ. Through him we have obtained access to this grace in which we stand, and we rejoice in our hope of sharing the glory of God' (Rom. 5: 1–2). 1 Peter 3: 15 also encourages the Christians always to be ready to account for the hope that is in them.

Historians, seeking to uncover and reconstruct the basis of this hope and to trace its earliest forms and first developments, must, to a certain extent, stand back from their own involvement in these matters, if they are to achieve an objective and accurate picture of the Christian hope reflected in the pages of the New Testament. But equally they must do justice to the novelty and the power of what came to expression there.

We shall begin with the preaching of Jesus; but, since the whole New Testament, including the Gospels, reflects the Easter faith of the disciples and the earliest Christian communities, it is not easy to discern the original message of Jesus himself. Skilful reconstruction is required if the post-Resurrection faith is not to colour our presentation of his preaching. One important task is to try to see it against the background of the hope of Israel that we were examining in Chapter 1, and to grasp what Jesus himself made of his Jewish inheritance, as he fashioned out of it a new understanding of the nature, acts, and purposes of God.

Jesus

It is generally agreed that the heart of Jesus's message is to be found in his preaching of the Kingdom of God. That in itself is clearly an eschatological notion only to be understood in the light of Jewish expectations. Moreover, it may surprise us to learn how close to the hope of Israel was Jesus's own expectation for the future. It seems that what was original and special in his preaching of the Kingdom was not so much the outer form of his future hope as rather the new and religiously compelling vision that he brought of what God's kingly rule actually meant. Unlike the Pharisees' insistence on the strict observance of the law, unlike the political messianism of the Zealots, and unlike the sectarian strictness of the Qumran community setting itself apart to await the end, the preaching of Jesus concerned God's unbounded love and forgiveness at work already among the poor and the outcast. Largely by means of evocative parables, Jesus taught that the power of God's future can be experienced now as men and women respond to him in repentance and faith. It was this teaching that evoked such unconditional response in many who heard his words. A further striking fact about the preaching is the way in which it simply assumed his own role in communicating God's forgiving love and healing power. It was not just a matter of the authority with which he spoke ('You have heard that it was said... but I say unto you...'); it was the calm assumption that people's ultimate future with God depended on their response to Jesus there and then.

We cannot, however, interpret Jesus's preaching of the Kingdom solely in terms of its presence here and now. The eschatological note, indeed the apocalyptic note, is too strong in the traditions about Jesus himself for us to be able to accept the hypothesis—attractive to anyone suspicious of Jewish apocalyptic—that Jesus himself rejected the apocalyptic ideas of late Judaism and preached a purely spiritual and ethical gospel of repentance and forgiveness. One has only to think of the Lord's Prayer to realize how implausible such a view would be. Admittedly, Jesus had given the current Jewish expectations a new slant and a new focus. There is evidence of a resumption of a more conventional apocalyptic framework on the part of the first Jewish Christian communities. But that Jesus himself to a considerable extent shared the current expectation is clear, both from his association with John the Baptist and from his own teaching about resurrection, the coming 'Son of Man', and the eschatological trials of the coming messianic age. The original features of his message, sketched above, certainly create a tension between present significance and future hope in Jesus's preaching of the Kingdom, and there is no doubt too that Jesus rejected fruitless speculation about the moment and the details of 'the end' (Luke 17: 20). But it is clear that, like his fellow Jews, he expected a relatively imminent end and the inbreaking of the messianic age. Even clearer is his endorsement, against the Sadducees, of the late Jewish hope of resurrection. God 'is not God of the dead, but of the living' (Mark 12: 27).[1]

Most, if not all, of the titles that the Gospels give to Jesus in their presentation of his significance reflect the experience and thought of the post-Easter communities. Some scholars believe that Jesus himself did not think in terms of his own return as 'Son of Man'.[2] Sayings such as Luke 12: 8 ('everyone who acknowledges me before men, the Son of Man also will acknowledge before the angels of God'), although they highlight the striking fact, mentioned above, that Jesus saw peoples' future as dependent on their reaction to himself, might suggest that he, like John the Baptist, looked forward to a transcendent eschatological 'Son of Man' along the lines of Daniel 7, by now interpreted, against its original sense (see p. 14 above) messianically. On this view, it was the early Church that identified Jesus himself as the Son of Man who would return to usher in the final eschatological drama. Other scholars think rather that it was Jesus who combined

---

[1] A thorough examination of the Kingdom of God in the preaching of Jesus may be found in John P. Meier, *A Marginal Jew: Rethinking the Historical Jesus*, ii (New York: Doubleday, 1996), chs. 15 and 16.

[2] See Morna Hooker, *The Son of Man in Mark: A Study of the Background of the Term 'Son of Man' and its Use in St Mark's Gospel* (London: SPCK, 1967).

the figure of Daniel 7 with the suffering servant of Isaiah 53 to fashion his own new conception of the role of the suffering Messiah that he saw himself called upon to undertake.[3] It is not necessary for us to try to settle these vexed issues of New Testament interpretation here.[4] It is enough if we can recognize the degree to which the hope of Israel was enhanced by Jesus's preaching of the Kingdom, by his conviction of the nearness of God and of God's love for the sinner. We have noted, too, the tension in his preaching between the present and the future, the sense of God's liberating power available here and now, and yet the still future expectation of the day of the Lord.

One further feature of the life and teaching of Jesus himself must be mentioned before we pass on to the hope of the first Christians, and that is his attitude to his own fate. It is clear that Jesus soon came to realize that his authoritative message of God's forgiving love and his own actions in eating and drinking with sinners, actions that broke the bounds of official religious behaviour, would bring him into conflict with the religious authorities and lead inexorably to suffering and death. Very possibly, Jesus himself went to his fate in the spirit of the suffering servant of Isaiah 53, and saw redemptive power in God's agent giving himself up to the worst people could do to him. Indeed, this conviction of the redemptive power of Jesus's death became a major factor in early Christian preaching. It adds its own weight and significance to the shifting of the balance between a purely future hope and a conviction of present fulfilment.

Paul and the Early Christians

This tension between present and future is everywhere apparent in the first Christian communities formed under the impact of Easter and Pentecost. The vindication of Jesus's preaching and life through his appearances to the disciples as risen and alive brought about a spiritual revolution in their lives that can only be described in terms of experience of salvation here and now. It was present experience of

---

[3] See C. H. Dodd, *The Founder of Christianity* (London: Collins, 1971).

[4] The dispute is discussed in Graham Stanton, *The Gospel and Jesus* (2nd edn.; Oxford: Oxford University Press, 2002), ch. 15.

life in the Spirit of Christ crucified and risen, understood as itself the fulfilment of the hope of Israel, that characterized the rapidly growing groups of Christians in Jerusalem and Antioch and within an astonishingly short time throughout the Mediterranean world as far as Rome. Yet at the same time the primitive churches were also characterized by a strong expectation of the return of Christ—the Parousia or 'coming' as they called it—at first, it seems, in the near future, within the lifetime of the first generation of Christians. All the resources of Jewish apocalyptic were taken over for the vivid depiction of this future hope.

Our earliest evidence for the form and content of this early Christian conviction and hope is to be found in the letters of St Paul. But we have to remember that Paul, although formerly a strict Jew, had become the leading apostle to the Gentiles. Already, before a single word of the New Testament had been written, the leaders of the Christian Church had come to realize that their message of present salvation and future hope was for all men and women, unrestricted by race. In fulfilling the hope of Israel, their risen Lord had become the hope of all the earth. It was Paul who grasped most thoroughly the necessity of this universalizing of the Christian gospel, and prevented the Jerusalem Church from slipping back into the status of a Jewish sect. Admittedly, in Romans 9–11, Paul struggled to preserve a special place for Judaism in the providence of God, even for the future, but the logic of his understanding of the universal scope of the salvation, achieved through the cross and resurrection of Christ, indicates a decisive and permanent break with Judaism and the birth of a new, universal religion. On the other hand, this problem of the continued resistance to the Christian gospel by the people of the old covenant may have helped Paul to come to terms with the delay in the Lord's return.

Paul's conviction of the saving power of Christ crucified and risen for the believer and for the Christian community here and now is worked out in what, despite recent questioning of its centrality,[5] is certainly one of his leading theological motifs—namely, justification by grace alone, appropriated through faith (Rom. 3: 21–6). For Paul, the Christ event with its saving power means that already the believer

---

[5] e.g. in Gordon D. Fee, *Paul, the Spirit, and the People of God* (Peabody, MA: Hendrickson Publishers, 1996), 5.

is a new creation (2 Cor. 5: 17). But, although men and women can experience forgiveness of sins and the spirit-filled life of being 'in Christ' here and now—the implications of this both for worship and for conduct are spelled out in some detail in his letters—Paul never forgets the continuing future dimension of the Christian hope. We who have the first fruits of the Spirit, he declares in Romans 8: 23–5, 'groan inwardly as we wait for adoption as sons, the redemption of our bodies. For in this hope we were saved. Now hope that is seen is not hope. But if we hope for what we do not see, we wait for it with patience.' One more quotation from Romans will underline this emphasis. As he approaches the final pages of his letter, he writes: 'May the God of hope fill you with all joy and peace in believing, so that by the power of the Holy Spirit you may abound in hope' (Rom. 15: 13).

In expounding this future hope Paul utilizes the framework and characteristic terminology of Jewish apocalyptic: the 'day' of the Lord (1 Thess. 5: 2) and, of course, resurrection, a topic on which he has more to say than any other biblical writer (see especially the Thessalonian epistles and 1 Cor. 15). For Paul, our future resurrection is anchored in the fact of Christ's resurrection from the dead (1 Cor. 15: 12–19).

Paul's treatment of the nature of resurrection introduces a subtle modification into the Hebrew conception of a literal bodily resurrection from the dead. Resurrection, he holds, is certainly an act and a gift of God. But it will involve transformation from a fleshly to a spiritual 'body' comparable to that of seed to flower (1 Cor. 15: 37). The comparison also brings out the continuity between the two—though we should not press this too far, in the light of Paul's insistence on transformation in verses 51–4. Moreover, Paul extends the resurrection hope to the whole creation. According to Romans 8: 2, 'the creation itself will be set free from its bondage to decay and obtain the glorious liberty of the children of God'.

Two further differences between Pauline and Jewish apocalyptic may be mentioned here. In the first place, the gift of the Spirit, experienced already in the believer who is 'in Christ', provides an 'earnest' or 'guarantee' of the Christian's future hope (2 Cor. 1: 22 and 5: 5).[6] And, in the second place, we find in Paul's letters a characteristic

[6] This is what Gordon Fee sees as the 'elusive center' of Paul's theology.

expression of that early Christian identification of the risen Lord himself as the heavenly figure who by his 'coming' or 'appearance' will usher in the last 'day' (1 Thess. 4: 16, 2 Thess. 2: 1–3).

We should note that it is Paul's teaching that the Christian *will* share in Christ's resurrection, not that he is raised with him already. One of the reasons why many scholars think that Colossians and Ephesians are not directly from Paul himself is that, perhaps in the light of the delay in the Lord's coming (the Parousia), these letters reflect the later idea that the Christian is already raised with Christ (e.g. Eph. 2: 6). If this is correct, we should suppose that Paul himself was careful to guard against an over-spiritualization of the gospel (such as the gnostics taught, largely relinquishing the future element (see pp. 40–1 below)) and to insist on what is still to come.[7]

In the course of this book we shall have to devote considerable space to the problem of the 'Parousia' expectation in Paul and other early Christian writers. It seems from the Thessalonian epistles that Paul, at any rate at first, expected the Lord's 'coming' to take place within the lifetime of the first generation of Christians. We should observe that there is no suggestion of 'millenarianism'—the idea that Christ will come to reign on earth for a thousand years—in Paul. The Lord's 'appearing' heralds the end, when both the living and the dead will be caught up, transformed, and taken to be 'always with the Lord' (1 Thess. 4: 17). Moreover, Paul's emphasis on justification and the spirit-filled life in Christ means that no special problem need arise for his theology and ethics from the Parousia's delay.

The Synoptic Gospels

We have already used the first three Gospels in our attempt to recon-struct the eschatological preaching of Jesus himself. We return to them now for what they have to show us of the Christian hope as it was at the times of their compilation—somewhat later than Paul's letters, but probably between the sixties and eighties of the first century.

---

[7] On the other hand, as we have seen, Paul certainly teaches that he who is in Christ is already a 'new creation', and it is *possible* that he himself developed this idea further in the light of the delay of the Parousia.

Mark's Gospel—generally agreed to be the earliest of the three—reflects very clearly the early Christian conviction of an imminent Parousia (see Mark 9: 1 and 13: 30). But the so-called Markan Apocalypse of chapter 13 shows how an apparent prophetic warning by Jesus about the fate of Jerusalem and its temple (as indeed took place with the city's destruction in AD 70, as Mark himself well knew) could be overlaid by apocalyptic imagery and turned into prophecies of the end.[8] We note especially Jesus's refusal to speculate about the timing of the end (v. 32) and also the practical lessons of readiness and watchfulness (vv. 33, 37) drawn from this endorsement of both prophecy and apocalyptic. But we can also see that, as with Paul, little is lost from Mark's eschatology when it is realized that expectation of an imminent end was mistaken. Indeed, Mark himself, through the lips of Jesus, insists that 'the gospel must first be preached to all nations' (v. 10).

Matthew includes this Markan material in his Gospel, heightening its apocalyptic content in chapter 24 and spelling out the Parousia doctrine very explicitly in terms reminiscent of Daniel 7. Matthew gives us our clearest picture of an early Jewish Christian community, probably not long after the fall of Jerusalem, when the problem of the Parousia's delay was beginning to be felt (see v. 48). The fact that no one knows the hour of the end is given even greater emphasis, and parables are told (the wise and foolish virgins, the master who goes on a journey) to reinforce the need for readiness and good use of the time before the bridegroom or the master comes. (For Matthew, these are parables about the Parousia; for Jesus himself, it is much more likely that they were parables about his 'first' coming.[9]) Again, as with Paul, there is no millenarian teaching. The coming of the Son of Man in glory will usher in the Last Judgement (Matt. 25: 31–46), the separation of the sheep from the goats. It is here that we find the most explicit teaching about eternal life and eternal punishment, which forms the basis for later Christian teaching about heaven and

---

[8] Its character as a later literary composition can be easily discerned from the aside at verse 14: 'let the reader understand.' For a brief and judicious discussion of the Markan Apocalypse, see Christopher Tuckett's commentary in John Barton and John Muddiman (eds.), *The Oxford Bible Commentary* (Oxford: Oxford University Press, 2001), 912–14.

[9] See C. H. Dodd, *The Parables of the Kingdom* (London: James Nisbet, 1935).

hell. Traditional Christian teaching about hell will be critically examined in Chapter 11 below.

Luke's two volumes—his Gospel and the Acts of the Apostles—present us with a very different picture. Written, it seems, for Gentile Christian communities some time after the fall of Jerusalem, these books reflect the virtual abandonment of expectation of an imminent end and a new conviction of the providential place of the Church and its mission. Luke does not renounce the Parousia expectation nor the use of apocalyptic imagery, but he separates them off from the prophecies of Jerusalem's fall, and diverts attention to present fulfilment and immediate tasks. In Peter's speech in Acts 2, Joel's prophecy about the pouring-out of God's spirit upon all flesh in the 'last days' is referred to Pentecost itself rather than the end, and we soon discover that the emphasis in Luke lies firmly on the new, spirit-filled, life of the Christian Church and its commission to preach the gospel. In Acts 1: 6–8, the risen Christ himself rejects all eschatological speculation, insisting only on the task of mission 'to the ends of the earth'. Similarly in Luke's Gospel (17: 20) Jesus says 'the Kingdom of God is not coming with signs to be observed; nor will they say "Lo, here it is!" or "There!"; for behold, the Kingdom of God is in the midst of you'. So in Luke we find the earliest form of what was to become the standard Church solution of the eschatological problem, a combination of emphasis on present fulfilment and present tasks with retention of a future, but distant Parousia and judgement.

John

It has long been recognized that the Johannine writings, especially the fourth Gospel, represent a very special strand in the New Testament witness to the events concerning Jesus Christ. To many readers, they constitute the most reflective and profound meditation on the meaning of Christ for the believer. Nowhere is their theological depth more apparent than in the way in which the eschatological dimension of early Christian preaching is reinterpreted and applied.

Admittedly, traces of the more common future expectation remain. In the fourth Gospel, we find on the lips of Jesus not only explicit teaching about the 'many rooms' in his Father's house, where he goes to prepare a place for his disciples (14: 2) but also references to 'the last day' (6: 39 and 12: 48) and to Jesus's coming again (14: 3) to take them to himself. There is also Martha's reference to 'the last day' in her conversation with Jesus about Lazarus in chapter 11. In the first letter of John we find confident expectation of a future day of judgement (4: 17) and a time of God's appearing when 'we shall be like him for we shall see him as he is'. There is even a trace in this letter of belief in an imminent end; and at 2: 18 John uses the language of apocalyptic, identifying the heretics as 'antichrists' and proclaiming that 'it is the last hour'.

Apart from the intriguing passage in chapter 21 explicitly dealing with the expectation that Jesus would return before John died (vv. 20–3),[10] these are the only references in John's writings to the 'end'. The dominant motifs of Johannine teaching, by contrast, are concerned rather with the meaning of Christ for the believer in the present. They form the clearest example in the New Testament of 'realized eschatology', a notion to which we shall return in our treatment of twentieth-century Christian theology (pp. 133–5 below). 'Eternal life' or just 'life' is perhaps the main theme of John's Gospel. 'I came that they may have life, and have it more abundantly' (10: 10). This abundant life *is* eternal life. 'Eternal' life, therefore, is chiefly a qualitative term, characterizing the kind of life enjoyed by the believer. This is most clearly expressed in 5: 24: 'He who hears my work and believes him who sent me has eternal life; he does not come into judgement, but has passed from death to life.' The 'realized' nature of this eschatology is brought out specifically in relation to the theme of judgement. At 3: 18 we read: 'He who believes in him is not condemned; he who does not believe is condemned already...' So not only the notion of eternal life but also that of judgement is focused on the present rather than the future. Even the notion of the Parousia is brought within this perspective. John 14: 3 ('I will come again and will take you to myself') was quoted above to show that the Parousia

---

[10] Chapter 21 is usually thought of as having been added to the Gospel after John's death. See Barnabas Lindars, *The Gospel of John* (London: Oliphants (Marshall, Morgan & Scott), 1972), 618–24, John Ashton, *Understanding the Fourth Gospel* (Oxford: Clarendon Press, 1991), 382, and René Kieffer, in Barton and Muddiman (eds.), *The Oxford Bible Commentary*, 999–1000. This view is challenged in Thomas L. Brodie, *The Gospel According to John: A Literary and Theological Commentary* (New York: Oxford University Press, 1993), 574–96.

doctrine is not absent from John's Gospel, but, as these farewell discourses proceed, it begins to look as if such language is being reinterpreted to refer not to Christ coming again at the end, but to his coming in the Spirit. Verse 18 of chapter 14 ('I will not leave you desolate; I will come to you') appears as a gloss on the preceding and subsequent verses (16–17 and 25–6) about the coming of the Paraclete or Comforter, the Holy Spirit. The same is true of 16: 7. Consequently, for the Johannine community, their present experience of the Spirit of the risen Christ is itself the fulfilment of the Parousia expectation.

It is a mistake, in our reading of John, to let this realized eschatology supplant the future hope entirely. But there is no doubt where the emphasis lies in the fourth Gospel. Perhaps the right balance between present and future is achieved if we consider the aforementioned dialogue with Martha in chapter 11. When Jesus says that Lazarus will rise again, Martha takes him to be referring to the end time. Martha said to him: 'I know that he will rise again in the resurrection at the last day.' Jesus said to her: 'I am the resurrection and the life; he who believes in me though he die yet shall he live, and whoever lives and believes in me shall never die...' (vv. 24–6). There is still a future reference here, but the future hope is brought right into the present and indeed, in the story, is symbolized by the actual raising of Lazarus there and then.

The presence of such a remarkable and religiously powerful reinterpretation of early Christian eschatology in the New Testament itself shows how, already in the apostolic age, the primitive expectations of an imminent return of Christ were being refashioned by the profoundest Christian minds.

Other New Testament Writings

Our brief consideration of Paul, Luke, and John will have shown something of the variety of ways in which the christianized apocalyptic of the primitive Church, with its expectation of an imminent Parousia to usher in the end, was modified within the New Testament period itself, partly on account of the Parousia's delay, but chiefly through the spiritual power of present experience of the risen Christ. Other New Testament writings show the same tendency. The Letter to the Hebrews, although it preserves the language of imminent Parousia expectation, gives much greater weight to the present possibility of access to the heavenly reality of Jesus, the mediator and high priest of the new covenant (8: 1–6). The Pastorals (1 and 2 Timothy and Titus) are closer to Luke's more distant Parousia expectation. 2 Peter, probably one of the latest writings in the New Testament, is the simplest and most direct of all. It has been called 'An Apologia for Primitive Christian Eschatology'[11] in that it sets out, quite explicitly, to answer critics who mock the Christians for their manifestly unfulfilled hope (3: 4: 'Where is the promise of his coming? For ever since the fathers fell asleep, all things have continued as they were from the beginning'). To this the writer replies, not with the profundity of Pauline or Johannine reinterpretation, but with the simple points that 'with the Lord one day is as a thousand years, and a thousand years as one day' (v. 8) and that the Lord is being forbearing, in order to allow people time to repent. He then reiterates the apocalyptic hope, urging his readers to wait and to be zealous (vv. 10–18).

Something must now be said about the main example of Christian apocalyptic in the New Testament, The Revelation of St John the Divine. This book has always stood out as exceptional among the New Testament writings. It draws quite explicitly on the main Old Testament example of this genre, the book of Daniel (see above p. 13), and can be understood only in the light of this peculiar tradition of late Jewish apocalyptic, with its pictorial and symbolic language, its sharp dualisms between the present age and the age to come and between the powers of darkness and the powers of heaven, and its conviction that the end is imminent and that the troubles of the present time are the beginning of the messianic woes heralding the last battle (Armageddon). For Revelation, like Daniel, was written out of vivid memories of violent persecution and designed to fortify the Christian churches against backsliding or lukewarmness. We need not go into the details of its number symbolism—a common feature of apocalyptic—except to note that 666, 'the number of the Beast' (13: 18), is generally agreed to refer to the Roman Emperor Nero, the great persecutor of the Christians. This figure of the great beast who makes war on the saints is clearly based on Daniel's symbolism (Dan. 7: 25).

[11] Ernst Käsemann, *Essays on New Testament Themes* (London: SCM Press, 1964), 169–95.

Later it was equated with Antichrist, a prominent figure in Christian apocalyptic and easily identified with any great persecutor of the Church, such as Nero. Here, in the book of Revelation, the term 'Antichrist' does not appear, but the great whore, Babylon (14: 8; 16: 19; 17 and 18), is clearly symbolic of the Roman Empire, and its doom is foretold in vivid picture language, reminiscent of Daniel's prediction of the overthrow of Antiochus Epiphanes (see p. 7 above). We note that the hope that comes to expression here is entirely concerned with God's dramatic intervention in a catastrophic future. There is no hope for this world in its present structures before the return of Christ.

Although Revelation is a typical example of apocalyptic, it is a thoroughly christianized example. It is the Lamb who was slain (5: 6–7) who alone is worthy to open the scroll, and who stands on Mount Sion with the redeemed as the last battle rages below (ch. 11). It is Christ with whom the risen martyrs reign for a thousand years, when Satan has been bound (ch. 20). Then comes the Last Judgement and a new heaven and a new earth, a new Jerusalem, where God and the Lamb are the temple and its light. Indeed, for this christianized apocalyptic, it is difficult to distinguish God and Jesus—both say 'I am the Alpha and the Omega, the beginning and the end' (21: 6 and 22: 13). The book ends with the eschatological prayer of primitive Christianity: 'Come, Lord Jesus.'

It has already been pointed out (p. 19 above) that the idea of the millennium that we find here in chapter 20 is but one example of a two-stage eschatology in which the more transcendent hope characteristic of the later apocalyptic is made to include within itself an element of the older Jewish hope for the vindication of God's people here on earth. The thousand years, in Revelation, symbolize the messianic age, a further 'day' in God's creative plan, each day of creation being symbolized by a thousand years. (This is based on Psalm 90: 4: 'a thousand years in thy sight are but as yesterday'.) In the book of Revelation, the notion of the millennium plays a relatively minor role, and while, as we shall see, it captured the imagination of a number of early Christian theologians, it gradually came to be excluded from, or at least radically reinterpreted in, the main stands of Christian eschatology. It can play no part in a serious modern attempt to recover the significance of apocalyptic for a Christian understanding of the world and its future.

Conclusion

We can now proceed to sum up the Christian hope in its first forms. Clearly the personality and message of Jesus himself and the overwhelming impact of his resurrection gave the first Christians a much more lively and specific hope than we find in anything that had gone before. Jesus's own preaching of the Kingdom of God, the vividly felt redemptive power of his death and resurrection, the present fellowship in the Spirit and 'in Christ'—all this provided an experiential basis for Christian hope of very great religious power and significance. It is not surprising that they expected an imminent Parousia, when they thought of themselves as the eschatological community in which the prophecies of Scripture were already being fulfilled.

It is a remarkable fact, however, that, despite the novelty and power of the early Christians' own experience of salvation through Christ and the Spirit, the outer form of their hope for the future remained very close to that of their Jewish contemporaries. The risen Christ may have taken over the central place in Christian eschatological hope, but the language and imagery in which it was expressed was largely that of late Jewish apocalyptic. Only in John's Gospel do we get the making of a profound reinterpretation of the notions of judgement and eternal life in the light of present experience of Christ. Here the question of the future appears to fade into the background.

The more common picture that we find in the New Testament remains highly coloured by apocalyptic imagery. Moreover, it is the transcendent, other-worldly, element in Jewish apocalyptic that comes to characterize the specifically Christian hope for the future. Again it is not surprising that the older Jewish hope for a historical, this-worldly, vindication of God's people on earth did not at first take root in Christian eschatology. For one thing, the break with Judaism and the universalizing of the Christian gospel meant the renunciation of a national, territorial focus for religious hope. And the power of the Roman Empire, the destruction of Jerusalem, and the experience of persecution left little room for hope for this world. Only the transformation of individuals and corporate experience of life in 'the body of Christ' were real possibilities now in the present, between the times, before the Parousia and the end. Admittedly, Jesus himself had taught the disciples to pray for God's will to be done on earth as it is in heaven, and Paul, in Romans 9–11, envisaged the conversion of the whole world, gentile and Jew, in the divine providential plan. But, for the most part, the early Church remained convinced that the world was doomed to war and disaster until the final battle. It was left to later generations of Christians to draw out the positive implications of the Christ event for the historical future of humanity as well as for the ultimate transcendent future.

Another element that is at most only implicit in the New Testament is its universalism in the further stronger sense of hoping for the eventual salvation of all men and women. The seeds of this view, whose development will be a major theme in later chapters of this book, are to be found in the letters of St Paul—in Romans 11: 12, for example ('for God has consigned all men to disobedience, that he may have mercy upon all'), and in his Adam/Christ typology: 'for as in Adam all die, even so in Christ shall all be made alive' (1 Cor. 15: 22). We may compare the words of Jesus at John 12: 32: 'and I, when I be lifted up, will draw all men to myself'. But it has to be said that the New Testament, including Paul, is too powerfully aware of people's freedom to reject the gospel and of the prevalence of darkness, sin and evil, for such an implicit universalism to be allowed to become explicit.

Part Two

The Classical Christian Hope

3
The Early Church

The First Century

The Christian hope, as found in the first Christian communities, has already been described in the chapter on the New Testament. It was hope for an ultimate future with Christ and with God in a new transformed creation. The basis for this hope was the Christian's present faith in Christ as saviour and the Christian's present love for God and the neighbour, as that faith and that love were experienced and acted out in the Christian communities themselves. The language in which Christian hope was expressed was largely that of Jewish apocalyptic and it varied greatly in the details of its speculation and in its symbolism. We have seen how its imminent Parousia expectation had soon to be modified, sometimes in favour of an even greater stress on present experience, more often in favour of recognition of an age of the Church's mission and life, of indefinite length, before the end. A common feature is the echoing of Jesus's refusal to specify the signs or the time of the end and his insistence on the need for constant vigilance and readiness.

We obtain no more than a few glimpses of the first-century Christian Church from sources outside the New Testament. Two in particular fill out our picture of the early Christian hope just a little. The first letter of Clement, who was bishop in Rome towards the end of the first century, is chiefly concerned with church order and moral teaching. But it reaffirms the scriptural (that is, Old Testament) teaching on the Lord's coming and the judgement that all must face, and it rather curiously tries to reinforce belief in resurrection (in very literal physical terms) by appealing to the analogy of nature (night and day, winter and spring) and also to the legend of the

Phoenix, the eastern bird alleged to rise again from death. Another early writing that may well come from the first century is the *Didache* (or Teaching of the Twelve Apostles), which concludes with a brief apocalypse, reminiscent of Matthew 24 and 2 Thessalonians, but lacking an imminent expectation of the end. Both these early writings illustrate the tendency for the Church, in the aftermath of the first enthusiasm, to use its standard eschatology of Parousia, resurrection, and judgement as a buttress for its moral teaching. The emphasis is on preparing for the coming of the Lord.

The Second Century

In the second century AD we find the early Church continuing to come to terms with the Parousia's delay and, in various ways, endeavouring to develop a Christian eschatology that steered a middle path between two extreme deviations—that of gnosticism, on the one hand, and that of what we may call, rather anachronistically for this early stage, adventism, on the other.

Gnosticism was itself a many-sided phenomenon, and it is probably a mistake to think of it just as a Christian heresy. Sects claiming esoteric 'knowledge' (gnosis), whereby men and women could achieve salvation, were common in the hellenistic world, with its mystery religions and theosophical systems. It was easy for gentile Christian communities in Greek environments such as those of Corinth or Alexandria to be tempted to interpret the Christian gospel as offering just such a secret, esoteric, saving knowledge. Already in the first century Paul had to oppose such tendencies among his Corinthian converts, and gnostic influences have sometimes been suspected behind John's radical and profound reflections on the knowledge of Christ that makes us free. For, while gnosticism did include an individualistic, futurist, eschatology of release from the body and the world at death, its main effect on Christianity was with regard to present experience of salvation and liberation. Sometimes this led to moral licence, more often to extreme asceticism and a thorough spiritualizing of Christian teaching. The gnostics thought of themselves as a spiritual elite, initiated into the true meaning of the gospel. It has often been thought that early Christians were tempted by gnostic versions of the faith as a reaction against apocalyptic in the face of the Parousia's delay. And, indeed, the gnostics treated both Jewish and Christian apocalyptic as symbolic, cryptic codes for spiritual, inner, knowledge. This then was one of the extremes against which the early Church had to take a stand. Notable among the second-century gnostic leaders, about whom we read from their Christian opponents, were Basilides in Alexandria and Valentinus in Rome.[1]

The other deviation, which, for the sake of a single identifying term, I call 'adventism', goes to the opposite extreme in embracing, literally, the imminent Parousia expectation in the light of some claimed special revelation of the true meaning of Jewish and Christian apocalyptic, particularly Daniel and Revelation. The leading second-century example of this tendency is Montanism. Montanus was a Christian convert in Asia Minor who fell into a trance and prophesied that the heavenly Jerusalem would soon descend to a plain in Phrygia. Many Christians left their homes and followed Montanus there to await its coming. Elsewhere Montanism became a sect practising extreme moral rigour and claiming special revelation from the Spirit. Its most notable supporter was Tertullian, one of the leading Christian theologians of the West, who became increasingly sympathetic to the sect early in the third century.[2]

Against these two deviating tendencies the Church of the second century tried, in its formulations of the Christian hope, to steer a middle path. Against gnosticism, it continued to affirm the future realities of Parousia, resurrection, judgement, and final consummation. Against adventism, it refused to countenance alleged special revelations, and developed instead the Lukan conception of a salvation history, including an age of the Church between Christ's resurrection and the Parousia. By and large the apocalyptic framework was retained, but there was considerable variety in its interpretation

---

[1] See Alasdair Logan, 'Gnosticism', in Adrian Hastings, Alistair Mason, and Hugh Pyper (eds.), *The Oxford Companion to Christian Thought* (Oxford: Oxford University Press, 2000), 268–9.

[2] Whether or not Tertullian actually left the Church and joined the sect, as Augustine asserted, is not clear. See D. H. Williams, 'Tertullian', in Ian S. Markham (ed.), *The Blackwell Companion to the Theologians*, I (Chichester: Wiley-Blackwell, 2009), 217–18.

and considerable freedom in speculation concerning the details of
the end.

The second-century 'Apostolic Fathers' provide some further evidence for the nature of Christian hope in this early period. Ignatius of
Antioch, on his way to martyrdom in Rome, wrote a number of
letters, in which, among other things, he speaks of his longing to
share Christ's sufferings and to 'attain to Jesus Christ'. The link
between present experience and future hope is manifest in his famous
teaching about the Eucharist as 'the medicine of immortality'.
Another second century text is the so-called Epistle of Barnabas,
mainly concerned to show that the chief tenets of Christianity were
prophesied beforehand in the Old Testament. These include Christ's
future coming to judge the living and the dead, and the thousand-
year rule (millennium) before the final new creation. A third example
is another apocalypse, known as *The Shepherd of Hermas*, which
contained depictions of the coming plagues and Last Judgement,
designed, as often in the sub-apostolic period, to reinforce the need
for penitence and a Christian way of life. There are other apocalypses
giving vivid descriptions of hell, and there are many Christian inter-
polations into Jewish apocalyptic texts as well.

Of the second-century apologists who set out to defend the Christian faith against its Jewish and Graeco-Roman critics (some being
addressed to the Roman Emperor in person), it is sufficient to
mention Justin Martyr, who, in his *Dialogue with Trypho*, argues,
like Barnabas, that, since the prophets' predictions of all the details of
Christ's life and resurrection had been fulfilled, there could be no
doubt that the prophecies of Christ's second coming and the Last
Judgement would also be fulfilled. Of particular interest is what he
says about the millennium. He himself has no doubt that the millennium has been prophesied as well, but he admits that many true
Christians think otherwise. This shows that millenarian belief was by
no means universal in the Church's eschatology at this time.

Millenarian belief was shared, however, by Irenaeus, probably the
most interesting of the second-century Christian theologians. From
his *Against Heresies* we get some idea both of the difficulties already
felt over Christian teaching about the last things and of the range of
speculation that creative Christian minds permitted themselves on
the subject. One set of problems that perplexed the early Christians
concerned the fate of those who had already died before the end-time

and the final resurrection. Texts from the Gospels and from Paul suggested that the faithful, at death, went straight to Christ; but the Parousia doctrine and the strongly physical belief in a future resurrection tended to prevail, and Irenaeus postulates an invisible place of sojourning, where souls await the resurrection. He makes an exception for the martyrs, however. They do go straight to Christ to return with him in glory at the Parousia. Millenarians, such as Irenaeus, were faced with a further problem. For they had to postulate two resurrections, one of the faithful, who would be raised to reign with Christ in a liberated and renewed creation, and a second, final, resurrection of all for the last judgement at the end of the millennial reign, after which redeemed men and women will receive a blessed immortality, fully restored to God's image and likeness. This picture was complicated by the suggestion, developed by subsequent writers, that the dead, awaiting resurrection, experience a foretaste of their eventual fate at the Last Judgement, a suggestion that tends, as we shall see, to make the idea of a single and final judgement somewhat redundant in the Christian scheme of things.

It might appear that what I have described as the second century's 'middle way' between the extreme deviations of gnosticism and adventism was closer to the latter than to the former; for the Church did not repudiate the Parousia doctrine, and the popularity of millenarian belief reinforces the impression of an adventist element in the teaching of the Church Fathers themselves. However, the Fathers did repudiate alleged private revelations concerning the place and date of the Lord's coming, and for the most part renounced belief in its imminence. Tertullian's support for Montanism suggested a definite break with the Church. Moreover, millenarian belief, as Justin Martyr noted, was not universal. The most important indication of this is that it found no place at all in the early Christian creeds that were in the process of formulation at this time, as we see from the *Apostolic Tradition* of Hippolytus at the beginning of the third century. Eventually, the so-called Apostles' Creed was content to conclude its section on Christ with the words 'from which he will come to judge the quick and the dead' and its final section with the words 'the resurrection of the body' (in its earliest form—'the flesh') and 'the life everlasting', admittedly without attempting to integrate these beliefs, but certainly with no mention of the millennium. Although, as we shall see, in the course of time millenarian belief (or 'chiliasm', to give it its Greek name) was repudiated and relegated to sectarian versions of Christianity, it is only fair to point out that, in the second century, it did provide a kind of this-worldly hope for Christians in addition to their ultimate hope of heaven. As indicated at the end of the last chapter, the experience of persecution and the hostility of the all-powerful Roman Empire left little room for hope for the historical future of human society. Only the Christian communities themselves provided a present refuge from the world and an anticipatory form of the transcendent, other-worldly, heavenly future. But millenarian belief could be taken to suggest some hope after all for this world. It pictured a transformed earthly future after the return of Christ, where the enemies of God would be defeated and a kingdom of peace and plenty established. As with late Jewish apocalyptic, Christian millenarianism flourished in times of persecution, when there seemed no hope for human society without drastic divine intervention. We shall see how, much later, after the conversion of Constantine, a more realistic hope for the future of humanity on earth began to be developed within the broader, transcendent, framework of the Christian hope of resurrection.

The Third Century

It is not necessary to trace here the thought of Hippolytus or Tertullian (before his move towards Montanism). These anti-gnostic writers pursued similar lines of thought on Christian eschatology to those of Irenaeus. But the third century, especially in the east, saw something of a swing back in the direction of gnosticism with the spiritualizing of eschatology, as in the hands of that great speculative thinker, Origen. It was not just the increasing implausibility, with the passage of time, of adventism in its more literal forms. One has to appreciate that the language of late Jewish apocalyptic, transferred from its original setting into the wider context of Hellenistic culture, had a very different and much stranger ring—as indeed it has for us today. It is not surprising that the gnostics sought to reinterpret its symbolism in terms of present esoteric knowledge. The Alexandrian scholars, Clement and Origen, influenced as they were by Platonist philosophy, also sought a symbolic interpretation of the language of

Christian eschatology, although, unlike the gnostics, they retained its future reference.

Clement of Alexandria, at the beginning of the third century, had already taught that souls endure remedial punishment and purification by 'fire' in a metaphorical sense. The righteous acquire, by the action of God, a growing likeness to God, until they find their place in the many 'mansions' of heaven. Only those who persist in stubborn unbelief incur the final condemnation. Origen went further than this. He too envisaged a probationary or intermediate state between death and the end of the world, but his treatment of Parousia and judgement constitutes a striking spiritualization of eschatology. Christ will not appear in a particular place. His divinity will be manifested to all, and by their reaction to his goodness men and women will bring judgement on themselves. Moreover the pains or 'fires' of hell cannot, in Origen's view, be everlasting. It follows from the goodness of God that in the end the whole creation will be restored into unity and the enemies of Christ finally overcome. By this he means that their enmity will be finally overcome, and it seems that he even included the devil within the scope of the final restoration of all things (the 'apokatastasis'—to give it its Greek name):

When it is said that 'the last enemy shall be destroyed', it is not to be understood as meaning that his substance, which is God's creation, perishes, but that his purpose and hostile will perish; for these do not come from God but from himself. Therefore his destruction means not his ceasing to exist but ceasing to be an enemy and ceasing to be death. Nothing is impossible to omnipotence; there is nothing that cannot be healed by its Maker.[3]

Thus we encounter the most remarkable instance of Christian universalism in early Church theology. Such universalism, mentioned in the previous chapter as implicit only in certain strands of the New Testament, is here brought out and developed to its logical conclusion. Needless to say, this view was exceptional, and much criticized at the time and indeed throughout the fourth century.

Origen's conception of the resurrection body and the final consummation is also of great interest. It will come as no surprise that he was opposed to literal, physical, spatio-temporal, conceptions of resurrection. For the same reason, he decisively rejects millenarian

[3] Origen, *De Principiis*, III.vi.5.

beliefs. Resurrection means the replacement of the fleshly body by 'a spiritual body, such as may be able to dwell in heaven'. It is not just the soul that bears the continuity between this mortal life and the resurrection life. The new body will have the same 'form' as the old, but its 'substance' will be spirit, not flesh and blood. There is an intriguing attempt to combine Pauline and Platonic thought at this point. In the final consummation or restoration, the redeemed creature will enjoy, through the vision of God, a union with God that can even be called 'deification'. This conception of the ultimate Christian hope was to have a central place in eastern Christian thought up to the present day.

Talk of restoration or restitution in Origen, as in Irenaeus, is suggestive of a cyclical rather than a linear view of creation and to that extent foreign to the Judaeo-Christian tradition. Origen was even prepared to consider the possibility that the redeemed, through their free will, might fall again, and that the whole process would have to be repeated. On the other hand, a surer instinct led him to affirm the opposite view:

And we learn from the Apostle what it is that restrains free will in the ages to come when he says 'Love never fails'... And John says, 'He who abides in love abides in God'. Thus love, which is the greatest of all things, will restrain every creature from falling. Then God will be all in all.[4]

Before we turn to the developments of Christian eschatology in late antiquity, it is worth pausing to consider one of the last flowerings of apocalyptic, millenarian, eschatology in mainstream Christianity, this time in the West. Lactantius' *Divine Institutes* was written soon after the beginning of the fourth century and before Christianity was declared the official religion of the Roman Empire. The work can hardly be called profound theology, but its seventh book on 'The Blessed Life' has become one of the classics of Western spirituality, and it is interesting to recognize here the power that apocalyptic undoubtedly still had to be the vehicle of a deeply felt Christian faith. Lactantius makes it clear that any who set themselves to find the path of virtue and the knowledge and worship of God should understand God's plan for the world and the reward of eternal happiness that God has in store for them. He spells out this plan and this reward in all the detail of apocalyptic millenarianism. Lactantius has no sense

---

[4] Origen, *Commentary on the Epistle to the Romans*, verse 10.

for the symbolic. He takes the apocalyptic entirely literally, the six, thousand-year, ages of the world corresponding to the six days of creation, the coming seventh millennium corresponding to the Sabbath day of God's rest, the increasing wars culminating in the appearance of two Antichrists, then the return of Christ. There will be two resurrections—that of the just to join in Christ's victories over the evil ones and reign with him in a fertile harmonious world—and then, after a renewed rebellion and a final battle, the second resurrection to the Last Judgement, the wicked rising to eternal punishment and the just to be like angels, as white as snow, always living in the sight of the Most High. Lactantius ends his book by reminding the reader that this secret knowledge is intended to encourage everyone to take up wisdom and true religion.

The Post-Constantinian Church and Late Antiquity

The conversion of Constantine and the eventual establishment of Christianity, towards the end of the fourth century, as the official religion of the Roman Empire made a considerable difference to Christian hope for this world. The ultimate Christian hope, of course, remained the same. But now for the first time the prospect was opened up of the christianizing of the whole known world. It is interesting to observe this change in the writings of the first church historian, Eusebius of Caesarea (c.260–c.340). In his panegyric on Constantine, as well as in his history of the Church, Eusebius develops a theory of the Christian empire. It was a theory, however, that drew as much on hellenistic political writing as on Paul's teaching about 'the powers that be' (Rom. 13: 1). Indeed, when compared with radical Christian apocalypticism, this new theology of a christianized world looks somewhat conservative, syncretistic, and temporizing. There are those who hold that the conversion of Constantine was a great disaster for the Christian Church. As its hope for the world became more realistic, it also became more worldly, and not surprisingly, under a Christian emperor, it took a politically conservative rather than a radical form. Not that the Church at large succumbed to the ideology of a christianized Roman Empire. Only sporadically did it identify the empire with Christ's Kingdom. When we turn, at the end of this chapter, to the dominant figure of Augustine (354–430), we shall find that the greatest Christian theologian of late antiquity, not least in the light of the troubles of the empire in his time, painted a much more negative picture of the earthly city.

But first, let us consider fourth- and fifth-century Christian thought about the more ultimate Christian hope—the ultimate framework within which Christian attitudes to the historical future developed and changed. This basic framework did not change. Indeed, no fourth- or fifth-century mainstream Christian theologian went as far as Origen had done in reinterpreting the great themes of resurrection, judgement, heaven, and hell. The influence of Origen was certainly great, but in both East and West reactions to his daring speculations set in. Reflection on 'the last things', we should recall, was by no means the chief preoccupation of Christian theology at this time. These were the centuries in which the Christian doctrines of the Incarnation and the Trinity were finally hammered out, often under considerable political pressure, against strong heretical movements, such as Arianism, which threatened to split not only the Church but also the empire. The great councils of Nicaea (325), Constantinople (381), and Chalcedon (451) were concerned with these more central Christian doctrines, not with eschatology. But the theologians of both East and West also turned their minds to the ultimate Christian hope, and it is worth summarizing what they had to say on resurrection, judgement, heaven, and hell.

Many writers in the East objected to Origen's views on resurrection. Appealing to God's omnipotence, they affirmed the crude belief that it is the very same material, earthly, body that will be raised to eternal life. Jerome (c.342–420) in the West also came to hold this view, and pressed it in great detail. Others tended to qualify rather than to contradict Origen. Cyril of Jerusalem (c.315–86), while stressing the identity of the resurrection body with the earthly body, taught also that it will be transformed and supernaturalized. Gregory of Nyssa (c.330–c.395) at times appears even closer to Origen in his treatment of the transformation involved, and in his recognition that bodily 'form' is more important than the specific 'matter'.[5] For Gregory, the resurrection body will be freed from those attributes, such as mortality

---

[5] Admittedly, Gregory does also, somewhat inconsistently, refer to the reconstitution of the same atoms. See Brian Daley, *The Hope of the Early Church: A Handbook of Patristic Eschatology* (Cambridge: Cambridge University Press, 1991), 82–4.

and susceptibility to injury and ageing, that were consequent upon the Fall. Closer to Cyril of Jerusalem were Western theologians such as Hilary of Poitiers (c.316–67), Ambrose of Milan (c.339–97) and his pupil, the great Augustine himself, who taught that our very fleshly bodies will be raised at the last day and clothed with incorruptibility. They will be perfect and mature (even the bodies of children who have died) and completely subject to the spirit. It is interesting to note that not even Augustine was able to accept the full implications of Origen's Pauline insight that 'flesh and blood cannot inherit the kingdom of God' (1 Cor. 15: 50, see above p. 27)—namely, that resurrection requires not a transformed body, but a transformed person with a new 'spiritual' body. Modern theology, as we shall see, has tended to follow Origen rather than Augustine here.

The necessity of a final judgement is affirmed by all the later Fathers, East and West. Often this necessity is argued on general grounds, as by John Chrysostom (c.347–407), appealing to the justice of God. Eastern Fathers, and Ambrose in the West, tended to follow Origen in suggesting that a person's own conscience, in the light of Christ's appearing, will be his own accuser. Some Western theologians toyed with the idea that the righteous and the wicked are judged already and only faltering Christians will require a final judgement, but Augustine insisted on a public vindication of God's justice for all at the end of time.

On heaven, the final destiny of the blessed, the Fathers expressed a diversity of views within the common conviction that the redeemed will enjoy everlasting life together with each other and the Lord. The Eastern emphasis was on 'divinization'. Here writers such as Gregory of Nazianzus (329–89), Gregory of Nyssa and Cyril of Alexandria (d. 444) followed Origen's usage of the language of deification in bringing out the meaning of union with God and participation in the life of Christ that the eternal life of heaven involves. But, despite the language, none of the Eastern Fathers went so far as to deny the basic distinction between Creator and creature.

In the West the dominant conceptions of the state of the blessed were those of the communion of saints (Ambrose and Jerome) and the vision of God (Augustine). For Augustine, men and women are made for the knowledge and love of God and, in the beatific vision, the blessed will finally realize their own true nature.

Hardly any Christian teacher in the fourth and fifth centuries agreed with Origen on the temporary and remedial nature of hell, although the two Gregorys are from time to time inclined in that direction, Gregory of Nazianzus on the plausible ground that eternal punishment seems unworthy of God. But, although we learn from Augustine that such ideas were common at the popular level in the West, the vast majority of theologians, including Augustine himself, affirm the everlasting anguish of the damned as the only view consistent with Scripture. Augustine, as is well known, darkened this picture of human destiny still further by a strong doctrine of predestination. (For comment on this profoundly pessimistic strand in Christian theology, see pp. 73–4 below.)

The prevailing hard-line teaching on hell is modified a little by the development of conceptions of purgatory, at least for Christian sinners. The uncertainty that we noted on the part of second-century writers over the interval between death and the final resurrection left some room for speculation over possible further purification during the interval. Prayers for the dead are justified along these lines by Eastern Fathers such as Cyril of Jerusalem and John Chrysostom, and purgatorial purification for Christian sinners is taught by Ambrose and Augustine in the West. The interval between death and final resurrection and judgement remained the greatest area of confusion in patristic eschatology. There was very little biblical material to which appeal could be made to settle the issue, and we shall see the problem recurring at later stages of Church history. But for Augustine, whatever scope there might be for purgatory between death and resurrection, the final judgement was certainly irrevocable and permanent.

What of the Parousia? While, as we shall see, it was no longer associated in the majority of Christian minds with a literally conceived millennium, belief in the second coming of Christ remained a cardinal feature of Christian eschatology, enshrined in the early creeds. Divorced from millenarian belief, it was now associated, as it had been for Paul and Luke, with the final resurrection and judgement and located at the end of history and the end of time. We have already noted the way in which the Lukan theology, embraced by many of the Fathers, envisaged a time of the Church and a more distant Parousia. Now the conversion of Constantine and a more positive Christian estimate of history added their weight to the case for a longer interval before the end. Located at the end of history, the Parousia was not so liable to be envisaged as occurring at a particular place. Christ would be manifest in judgement to the whole world. Here Origen's view tended to prevail, and Augustine lent it his great authority.

The demise of literal belief in the millennium was partly due to the influence of Origen and the spiritualizing arguments that weighed with him, but much more to Augustine's decisive identification of the millennium with the age of the Church. Augustine quotes Mark 3: 27 ('No one can enter a strong man's house and plunder his goods, unless he first binds the strong man') as showing that Satan was already bound with the first coming of Christ, and then applies Revelation 20 to the Church's life, which, he holds, will culminate in the final apostasy and battle with Antichrist, before the end. This acceptance of an element of apocalyptic indicates how Augustine was not prepared to christianize the Roman Empire in the manner of Eusebius. Indeed, it was the troubles of the Empire and the sack of Rome in 410, interpreted by pagans as evidence of the folly of a Christian empire, that prompted him to write his treatise on the relation between time and eternity, history and the Kingdom, in his famous book *The City of God.*

Augustine's book has been described as a theology of history, but it must be said that it remains a pretty negative contribution to the topic of this-worldly hope. Over against the earthly city of man, Augustine sees the heavenly city of God, represented by the Church, as the only sure basis for a lasting hope. Yet the Church exists in history and engages with the earthly city, rebuking it in the name of justice. Augustine has a very negative view of the basic dynamics of the earthly city. It is the city of Cain and ultimately of the devil, but in its actual forms in history it is open to criticism and influence by the heavenly city, embodied partially and fitfully in the Church. Consequently there remains some hope of improvement even in the earthly city. To that extent Augustine is recognizably a post-Constantinian theologian. But he is too aware of human wickedness and fallenness to allow much positive hope for humankind apart from participation, by God's grace, in the life of the transcendent heavenly city of God.

Conclusion

We have briefly traced the history of Christian eschatology in the early Church, noting its temporary flirtation with adventism and its more persistent, because more profound, flirtation with gnosticism. But against both extremes, the Christianity of the early creeds came to include a more or less standard eschatology of Parousia, resurrection, judgement, heaven, and hell. If millenarian belief and apocalyptic imagery tended to fall away, speculation continued over the nature of resurrection and our ultimate destiny. In the East, this was thought of in terms of divinization, in the West in terms of the vision of God, although, in both, the communion of saints was also an essential element. Until the conversion of Constantine, little hope was entertained for the secular world. Christian hope was a transcendent hope, anchored in the present experience of Christians in the Church, but directed to a heavenly future beyond death. For a time the picture was complicated by millenarian belief, but this did not last in mainstream Christianity. The conversion of Constantine opened up new possibilities for Christian hope for the historical future, but, in the light of the decline of Rome in the fifth century, the profound theological mind of Augustine reasserted the primacy of the heavenly city as the focus of Christian hope and the basis of Christian life. The State was no longer thought of as beyond the influence of the Church, but it was the Church that was at least the partial embodiment on earth of the heavenly city or kingdom.

A recognition of the variety of Christian thought about the last things in these early centuries, and of the problems of eschatology that remained unsolved, even in the Christianity of the creeds, will lead us to expect comparable freedom of interpretation and new developments in the Christian eschatology of subsequent centuries down to our own time. We may expect to discern a basic characteristic shape to the Christian hope, but, where details are concerned, we should not be surprised to find continuing diversity, uncertainty, and innovation in this of all areas of Christian theology. If one thing has emerged from our study of eschatology in the early Church, it is that here, especially, in Paul's wise words (1 Cor. 13: 12), 'we see in a glass darkly'.

4

The Middle Ages

Introduction

In our brief and selective sketch of the history of Christian eschatology, we now move on across some four or five centuries of consolidation (at least in Western Christendom) to look at the Christian hope as it had come to form part of the settled belief-system of the vast majority of men and women in the Christian West in the period we call the Middle Ages.

Once again we shall be concentrating on the ultimate Christian hope—on beliefs about the final destiny of men and women. But we shall also consider attitudes to the historical future; for, in different ways, historical developments in both State and Church led to changed expectations of what could be achieved in human society here on earth. Pope Gregory the Great (c.540–604), 'the father of the medieval Papacy', shared something of Augustine's pessimism about the earthly city, but by the time of the coronation, by Pope Leo III, of Charlemagne (c.742–814) as the first 'Holy Roman Emperor' in St Peter's, Rome, on Christmas Day 800, we find a much more positive appraisal of the political future. Indeed, in the panegyrics of Alcuin of York (c.735–804), an influential member of Charlemagne's court, we find echoes of Eusebius on Constantine. And the very concept of a Holy Roman Empire represents a new gloss on the worth and possibility of political power and organization. At the same time the Church itself was becoming more worldly and political, and this assimilation of the actual historical embodiments of both the earthly and the heavenly city led to a very different perspective on God's will for human society here on earth from what had prevailed in the pre-Constantinian early Church. There the Church had been seen as an ark of salvation from a doomed world. Now it was working together with emperors, kings, and princes to order and govern people's temporal as well as their spiritual life on earth. We shall note both developments of and reactions against this newer perspective in our treatment of the Middle Ages.

Popular Beliefs about the Last Things

There were, of course, in any view, distinct limits to what could be hoped for on this earth. First and foremost, there was the ever-present inexorable fact of death—the death of children, death by plague, death in battle. Moreover, for all its growing political involvements, the Church continued to teach the basic framework of Christian eschatology—Parousia, resurrection, judgement, heaven and hell—that it had inherited from Augustine and Gregory the Great. We shall shortly be considering some striking revivals of millenarian belief in the Middle Ages, but, even where Augustine's view prevailed, the old apocalyptic imagery continued to impose a limit on positive expectations for the historical future. The Parousia and the End would still be preceded by the appearance of Antichrist and the terrible wars and disasters of the end-time.

The common framework of belief about the end that came to form part of the settled consciousness of the whole medieval world is best seen in the exquisite sculpture and painting that adorn the Romanesque and Gothic cathedrals and churches of Europe. These works of art were both expressions of and visual aids to reinforce the Church's standard teaching on these matters. The twelfth-century Romanesque tympanum at Conques and the thirteenth-century central portal at Bourges, both in France, may be taken to illustrate the genre. They both exemplify the imaginative delight in spelling out the details of biblical and church teaching characteristic of the medieval mind. The tympanum at Conques is the more complicated of the two. It contains two main rows of sculpture. In the lower part of the bottom row, we see the fate of the just and of the wicked at death. In the left-hand portion, souls of the just are being led before a row of seated figures of whom the central one is Abraham. Here, we understand, they will enjoy a period of rest and refreshment before the final resurrection and judgement. To the right the wicked are being pushed through the gaping mouth of hell where devils torture them. Above these scenes, but still in the lower of the two main rows, the final resurrection is depicted, with the dead rising from their tombs. Above, in the upper row, sits Christ in judgement, in front of a large cross, held by angels. To his left—our right as we look at the scene—is another depiction of hell, now the permanent fate of the wicked, while to his right the redeemed are welcomed into paradise. (The artist, here as elsewhere, created less vivid portrayals of heaven than of hell.)

The portal at Bourges is a rather simpler affair. There is no clear depiction of an intermediate state. The lintel shows, in vivid detail, the dead rising from their tombs. Above, Christ sits in judgement. At his feet an angel weighs souls in the balance. To his left the damned are precipitated into hell, whose gaping mouth contains a burning cauldron. To his right, St Peter leads the blessed past the seated figure of Abraham (with a napkin full of souls in his bosom) to the beatific vision, symbolized by angels holding crowns.

The uncertainty over the fate of souls between death and the final resurrection, which we have noted at earlier stages in this study, is reflected in these works of art, both in the ambiguous place of Abraham in the Bourges portal and in the double depiction of hell at Conques. We note that, even where, at Conques, an intermediate state is portrayed, the theme of purgatory is absent. But in the later Middle Ages, as we shall see, the doctrine of purgatory was developed and encouraged to an extraordinary degree, and in later paintings, such as the altarpiece at Avignon (1453), we find the fires of purgatory from which an angel finally releases the purified soul.

Church teaching on the last things, thus depicted in painting and sculpture, certainly informed the minds and imaginations of medieval men and women. But we should not forget the imperfect control of the Church over popular belief, even in the Christian West. Powerful heretical movements established themselves in parts of Europe between the eleventh and thirteenth centuries. A fascinating glimpse into the minds of such people, in this case the Albigensian Cathars at the turn of the twelfth and thirteenth centuries, is provided by the records of the Inquisition into heresy at Montaillou, a village on the French side of the Pyrenees.[1] These give a vivid picture,

---

[1] See Emmanuel Le Roy Ladurie, *Montaillou: Cathars and Catholics in a French Village 1294–1324*, Eng. trans. (London: Scolar Press, 1978).

in the recorded testimonies of the villagers of Montaillou, of the heretical belief that the souls of the dead rush about among the living until the 'second death' admits them to the place of rest. There 'every soul will have as much wealth and happiness as every other, and all will be as one. And the souls will love one another as if they loved the soul of their father or of their children.' Ladurie comments on the absence of any talk of the beatific vision. 'The sacred is only the social transfigured.' It is worth considering how far this comment applies to orthodox popular belief as well.

There was much discussion in the Middle Ages, both at the popular level and in the monastic orders, as to when the world would end. There is no evidence, as used to be asserted, that there was a widespread expectation that the world would end in the year 1000. But prophecies of the coming of Antichrist were common at a later stage, a favourite date being 1260, in the light of Revelation 11: 3 and 12: 6, both of which verses mention 'a thousand, two hundred and three score days'. Popes and theologians discouraged such speculation, just as Augustine had done, but numerous other examples can be found.

Medieval Theology

The theology of the medieval schools, known as scholasticism, was remarkable for the thoroughness with which the details of Christian doctrine were worked out and systematized. This was as true of eschatology as it was of other areas of doctrine. Probably the main feature of medieval eschatology is its strongly juridical conception of God's righteousness in the exercise of judgement and the issuing of rewards and punishments.

The biblical data, often somewhat literally conceived, were fused with a picture of the cosmos largely derived from Aristotle into a comprehensive vision of God's unseen world beyond the grave, both in its present and in its future dimensions. In this sketch of medieval eschatology, we shall chiefly rely on Thomas Aquinas (c.1225–74), the greatest of the scholastic theologians.

By the time we reach the high Middle Ages, the distinction between what happens at death and what happens at the final resurrection has been sharpened and clarified, even if some of the details were still in dispute. At death will come the Particular Judgement, determining the fate of the individual in the intermediate state between death and the final resurrection at the time of the coming of Christ. Then will follow the General Judgement and the final consummation of all things.

Let us first consider the intermediate state. The initial point to note is that belief in the survival of the soul between the death of the body and the general resurrection requires some conception of the immortality of the soul. Despite Thomas's preference for Aristotle's understanding of the soul as the form of the body over Plato's doctrine of the soul's immortality, he nevertheless believed the human soul to be a spiritual reality capable of surviving the death of the body. Nevertheless its disembodied state is not its natural state, according to Thomas. It cannot fulfil all is potentialities, and, as F. C. Copleston puts it, it 'retains a natural orientation towards informing the body'.[2] The Particular Judgement at death establishes the direction of a person's will, and that, Thomas held, could not be changed. The redeemed cannot fall away again. Moreover, some of the redeemed—those, such as the saints, whose will is already purified—despite their temporary separation from the body, will be given at once their heavenly reward, the beatific vision of God, which is, in Thomas's terminology, our last end, that for which we were created. Thomas, not surprisingly, provides some rather tortuous arguments to show how the soul, before the final resurrection (and thus lacking some of its full potentialities) could nonetheless enjoy the beatific vision. The question became very much a debated issue in the fourteenth century. Pope John XXII astonished the theological world in 1331 by announcing, in a sermon, that at death the souls of the redeemed did not immediately enjoy the vision of God, but must wait 'under the altar of God' until the general resurrection. In this period they would be confronted only with the humanity of Christ. This teaching was reversed by the next pope, Benedict XII, in an official Bull of 1336, in which he asserted that the souls of the elect see God face to face immediately after the death of the body.

For Thomas Aquinas the fate of the damned was also fixed at death. There could be no further change for those who died with their wills set against God. They would immediately experience the fires of hell. Even

[2] F. C. Copleston, *Aquinas* (Harmondsworth: Penguin Books, 1955), 165.

more tortuous arguments were required to show how disembodied souls could suffer from physical fire! There is no need for us to go into these implausible aspects of the great doctor's teaching.

Not all the redeemed, however, despite the unchangeable direction of their wills, are sufficiently purified at death to be able to enjoy the beatific vision immediately. Thomas marshals a whole range of arguments from scripture and the Church's universal practice in praying for the dead, in favour of the doctrine of purgatory. It is interesting to note that, for Thomas, the pains of purgatory are intended solely to purge away the remaining effects of 'venial' sin (that is, sin that is not so deadly as to deprive the soul of grace altogether) in those already redeemed from the guilt of sin. The doctrine of the communion of saints encouraged Thomas to hold that the faithful may help the dead through this purifying process by prayers and by Masses said on their behalf.

The main reason why the doctrine of purgatory became so suspect in the later Middle Ages and at the time of the Reformation was not so much the notion as expounded by Thomas Aquinas, but rather the practice that grew up in the fourteenth and fifteenth centuries, first of the granting, and then of the sale, of indulgences, remissions by the Church of the temporal penalty for sin. These could be acquired by the living, both on their own behalf, so that they could look forward to a shorter time in purgatory, and on behalf of those already there—though only as a form of prayer, since the jurisdiction of the Church on earth was held not to extend beyond death. In the words of David Knowles, commenting on the increasing abuse of this practice, the faithful in the Middle Ages 'regarded indulgences in a legalistic and mechanistic way as providing passports to heaven, an illusion which encouraged and was stimulated by all kinds of unworthy and sacrilegious traffic'.[3]

The medieval conception of the afterlife was not confined to heaven, purgatory, and hell. The problem of those who died before Christ, especially the Old Testament saints, and the problem of unbaptized infants who died before incurring any guilt, led to the postulation of 'limbo'. As far as the Old Testament saints were concerned, this was a temporary abode or condition, from which they would be redeemed by Christ at the general resurrection. As far as unbaptized infants were

[3] See Hubert Cunliffe-Jones (ed.), *A History of Christian Doctrine* (Edinburgh: T. & T. Clark, 1978), 241.

concerned, this was an everlasting state, a happy state according to Thomas Aquinas, but lacking the supernatural beatific vision in store for the redeemed. The reader may well be disposed to think that there is little to be said for these ideas.

We must now pass on in this survey of medieval eschatology to consider the last things themselves. The medieval picture of the catastrophic events attending the end of the world and the return of Christ contains some features that we have already met and some that are relatively new.

Thomas Aquinas held that Antichrist, the embodiment of evil, will undoubtedly appear, but he was sensibly reserved about precisely when and for how long. But there is no reserve in his discussion of the very drastic happenings that will immediately proceed the advent of Christ, the resurrection of the dead, and the General Judgement. The celestial rotation of the heavens (a cosmological conception that Thomas took over from Aristotle) will stop, and a great conflagration will occur. As with the Flood of old, all men and women will perish in the Fire, so that all may be raised to judgement. (This notion of universal conflagration is based on a very literal acceptance of the apocalyptic imagery of 2 Peter 3: 10.) Curiously, in view of his earlier reserve, and in view of the universal cosmic nature of the final catastrophe, Thomas was prepared to speculate about the precise location of the General Judgement. He thought it most probable that it will take place in the valley of Josaphat by Mount Olivet, where the Ascension took place (Acts 1: 12).

As for the nature of the resurrection body with which all souls will now be clothed for all eternity, although in early scholasticism there was some uncertainty over its material or fleshly nature, by the time of Thomas Aquinas it was agreed that the very same fleshly body that had died would be raised (even reassembled, if necessary) and reunited with its soul. But it would also be transformed by God, becoming incorruptible and immortal, in accordance with God's original intention for bodily persons. (Here Thomas dealt at length and in astonishing detail with many particular difficulties, such as that of bodies consumed by cannibals.) Such risen bodily persons, Thomas taught, will not need those things that subserve the corruptible life, such as food and sex. The latter point reflects the fact that there will be no new human beings in heaven. Risen persons remain differentiated as men and women, however.

At the Last Judgement, the risen dead will finally be separated into the blessed and the damned (the only exception being that of unbaptized infants who remain in limbo). The risen bodies of the damned will, despite their incorruptibility, increase the damned souls' affliction. The details added here are among the least plausible as well as the most deplorable of Thomas's speculations. But his portrayal of the glorified bodies of the blessed in heaven contains many interesting and suggestive features. We need not pursue what he said about their location among the celestial bodies (an idea that depends on the Aristotelian conception of the universe), but his treatment of the perfected incorruptible bodies of the blessed, completely under the control of the souls whose proper embodiment they are, is well worth pondering. Perfectly embodied, the souls of the blessed are now able to exercise all their potentialities in their enjoyment of God in the beatific vision. And Thomas had a beautiful answer to the objection that the vision of God must ultimately become tedious:

Nothing that is contemplated with wonder can be tiresome, since as long as the thing remains in wonder it continues to stimulate desire. But the divine substance is always viewed with wonder by any created intellect. So it is impossible for an intellectual substance to become tired of this vision.[4]

The doctrine of the beatific vision may be regarded as the high point of the medieval understanding of the last things. Here the various strands of medieval theology and spirituality, drawing particularly on the Augustinian tradition, come together. Reference to spirituality reminds us of the role of experience in shaping this theology. Bernard of Clairvaux (1090–1153) in the twelfth century and the Franciscan theologian Bonaventure (c.1217–74) in the thirteenth both insisted that the ecstasy of Christian mystical experience constitutes a foretaste of the beatific vision of the God who is Love, and who made men and women for eternal union with himself.

The Revival of Millenarianism

The sculpture of the great cathedrals and the theology of Thomas Aquinas sum up, in their different ways, the standard eschatology of the Middle Ages. With some embellishments and modifications they

---

[4] Thomas Aquinas, *Summa contra Gentiles*, bk. III, ch. 62.

illustrate the ultimate Christian hope as taught in the Church from the time of Augustine. But now we must consider the question of this-worldly hope, of hope for a better ordering of human life on earth in the historical future before the cataclysmic events that will herald the end. Here the Middle Ages saw some striking revivals of millenarian belief.

Augustine's view that the notion of the millennium referred to the age of the Church tended to prevail from the fifth century onwards. We do not encounter the millennium in medieval sculpture and painting, nor in most scholastic theology. But revivals of millenarian belief, albeit in somewhat different forms from that of the early centuries, did also occur in the Middle Ages and gained widespread popular support. They can be divided into two categories—'political' millenarianism and 'spiritual' millenarianism. What differentiates both forms from early millenarianism is that dramatic changes and improvements in human life on earth were now expected before rather than after the return of Christ.

It was suggested in Chapter 3 that millenarian belief did provide a kind of hope for this world prior to the end, but only through the large-scale divine intervention of the return of Christ and the first resurrection—that of the redeemed—to reign over the earth after the defeat of Antichrist. The most implausible aspect of this view was its doctrine of the two resurrections, one, of the saints, at the beginning of the thousand-year reign and the other, of all, for the Last Judgement. The great attraction of Augustine's view was that it did away with the idea of two resurrections, interpreted the millennial age as that of the Church following upon Christ's first coming, and located the Parousia, resurrection, and judgement at the end of history. But, as the centuries passed and the Church became established, with an increasingly worldly structure in the midst of more or less secular empires and kingdoms, Augustine's view itself acquired a certain implausibility. For it failed to match the dynamism of biblical apocalyptic and its concern for universal history under the providence of God. Drastic change was looked for only at the end.

Reactions against the standard medieval eschatology took the form of much more concrete expectations of a new age of peace and equality before the end—an age, admittedly, like Augustine's, prior to the Parousia and the resurrection, but something very different from peoples' present experience of political and ecclesiastical life.

In its more political forms, medieval millenarianism envisaged a messianic emperor who would unite Christendom in a single empire of peace, which would last until the coming of Antichrist. This theory, widely used to support the ideology of the Crusades, was fuelled in the twelfth century by the popularizing of certain earlier tracts (the Tiburtine Sibyl from the fourth century and Pseudo-Methodius from the seventh century) that prophesied a last great Roman Emperor who would defeat the enemies of Christ and establish a glorious reign of peace. These tracts were supplemented by new prophecies, more specifically related to the times, focusing these political hopes on figures such as the Holy Roman Emperor Frederick II, who recovered Jerusalem for the West in 1228 and proclaimed himself the instrument of God. At later stages, other rulers became the focus of these hopes.

Apocalyptic millenarianism was here being used in a this-worldly sense, reminiscent of the Old Testament expectation of a messianic king. It was hardly at this stage a vehicle of revolutionary sentiment, as it was to become later. It was closer to the imperial ideology of Constantine and Charlemagne, and, as already mentioned, it was employed to gain support for the Crusades. It did not simply sacralize the status quo. Its future-oriented, idealistic, hope for a reign of universal peace and plenty could easily be transferred to more radical uses. Such radical political millenarianism may have been an element in the Peasants' Revolt in England in 1381.

Even more significant as a reaction against the standard Augustinian eschatology of the Middle Ages was the spiritual millenarianism of Joachim of Fiore (c.1132–1202) and the spiritual Franciscans. This too involved a rejection of Augustine's conception of the Church as the fulfilment of the prophecies of Revelation 20. But, unlike the political millenarians, Joachim and his followers did not expect an age of peace before the coming of Antichrist. Rather they thought that Antichrist was imminent or here already. The new age would dawn with his overthrow and last for a greater or lesser time between the defeat of Antichrist and the Parousia. Moreover, the new age, they held, would be a spiritual not a political phenomenon. It would entail the purification of the Church and the conversion of the heathen.

A number of earlier writers had taken up the possibility—against what I have called the standard eschatology—of interpreting the interval between the defeat of Antichrist and the return of Christ as longer and more significant than the usual exegesis of Daniel and Revelation allowed. Joachim developed this idea into a striking three-fold (trinitarian) theology of universal history. Joachim was a monk and visionary who founded a monastery at Fiore in Calabria. He was encouraged by the Pope to write down his apocalyptic interpretations of scripture. In his *Book of Concordance* and in his *Exposition on the Apocalypse* we read of three periods or ages: the age of the Father, corresponding to the Old Testament dispensation; the age of the Son, the New Testament dispensation of Christ and the Church; and the age of the Spirit, in which new religious orders would arise to reform the Church, convert the world, and establish spiritual peace and unity on earth. Each age, he held, was of forty-two generations (a generation being thought of as thirty years), and he expected the age of the Spirit to begin in the year 1260. Since he seems to have equated the age of the Spirit with the millennium after the defeat of Antichrist, it would follow that Antichrist was already born and would shortly raise his head. In a celebrated interview in Sicily with Richard 'Lion-heart', who was on his way to Palestine on the third Crusade, Joachim said that 'Antichrist is already born in the city of Rome, and will be elevated to the Apostolic see'. As far as we know, this is the first association of Antichrist with the Pope of Rome. Joachim can hardly have meant to identify the actual Pope with Antichrist, since he remained on good terms with the popes of his day. Probably he envisaged some kind of usurpation of the papacy by the enemies of Christ in the course of the conflict that would usher in the new age. But later millenarian groups, including some of the more radical Franciscans, began to see in the papacy itself the heart of opposition to a truly spiritual Church, and this idea, identifying Rome with the whore of Babylon (Revelation 17) and the Pope with Antichrist was to have a powerful future at the time of the Reformation.

It is not surprising that some of the Franciscans of the thirteenth century should have seen their founder (St Francis of Assisi, *c.*1181–1226) and their new order as a fulfilment of Joachim's prophecies and as the inauguration of the new age. The radical Franciscans, known as the Spirituals, may not have gone as far as Gerardo of Borgo San Donnino, who issued an interpretation of Joachim's works in 1254 identifying the Pope with Antichrist and prophesying the overthrow of the institutional Church in 1260. But spiritual Franciscans, such as Peter Olivi (*c.*1248–98), wrote apocalyptic tracts very hostile to the 'carnal' Church, as they called it, and the result was the suppression of the Spirituals by Pope John XXII in 1318.

It will readily be seen that these revivals of millenarianism, whether in the political form of a universal empire of peace prior to the coming of Antichrist or in the spiritual form of a spiritual age subsequent to the overthrow of Antichrist, represented very different kinds of Christian hope from the standard eschatology of Thomas Aquinas. Without rejecting in any way the more ultimate hope of a future with God beyond death, they held out a more immediate and concrete hope of a better earthly future for humankind in history. The power of apocalyptic imagery to evoke and sustain increasingly radical, even revolutionary, hopes for a social life on earth will be further illustrated in the next chapter.

The Divine Comedy of Dante Alighieri

It is fitting to conclude our picture of the Christian hope in the Middle Ages by returning to the standard eschatology as presented in one of the greatest works of literature of all time, Dante's *La Divina Commedia*.

Dante Alighieri (1265–1321) was an Italian poet and philosopher, who certainly held strong views on the need for a universal monarchy and for an unpolitical Church, but the crown of his work was the great poem, composed in the last period of his life, in which he presents his vision of the future beyond death. It is at the same time an allegory of grace and salvation both for the individual and for the community in this present life, but the vision gives us as vivid a picture as there could possibly be of the framework of belief and hope within which medieval men and women lived out their days.

The vision is set at Easter in the year 1300, and Dante is led from a dark wood into the bowels of the earth by the pagan poet Virgil, who acts as his guide through hell and purgatory. The nine circles of hell down to the centre of the earth where Satan dwells reflect the deepening degrees of evil that ensnare the soul, and the concomitant torments brought upon itself. 'Abandon hope, all ye that enter here' is the last line of the inscription on its gate. The first circle of hell is that of limbo, the region of the unbaptized and the virtuous pagans. This and this alone is the circle of hell visited by Christ in 'the harrowing of hell' when, in the time between his crucifixion and his resurrection, he came to rescue the souls of the Old Testament patriarchs. There is no torment here in limbo, only grief for 'loss undying'. In the second circle, Dante finds the lustful, including the famous lovers such as Helen, Cleopatra, Dido, and Paolo and Francesca, all tossed for ever in a howling wind. In the third circle the gluttonous lie wallowing in the mire; in the fourth the hoarders and the spendthrifts roll rocks against each other. The fifth circle, the last of upper hell, contains the wrathful, some tearing each other with their teeth, others lying sullen in black mud. Only in nether hell, beyond the red-hot walls of the city of Dis across the river Styx (Dante builds the myths of Greece and Rome into his picture), do we encounter fire. The sixth circle here is that of the heretics, who lie in burning tombs. The circles now become more complex. The seventh contains three rings for the violent against others, against themselves, and against God. Then, beyond a great barrier, are found the ten trenches of the eighth circle, where perpetrators of different kinds of fraud suffer a variety of torments. Here several popes are found. The ninth circle, a deep well at the bottom of the abyss guarded by giants, contains the traitors, ranging from traitors to their kindred plunged in ice to the three figures of Judas, Brutus, and Cassius, traitors to God and the Empire, who are perpetually devoured by Satan himself.

Dante and Virgil emerge from hell on the opposite side of the earth from Jerusalem and climb the mount of purgatory. Here those who have repented are brought on the 'ship of souls' to expiate their sin. First, outside the gate are found the excommunicate, the late repentant, and the unshriven. The gate of purgatory is Peter's gate, for the ascending souls are on their way to heaven. On seven terraces the penitent sinners expiate the seven deadly sins, from pride up to lust. At each stage an angel commends, with examples, the opposite virtue, from meekness up to chastity. At the top of the mountain is a sacred forest—the earthly paradise of innocence, where Virgil can lead Dante no further. His new guide, come down from heaven to show him the way, is Beatrice, the girl he had loved in Florence as a child, who had died in 1290, and who had long since been idealized in the poet's imagination.

Beatrice and Dante gaze towards the sun and ascend from the earth into the celestial spheres. In each of the nine concentric heavens, from that of the moon to that of the 'Primum Mobile' beyond the fixed stars (the Ptolemaic Aristotelian picture of the universe, as adopted by Thomas Aquinas, is presupposed), Dante converses with the blessed at their various levels. In the fourth heaven, that of the sun, for example, Dante meets St Thomas Aquinas, who tells him the story of St Francis and instructs him in the mysteries of creation. Already at the fifth heaven, the heaven of Mars, where Dante encounters warriors such as Charlemagne and Roland, he is given a vision of Christ and his cross, and at the eighth heaven, beyond the just and the contemplatives of the sixth and seventh heavens, he beholds the Church Triumphant, the Virgin Mary, and the saints, and, for a moment again, the brightness and the glory of Christ. St Peter examines Dante on the theological virtues of faith, hope, and love, before they ascend to the ninth heaven, the Primum Mobile, where Dante is given a vision of the nature of time and creation. Finally, Beatrice, transfigured, leaves him to resume her place in the highest heaven, the Empyrean, encompassing all the others, where Dante is now led by St Bernard towards the vision of God. The Empyrean is contemplated under the figure of a snow-white rose. Beatrice is glimpsed enthroned. The blessed and the angels and, again, the Virgin Mary are seen amid the countless petals of the rose. Then Dante looks towards God. He sees the whole universe in God and finally the triune God himself:

> Within the being—lucid, bright and deep—
> of that high brilliance, there appeared to me
> three circling spheres, three coloured, one in span.
> And one, it seemed, was mirrored by the next,
> twin rainbows, arc to arc. The third seemed fire,
> and breathed to first and second equally.[5]

As he gazes, the second, mirrored, sphere acquires within itself a human form. The divine light floods his mind as it struggles with these mysteries and he finds his will and his desire moved solely now by the love of God, 'the love that moves the sun and the other stars'.

---

[5] Dante Alighieri, *The Divine Comedy 3: Paradiso*, trans. and ed. Robin Kirkpatrick (London: Penguin Books, 2007), 325.

Conclusion

Whether we consider the sculpture of Bourges Cathedral, the theology of Thomas Aquinas, or the sublime poetry of Dante Alighieri, we are likely to find the accepted framework of Christian belief and hope, within which medieval men and women lived their lives, extremely impressive in its scope and detail, as well as in the confidence with which it was clearly held.[6] Nevertheless, the eschatology of the medieval Church cannot be contemplated without considerable reservation. It is not just a question of the excessive juridical emphasis on rewards and punishments that characterized religion in the Middle Ages. The whole medieval world view strikes us as fixed and static, and its eschatological horizon seems distant and static too, affecting everyday life only in terms of a distant threat or promise. The sense of urgency and immediate import characteristic of Pauline or Johannine eschatology seems absent here, as does the moral sense of Origen or Gregory of Nazianzus that everlasting punishment is unworthy of God.

The more we examine the medieval framework of belief in the last things, the more problematic it appears. For one thing, no modern theologian, trained in the critical study of the Bible and Christian tradition (the significance of which will be examined in Part Three of this book) would suppose that we are in a position to set out the destiny of humankind as precisely and in such detail as Thomas Aquinas thought he could. But even the general features of medieval eschatology contain some theologically implausible elements. Admittedly, the various interpretations of the millenarian language of Revelation 20, whether as referring to the Church or to the Empire or to a political utopia or to a new age of the Spirit, all involved the abandonment of the idea of two resurrections. Nevertheless, medieval eschatology was still firmly committed to belief in two judgements—the Particular Judgement at death and the General Judgement at the coming of Christ and the general resurrection. In subsequent chapters we shall see how

---

[6] Its power to capture the religious imagination could be illustrated further by the thirteenth-century poem the *Dies Irae*, still found in the Latin Requiem Mass.

Christian theologians have tried to work out a more unified picture of human destiny.

As for the millenarian revivals themselves, whether in their political or in their spiritual form, the modern historian may well be struck by their utopian and unrealistic nature. But the historian will also have to recognize something of their power—the continuing power of apocalyptic, that is—to evoke movements of reform against a static, worldly, Church, or even of revolution against a feudal world picture.

5

The Reformation

Introduction

In turning to the Reformation of the sixteenth century, we encounter
one of the major factors making for the breakdown of the Middle
Ages. The reformers did not reject the overall framework of the fear of
hell or the hope of heaven (though purgatory was denied decisively
on both theological and practical grounds[1]). But within that framework they found a more urgent and dynamic sense of the new age in
which a Christian man or woman is already living. In their recovery
of the Bible and of the impact of the original gospel, they came to give
much greater emphasis to the eschatological tension between the
'now' and the 'not yet' that was characteristic of New Testament
hope. And, as we shall see, they applied it to their understanding of
the Church and of human history in much more theologically
searching and profound ways than had been the case with Joachim
of Fiore and other Pre-Reformation critics of the medieval Church.

The reformers' onslaught on the medieval Church—their denunciation of Rome and of contemporary clergy for worldliness and
immorality—had indeed been anticipated by the spiritual Franciscans and by many others. John Wycliffe (c.1330–84) in fourteenth-
century England, for example, closely prefigured the reformers in his
insistence on the authority of the Bible and its availability in the
native tongue. Moreover, his sense of the eternity of God, present in
power to all times, past, present and future, can be seen as a form of
'realized' eschatology, more concerned with the faith of the believer

---

[1] The Reformers not only denounced the abuse of the sale of indulgences
(see p. 58). They also held purgatory to be incompatible with the doctrine of
justification by faith.

and with immediate reform than with any ultimate future hope. John Hus (c.1372–1415) in Bohemia was influenced by Wycliffe's teachings, but, as with some of Wycliffe's followers in England, the Lollards, that influence had much more radical effects. Moreover, in Bohemia, the apocalyptic tradition was drawn upon for the preaching and enactment of social revolution. The more radical Hussites known as Taborites from their mountain stronghold south of Prague (named after the biblical Mount Tabor) embraced a form of apocalyptic millenarianism that led to violent revolt, the abolition of property, and the setting-up of anarchic communes. They were suppressed by force in 1434. By contrast, the Dominican friar Girolamo Savonarola (1452–98) at the end of the fifteenth century in Florence, while denouncing papal abuses in passionate apocalyptic imagery, went back to an older form of political millenarianism in focusing his hopes on Charles VIII of France. Savonarola was himself denounced as Antichrist by the Italian humanist Marsilio Ficino (1433–99).

At the end of this chapter we shall consider the radical millenarians of the Reformation itself, but it is important to realize that the great reformers did not adopt millenarian views, nor did they encourage radical social change. They certainly used apocalyptic imagery in denunciation of Rome as the whore of Babylon and of the Pope as Antichrist. But their positive teaching in eschatology as in other areas of doctrine represented an inner spiritual rediscovery of the biblical experience of a living God active in history and bringing the dimension of eternity to bear immediately upon the problems of time.

The Eschatology of the Leading Reformers

Martin Luther (1483–1546)

Luther's eschatology was called by Gordon Rupp an eschatology of faith.[2] By this he meant that, for Luther, eschatological hope is determined and controlled by one's experience, in faith, of God's justifying grace in Jesus Christ. This is an indication of the priority for Luther of his rediscovery of Paul and the Gospels over apocalyptic

---

[2] Gordon Rupp, *The Righteousness of God: Luther Studies* (London: Hodder and Stoughton, 1953), 255.

speculation based on the book of Revelation. Luther learned from Paul that the decisive events of ultimate significance for humanity and the world had already happened and could be appropriated in faith, so that, while still in time, we are caught up into God's eternity. The eschatological moment is the moment when one accepts what God has done for us in Christ. So Luther rejects the idea of time and eternity as stretching in linear relationship into a distant future. He does not deny the future consummation or our eternal destiny in heaven or hell. The tension between 'now' and 'not yet' is vivid in his experience and in his theology. But the relationship between time and eternity is a dialectical one. The sinner experiences hell in his conscience now. The believer is already raised with Christ. There is no place for purgatory or an intermediate state of temporal duration in Luther's eschatology. At the last day, when all will be raised to judgement in the sight of God, it will be as if Adam and the fathers had been living only half an hour before.

This powerful sense of the Christian as existing on the boundary of time and eternity, and of the Church as the eschatological community already living in the end-time, determined Luther's basically pessimistic attitude to the secular world. At one point, he thought that Christ's return would surely occur before he had finished translating the Bible into German. His eschatology of faith, we realize, set him in powerful opposition alike to the settled world view of medieval Catholicism and to the future hopes of every kind of millenarian. And yet his detailed concern for the ordering of human life and his continued advice to the German princes indicate again that we must read him dialectically and avoid a one-sided emphasis on the Christian's inner world of faith.

This dialectic is clearly seen in Luther's well-known doctrine of the two kingdoms, a direct descendant of Augustine's teaching on the city of God and the earthly city. For Luther, the kingdom of Christ is the sphere of the gospel, the kingdom of faith where Christians live in the eschatological dimension of the righteousness of God. But Christians also live in the kingdom of the world, and Christian princes bear a responsibility for Christians and non-Christians alike. Moreover, the world remains God's world, even in its fallen state, and God has ensured, through the institutions of State, family, and Church, that the world does not collapse into chaos. Luther takes further than Augustine had done the idea that God's sovereignty is exercised through secular powers. Moreover, the sphere of the gospel, the true reformed Church of the kingdom of Christ, can act as a catalyst for reform in the world, the sphere of law. However, Luther condemned both the direct application of the gospel to the secular world (the error of the millenarian enthusiasts) and the direct application of the law to the kingdom of Christ (the error of the Catholics). The dialectic is subtle, and Luther did not always succeed in sustaining it. One can appreciate the accusation of political conservatism that has been brought against him, especially over his brutal endorsement of the crushing of the Peasants' War in 1525.

John Calvin (1509–64)

Calvin's eschatology has been called by T. F. Torrance an eschatology of hope.[3] Torrance points out the much greater stress in Calvin's theology on resurrection and on participation by the Church in the heavenly peace of the risen Christ. Moreover, Calvin's thought on these matters is less centred on the individual. It is the Church that is built up as the body of Christ towards the ultimate unveiling of Christ's glory. As the body of Christ, the Church participates by the Holy Spirit in Christ's ascension and looks for his return. The Christian, as a member of that body, is encouraged to meditate on the future life 'as part of the life and exercise of daily faith'.

But Calvin shares with Luther the ever-present tension between the two ages, the old age and the new age initiated by the death and resurrection of Christ. As with Luther's two kingdoms, the two ages overlap and, because of the overlap, the kingdom of Christ exists in two conditions, its present state of concealment in the pilgrim Church and its future state of glory, manifested to all. But Calvin does not narrow down the relation between eternity and time to the moment of decision, as Luther tends to do. He recognizes the time of the Church's earthly pilgrimage and mission as playing an essential role in the providence of God. He is more confident than Luther in the historical mission of the visible Church, and more confident in the positive role of the Church in the ordering of human society in general. He sees the task of the Church as being that of expansion throughout the world,

---

[3] Thomas F. Torrance, *Kingdom and Church: A Study in the Theology of the Reformation* (Edinburgh: Oliver & Boyd, 1956), ch. 4.

filling all creation with the kingdom of Christ, thus realizing on earth more and more the triumph that Christ has already won.

In his meditations on the future life, Calvin affirms both the immortality of the soul and the resurrection of the body. He rejects the analogy between death and sleep and teaches that the faithful dead 'are gathered into rest, where they await with joy the fruition of the promised glory'. Similarly the reprobate are 'chained up like malefactors until the time when they are dragged to the punishment appointed for them'. At the second coming Christ will be manifest to all the living, and all the dead will be raised to join them for the final judgement. Calvin is reticent in his use of the biblical imagery to characterize the ultimate states of heaven and hell:

Though the Scripture teaches that the Kingdom of God is full of light, joy, felicity and glory, nevertheless all that is said about it is far above our intelligence, and as though wrapped in imagery until the day shall come when the Saviour will explain himself to us face to face.[4]

We cannot leave the eschatology of Calvin without some consideration of the topic, postponed from our study of Augustine, of predestination. For Calvin is the leading theologian in that strand of Christian theology down the ages that, convinced of the absolute sovereignty of God and yet faced with the manifest fact that only some accept the preaching of the gospel, maintains the awesome doctrine that some men and women are eternally elected to salvation and some, of necessity, to perdition. It must be admitted that Calvin's logic in his acceptance of double predestination is more consistent than that of Augustine, for whom only the destiny of the elect is foreordained by God, while the reprobate are allowed to fall away by their own sin. But, in either case, this deeply pessimistic doctrine is likely to render Christian eschatology unacceptable. It is hard enough to hold the view that the glory of God is equally subserved by the bliss of the redeemed and by the suffering of the damned; but, if both those states are results of divine decree, then such a doctrine of God's sovereignty is morally incredible.

It is sometimes argued that Calvin did not really teach double predestination in such a stark and uncompromising form. Certainly, when we come to the teaching of the great Calvinist theologian Karl

---

[4] John Calvin, *Institutes of the Christian Religion*, III. 25. 10.

Barth in the twentieth century, we shall find a radical reinterpretation of the doctrine of predestination, less open to moral objection. But to read Barth back into Calvin himself is not very plausible; and it is better simply to reject, without qualification, this element in the Augustinian and Calvinist tradition.

Other Reformers

The Swiss reformer Ulrich Zwingli (1484–1531) needs little separate consideration where eschatology is concerned. His conviction of the elect individual's participation in the kingdom here and now led him to place less emphasis on the final cosmic judgement and, like Calvin, to reject the analogy between death and sleep. He went even further than Calvin did in working (and fighting) for a reformed theocracy here on earth.

Philipp Melanchthon (1497–1560), a close follower of Luther, was the chief architect of the *Augsburg Confession* (1530), one of the main Reformation statements of faith. It has often been remarked how this (and still more the other Reformation Confessions) have little explicit treatment of eschatology. But Edmund Schlink has shown that in fact the whole statement of Christian faith is made from an eschatological perspective.[5] This is what we would expect from Lutherans with their strong sense of already living in the new age. But the *Augsburg Confession* does contain, in its seventeenth article, a statement about the Last Day, and the unveiling of Christ's kingdom. All will be raised, and judged. Everlasting punishment for the wicked is affirmed, but the stress is on the eternal life and everlasting joy of believers.

The eschatology of Martin Bucer (1491–1552) has been described as an eschatology of love, and in many ways it is Bucer, of all the reformers, who presents the most rounded and unified conception of the Christian hope. Within the framework of divine election, the kingdom of Christ has been established on earth in the Church, the spirit-filled community of love. This reign of Christ is to be extended throughout the world, transforming the secular realm into a godly commonwealth, until the coming of Christ, when the whole creation

---

[5] Edmund Schlink, *Theology of the Lutheran Confessions*, Eng. trans. (Philadelphia: Muhlenberg Press, 1961), ch. 8.

will be renewed in accordance with the purpose of divine love, and God will be all in all.

Exiled from Strasbourg, Bucer came to England, where he became an important influence on many of the future English reformers. The latter, however, made few original contributions to Christian eschatology, at least in the sixteenth century. The views of Thomas Cranmer (1489–1556) are best gathered from the Edwardian Prayer Books (1549 and 1552) that lie behind the *Book of Common Prayer* (1662). The Burial Service has often been criticized for its negative assessment of this sinful world, out of the miseries of which it has pleased God to take the deceased, but the service also expresses finely the sure and certain hope of resurrection that characterizes a faith rooted in the New Testament. Nevertheless, the English reformers had little hope for the historical future. Nicholas Ridley (1500–55) and Hugh Latimer (*c*.1485–1555) believed that the end of the world was near. They both shared Luther's relatively pessimistic views about the scope of the kingdom of Christ on earth. A sober realism characterizes the writings of John Bradford (*c*.1510–55), who declared against Anabaptist enthusiasm (see pp. 81–2 below) and papal glorification of the Church that the sheep and the goats would coexist until the day of judgement. While tending to share the Augustinian identification of the millennium with the age of the Church, some English writers, such as John Foxe (1516–87), author of the *Book of Martyrs*, dated the beginning of the millennium with the conversion of Constantine, and made other, more or less far-fetched, identifications of figures from the book of Revelation with historical or contemporary events. We are reminded that we are still very much in the pre-critical age of biblical interpretation.

The Protestant Synthesis

A leading characteristic of Protestantism was its attempt to set out the Christian faith in confessions and catechisms. These sought to define, against both Rome and the extremists, the heart of the rediscovered biblical faith. Mention has already been made of the *Augsburg Confession* of 1530. One of the most influential Protestant catechisms was the *Heidelberg Catechism* of 1563, a basically Calvinist document, modified somewhat eirenically in a Lutheran direction. Its focus is intensely personal, capturing the Reformation's stress on the comfort of faith in Christ for the individual Christian. Its stress is on salvation and the assurance that, when Christ comes as judge, he will take the believer 'with all His chosen ones to Himself, into heavenly joy and glory'. The comfort of the credal articles on resurrection of the body and life everlasting is said to be that 'this flesh of mine ... shall again be united with my soul, and shall be made conformable to the glorious body of Christ' and that, 'since I now feel in my heart the beginning of eternal joy, I shall possess after this life complete blessedness such as eye has not seen, nor ear heard and which has not entered into the heart of man, therein to praise God for ever'.

One of the most substantial seventeenth-century confessions was the *Westminster Confession* of 1648, setting out a uniform understanding of the faith for the (Presbyterian) Churches of Scotland and England. Its last two chapters deal with eschatology. Unlike the *Heidelberg Catechism*, the *Westminster Confession* spells this out with sober objectivity, and the problems of such a statement stand out all the more clearly. Chapter XXXIV is entitled 'Of the State of Man after Death, and of the Resurrection of the Dead'. It first affirms:

The bodies of men, after death, return to dust, and see corruption; but their souls (which neither die nor sleep), having an immortal subsistence, immediately return to God who gave them. The souls of the righteous, being then made perfect in holiness, are received into the highest heavens where they behold the face of God in light and glory waiting for the full redemption of their bodies, and the souls of the wicked are cast into hell, where they remain in torments and utter darkness reserved to the judgement of the great day. Besides these two places for souls separated from their bodies the Scripture acknowledgeth none.

We note the rejection of purgatory and limbo, the insistence on the immortality of the soul, and the two recurring difficulties of a particular judgement that seems to render a final judgement redundant and of a 'perfected' soul still waiting for its body. The *Confession* then goes on:

At the last day, such as are found alive shall not die but be changed: and all the dead shall be raised up with the self-same bodies and none other, although with different qualities, which shall be united again to their souls for ever. The bodies of the unjust shall, by the power of Christ, be raised to dishonour, the bodies of the just, by his Spirit, unto honour, and be made conformable to his own glorious body.

The difficulties here concern (a) the meaning of 'self-same bodies... with different qualities' and (b) the point of raising the unjust to 'dishonour'.

The *Westminster Confession* ends with a chapter entitled 'Of the Last Judgement'. It affirms that God has appointed a final day of judgement. Angels as well as men and women will be called to give an account of their thoughts, words, and deeds, and will be judged accordingly. Everlasting life for the righteous and everlasting damnation for the wicked are clearly affirmed. The *Confession* ends by insisting that it is God's will to have that day, though preordained and certain in itself, unknown to us as to its hour. In addition to the problem of the final judgement's apparent redundancy, we may also point out the individualism of the *Confession*. No mention is made of Christian fellowship in heaven. Moreover, judgement according to works is not easily reconciled with the leading Reformation motif of justification by faith.

The *Westminster Confession* was accompanied by two catechisms, the Larger and the Shorter. The *Larger Catechism* fills out the propositions of the *Confession* in further detail, especially in answer to the question 'What shall be done to the righteous on the day of judgement?' The answer tells us that in heaven 'they will be filled with inconceivable joys, made perfectly happy both in body and soul, in the company of innumerable saints and holy angels, but especially in the immediate vision and fruition of God ...'. So at least the *Catechism* corrects the individualist stance of the *Confession*.

With the late sixteenth and seventeenth centuries, we come to what is known on the Continent as the era of Protestant orthodoxy, in which a number of theologians attempted to systematize the Reformed faith in ways comparable to those of medieval scholasticism. As an example we may take *The Substance of the Christian Religion* by Amandus Polanus, an English version of which appeared in 1600. Polanus was a Calvinist theologian teaching in Basle, Switzerland. Unlike the *Westminster Confession*, however, Polanus had little to say about judgement at death.[6] In the chapter entitled 'Of God's Works after this Life'

---

[6] It is true that he speaks of the first and second death, but by this he means the death of the body and the death of the soul, the latter being the fate of the damned cast away from God.

he deals with the last coming of the Lord, the general raising up of all the dead, the Last Judgement, and the manifesting of God's glory in all eternity. These themes are first expounded largely in biblical terms, although the Lord's last coming is glossed with the words 'in the end of the world' (that is, no trace of millenarianism). But the most interesting paragraphs are those that spell out what the Last Judgement will mean for the damned and the blessed respectively. Here he deftly relates the final judgement both to present experience and to what happens immediately after death. He refers to the everlasting punishment of the damned 'the beginnings whereof they do indeed feel in this life, but shall fully feel the increase thereof in their souls separated from the body'. Similarly he says:

Life eternal is that blessed state of the elect after this life: whereof verily they receive some taste even in this life, and a greater in their souls separated from the body, but they shall receive, full and perfect, after the universal rising of the bodies, and when they shall again be joined to their souls, namely when in body and soul, they shall be received into heaven, and shall with Christ and the blessed Angels be freed from all miseries, and enjoy eternal blessedness.

Then follows a paragraph spelling out what the manifestation of God's glory to all eternity will mean both for the souls and for the bodies of the elect. For the soul, it will mean its beautifying with the perfect sight and knowledge of God and all his mysteries, and also with the unchangeable uprightness of the will. For the body it will mean its being made spiritual, incorruptible, immortal, impassible, and conformable to the glorious body of Christ. Polanus insists that a spiritual body is not just a spirit, but rather a raised body endowed with new qualities. In the sequel, we shall have to press the question what this kind of talk might mean.

The emphasis on the last things and the assimilation of the intermediate state to the foretaste of one's eternal destiny already felt in this life certainly result is a more unified eschatology, the problems of the particular judgement at death and the actual state of souls separated from the body being more or less ignored. Nevertheless, since Protestant orthodoxy firmly resisted any suggestion of change or repentance after death, the moment of death becomes all the more important, and consequently we find in seventeenth-century Protestantism a great emphasis on the need to make a good death, since that is the moment when one's eternal destiny becomes irrevocably fixed.

The Church of England in its formative years, as was pointed out above, simply followed the eschatology of the continental reformers. The *Thirty-Nine Articles of Religion*, finalized in 1571, has very little to say on the subject, restricting itself largely to giving guidance on more controversial subjects. Purgatory is one of the 'Romish doctrines' decisively rejected in article XXII and a very careful article (article XVII—one of the longest) commends, to godly persons only, consideration of God's everlasting purpose in predestination to Life (glossed as everlasting felicity). Similarly Richard Hooker (1554–1600), probably the greatest of the Anglican divines, is much more concerned, in his *Treatise on the Laws of Ecclesiastical Polity*, with the ordering of the Church on earth (and in particular with answering critics of the Elizabethan settlement) than with our state beyond death. But we can gather from his answers to particular objections to the Elizabethan *Book of Common Prayer* the balanced and positive approach that he maintained towards the Christian hope. For example, his defence of prayer for 'mercy upon all men' is a model of Christian charity, in accordance with God's desire for 'all men to be saved' (1 Tim. 2: 3), as is his insistence on the comfort brought by decent Christian burial, with its 'outward testification of the hope which we have touching the resurrection of the dead'.

The late sixteenth- and seventeenth-century Puritans in England show a strange mixture of pessimism and optimism in their attitude to the future. On the one hand, they saw the world and the Church as incurably corrupt, and their own congregations as islands of purity in the storm, awaiting the return of Christ. This side of English Puritanism is reflected in Milton's *Paradise Lost*, where a survey of world history is given to Adam by the Archangel Michael. After the coming of Christ and the apostolic age, apostasy, superstition, and greed will set in. The just will suffer persecution at the hand of the wicked until the Saviour returns

> to dissolve
> Satan with his perverted world, then raise
> From the conflagrant mass, purged and refined
> New heavens, new earth, ages of endless date
> Founded in righteousness, and peace and love,
> To bring forth fruits, joy and eternal bliss.[7]

---

[7] John Milton, *Paradise Lost*, bk. XII, ll. 546–51.

John Bunyan (1628–88), on the other hand, was much more optimistic about the historical future. Somewhat in the manner of the spiritual millenarians of the later Middle Ages, and by dint of conflating the imagery of Revelation 20 (the millennium) and Revelation 21 (the end), he describes a future converted Christian world in which 'a great harvest of sinners shall be gathered by the grace of the Gospel'.[8]

It was this more optimistic side of English Puritanism that led the Pilgrim Fathers, under the conviction of divine providence, to establish godly settlements in the New World. The Puritan movement reached its zenith with the overthrow of the monarchy in England and the establishment of the Commonwealth. It was at this time of their strength and influence that the English Presbyterians were joined by the firmly established Scottish Presbyterians in drafting the *Westminster Confession*, considered above.

The Extremists of the Reformation

The leading reformers were all attempting in their various ways to re-emphasize the urgency and immediacy of the New Testament hope—a hope based on God's action and availability in Jesus Christ. Their eschatology involved a sense of the dimension of eternity breaking into that of time. This was a thoroughly theological approach to the topic of Christian hope. The implications of such convictions for the historical future were variously conceived, but none of the reformers actually identified the Kingdom of Christ with any specific worldly phenomenon or worldly hope. They were as much opposed to the extreme views of the millenarians as they were to the Church of Rome. It is this that gives a note of pessimism to their expectations for the world.

It remains to consider some of these extremists of the Reformation, the so-called radical Reformers, and to note their difference from the main lines of Reformation eschatology. The first of these was Thomas Münzer (c.1489–1525), formerly a priest, then for a short time a follower of Luther, but soon embracing a much more radical, political,

---

[8] A quotation from John Bunyan's *Holy City or The New Jerusalem*.

millenarianism that he caught from remnants of the Taborites near the borders of Bohemia. Claiming (like the Montanists of old) a special revelation from God, he taught the imminent Parousia and millennium together with the need to prepare its way by rising in a war of extermination against the rich. True 'spiritual' Christians, according to Münzer, were those who allowed themselves to become vessels of the Holy Spirit, enduring every kind of worldly suffering, in order to become God's instruments in 'putting down the mighty'. Münzer's preaching, based on Daniel and Revelation, demanded the overthrow of tyrants, and pictured the coming millennium in terms of an egalitarian community of the poor. Now denouncing Luther as the beast of the Apocalypse for his support of the German princes, Münzer joined in the Peasants War of 1525 and was captured and beheaded after the catastrophic defeat of the peasants at Mühlhausen. Honoured by Marxists as an early social revolutionary, Münzer was in fact an apocalyptic dreamer. He had no interest in the material well-being of the poor. His actions exemplify the terrible power of the millenarian tradition, divorced from any serious theological insight, to feed religious fantasy and precipitate unreason and violence.

Thomas Münzer is often described as an 'Anabaptist'—a nickname given to a wide variety of individuals and movements on the 'left' of the Reformation, who refused to recognize infant baptism as legitimate. However, the term 'Anabaptist' should not be too closely associated with views such as those of Münzer. Most Anabaptists preached non-violence and sharing of goods, and a number of important extant movements, such as the Quakers and the Mennonites, have their roots in this strand of the sixteenth-century Reformation.

The most extraordinary example of extreme millenarianism among the Anabaptists of the Reformation was the revolution that occurred in the north German city of Münster in 1534/5. The story makes sober reading. Anabaptist groups had already gained control of the city council and made Münster a haven for Anabaptist refugees from north Germany and Holland. Fanatical preaching about the imminence of the Second Coming and the millennium, and about the holding of all things in common, won an enthusiastic response. The well-to-do citizens began to leave the city. By February 1534 two of the newcomers, the Dutchman Jan Matthys and Jan Bockelson (known as John of Leyden), had gained supreme power in the Anabaptist council, and all inhabitants of Münster who refused to be re-baptized were banished from the city. Meanwhile the Catholic Bishop of Münster was gathering an army of mercenaries and preparing for a long siege of what was now entirely an Anabaptist stronghold. At first, under the leadership of Jan Matthys and in face of the siege, private money was abolished and food and shelter organized on a common basis. At the same time, all books except the Bible were burned. After Matthys's death in a hopelessly unrealistic apocalyptically inspired attempt to relieve the siege, John of Leyden began to impose a dictatorial regime in the city, eventually having himself proclaimed messianic king. Not only was any opposition ruthlessly suppressed, but also a regime of terror was begun, with almost daily executions, even for refusal to comply with the newly instituted polygamy. Until the siege became entirely effective, millenarian propaganda was sent out of Münster, extolling the new Jerusalem there and encouraging the Anabaptists in other towns to rise and exterminate the enemies of Christ. Münster was finally captured in June 1635 and the Anabaptists massacred.

One more example of militant millenarianism, this time from the seventeenth century, may be mentioned here. Reference has already been made to the Puritans in England, whose most notable, if temporary, triumph was the establishment of the Commonwealth in 1649. Oliver Cromwell (1599–1658), although believing himself to be the instrument of divine providence, was no millenarian. But his one-time commander-in-chief in England, Thomas Harrison (1616–60), was. A leading member of the Fifth Monarchy Men, he held that the reign of Christ, identified as the fifth monarchy of Daniel 2: 44, was presaged by the execution of Charles I, and would soon begin. Turning against Cromwell, the Fifth Monarchy Men came to think of him as the 'little horn' of Daniel 7: 8, and of the Protectorate as the final phase before the millennium. Unsuccessful risings took place in 1657, and again in 1661 after the execution of Harrison (in 1660) at the Restoration of the Monarchy. This fanatical movement then died out.

The story of these extreme groups is a sad one. It may be a matter of some sociological interest to see how the visionary language of apocalyptic could by now be used to foment and sustain unrealistic revolution. And, as leaders of protest by the dispossessed against the rich and powerful, the extremists of the Reformation may retain some symbolic significance in a more revolutionary age. But both from a religious and from a practical point of view, these fanatical movements can only be condemned. Compared with the deep religious and theological insight of Luther and Calvin, the visionary transports of Thomas Münzer and John of Leyden must be deemed to belong only to the pathology of religion.

Conclusion

The eschatology of the leading Reformers was first and foremost a spiritual phenomenon. The recovery of a biblical sense of the impact of eternity on time and of authentic Christian life in the new age was a matter of faith and hope as experienced by individual men and women in a reformed Church. The primary object of the reformers' criticism was the late medieval Church itself, grown worldly and corrupt.

On the other hand, the Reformation could not go back to the political quietism of the New Testament and the early Church. The reformers could not ignore the immense changes that had taken place with the conversion of Constantine and the development of medieval Christendom. The possibility of a Christian shaping of the secular world was undeniable, and, for the most part, the Churches of the Reformation saw ways in which the rule of Christ could make its impact on the social and political order in general. The leading reformers, for all their vision of a Christian world, remained realistic and even pessimistic in their assessment of what could actually be done. Their sense of humanity's sinfulness and of the inevitability of coercion and war prevented them from attempting or endorsing any utopian scheme of social and political reform, still less revolution.[9] The appalling fanaticism and unrealism of the millenarians could only confirm them in this stance, and indeed the reformers tended to renounce the apocalyptic tradition at this point, preferring Augustine's insight into the resources of non-apocalyptic Christianity for the ordering and bettering of the state. Only the Puritans in England and

[9] The term 'utopia' (literally meaning 'no place') goes back to the influential book *Utopia* (1516) by Sir Thomas More, which had described an imaginary island where a perfect social and political system prevailed. More himself was probably writing in ironic vein. His book had certainly not been offered as a political programme.

America achieved some partial success in translating the apocalyptic tradition into a more realistic programme of social revolution or reform.

Where transcendent eschatology was concerned, the Reformation had little to add to the received scheme of things. Purgatory was rejected and the intermediate state played down. It is true that men and women were made more immediately aware, in present religious experience, of the realities of heaven and hell. But Parousia, resurrection, judgement, heaven, and hell remained the ultimate framework and future horizon of the Christian hope—and fear.[10]

[10] For a thorough study of the whole Reformation period, see Diarmaid MacCulloch, *Reformation: Europe's House Divided 1490–1700* (London: Allen Lane (Penguin Books), 2003).

Part Three

The Christian Hope in the Modern Age

6

The Enlightenment

Introduction

The first two parts of this book, in tracing the development of Christian eschatology up to the seventeenth century, had little occasion to look outside the world of Church theology and the framework of belief in terms of which the churches taught men and women to experience the world and God and to hope for the future under God. Deviant, extremist, groups too were nurtured in even more closed worlds of 'adventist' biblical interpretation. But now we come to the beginnings of the modern world and in particular to the eighteenth-century Enlightenment, where it is no longer possible to restrict attention to the Church; for the seminal thinkers now were secular philosophers, many of them still religious believers but not Church theologians; and the Church's teachers themselves came to be deeply influenced by the independent secular thought of the day. Christian hope in the modern age has been greatly affected—both for good and for ill—by the various philosophies of the 'world come of age'.

The roots of that phase in Western cultural history that we call the Enlightenment, with its new insistence on the independence of human reason, lie far back in the fifteenth- and sixteenth-century Renaissance. Its first full flowering was the seventeenth-century Age of Reason. For the seventeenth century was not only the age of Protestant Orthodoxy and Puritanism (and the consolidation of the Counter-Reformation too), but also that of the rationalist philosophers, such as Descartes, Leibniz, and Locke, who made a great impact on human science, politics, morality, and religion, by their unfettered use of reason and experiment. These men were not hostile to religion. Few in the seventeenth century were, although reaction against the wars of religion increased the desire for more tolerant, open-minded, rational, forms of religion. Even Thomas Hobbes (1588–1679), whose writings seemed to many to smack of atheism, defends what he calls 'true religion', subject to the sovereign who preserves the State from anarchy.

The seventeenth-century rationalists affected the understanding of Christian hope in two main ways. As far as hope for the historical future was concerned, their confidence in human powers led them to look for progress through education and through political theory and action rather than specifically through the Church or through some spiritual elite (still less through divine intervention). As far as the ultimate future was concerned, they tended to reduce the eschatological dimension of Christianity to belief in the immortality of the soul, argued on philosophical grounds. Once again the result was to accentuate the loss of the urgency and the immediacy that had characterized Reformation eschatology.

These trends in the seventeenth-century background to the Enlightenment may be illustrated by considering the views of some of the leading rationalists themselves.

The French philosopher René Descartes (1596–1650), the father of modern philosophy, is mentioned here only because his conception of the soul as a simple unextended thinking substance lent plausibility to the idea of the soul's immortality. For Descartes, only God who created it could annihilate the soul.[1] Similarly, the greatest of the rationalists, the German philosopher Gottfried Wilhelm Leibniz (1646–1716), despite his denial of an ultimate dualism between mind and matter, argued that the human soul is indestructible (except by miracle) and spoke as scathingly of the view that our immortality was 'but a miraculous grace of God' as he did of the view that souls are absorbed 'in the ocean of divinity'.[2] Indeed, in his *Discourse of Metaphysic*, Leibniz extols the excellence of minds, and praises the Gospel of Jesus Christ for making known to us 'the Kingdom of Heaven or that perfect commonwealth of minds which deserves to be called the City of God'. He sums this section of the *Discourse* up as follows: 'God is the monarch of the most perfect

---

[1] See René Descartes, *Meditations on First Philosophy* (1641), *passim*.
[2] See G. W. Leibniz, *Philosophical Writings* (Everyman's Library) (London: J. M. Dent, 1934), 155–6.

commonwealth of all minds and the happiness of the City of God is His chief design.'[3] It is in keeping with this philosophical eschatology and with the spirit of the age that Leibniz strove to bring together Catholics and Protestants by setting out the beliefs they held in common.

The English philosopher John Locke (1632–1704) was taken to task by Leibniz for his failure to assert the natural immortality of the soul. Locke's *The Reasonableness of Christianity* sets out to defend by reason the truths of Christianity, but allows that some of these, including resurrection, are beyond the scope of reason alone, requiring revelation to disclose them to our minds. But, once disclosed, they can be recognized to yield quite rational beliefs.[4] If, in this respect, Locke was less than typical of the Age of Reason, in other respects he was its leading figure. His insistence on toleration and his enormously influential political philosophy, urging the ultimate sovereignty of the people and government on the basis of a kind of social contract, were among the most important factors shaping the historical future of the modern Western world.

It is worth considering how the Age of Reason impinged on some, at least, of the Church's theologians. By contrast with the figures and movements mentioned in the last chapter, the so-called Cambridge Platonists of the mid-seventeenth century, despite their nurture in Puritan religion, reacted against its narrow dogmatism, its doctrine of predestination, and its depreciation of reason, to produce an attractive marriage of philosophy and theology. They were aware of the danger of contemporary thought—the figure of Hobbes was held to be a threatening one—but they found in the legacy of Platonism resources for a more positive rational defence of the truths of Christianity. One of the Cambridge Platonists, John Smith (1618–52), Dean of Queens' College, wrote *A Discourse Demonstrating the Immortality of the Soul*. Its combination of religious and philosophical argument is striking. Smith's preparatory considerations are three in number: the universal prevalence of belief in immortality, the importance of self-knowledge for a proper appreciation of the arguments for immortality, and the basic principle 'that no substantial and indivisible

---

³ G. W. Leibniz, *Philosophical Texts*, trans. and ed. R. S. Woolhouse and Richard Francks (Oxford: Oxford University Press, 1998), 88.

⁴ See John Locke, *The Reasonableness of Christianity*, ed. I. T. Ramsey (London: Adam and Charles Black, 1958), 25–77.

thing ever perisheth'.[5] Smith then gives four arguments for immortality from the incorporeality of the soul, its spontaneity or freedom, its power of framing necessary truth, and its recognition of a source of goodness that will not let it go. It is clear, especially from consideration of Smith's treatment of the last of these four arguments, that we are dealing with a deeply felt and thoroughly Christian framework of belief, but the difference from the style and conviction of the Reformers is very great.

If we turn to the writings of the Cambridge Platonists on political society and the historical future, we find a comparable combination of Christian principle with belief in progress under civil government. Ralph Cudworth (1617–88), the greatest of the Cambridge Platonists, in his *The True Intellectual System of the Universe*, argues powerfully against Hobbes's doctrine of the absoluteness of political sovereignty and in favour of the primacy of conscience and the laws of God, but at the same time it is civil government, under God, that will improve the lot of men and women and bring about the good of society. Cudworth, like Luther, held government to be an ordinance of God and denied the legitimacy of rebellion. But he had a much more positive view than Luther of the scope of government in promoting the common good.

The Enlightenment in England

The age of the Enlightenment proper is the eighteenth century. It was in these years that the influence of John Locke's political philosophy spread throughout Europe and America, together with his belief in education and its power to improve, if not to perfect, the human condition. Locke's *Some Thoughts Concerning Education* had been published in 1693 and was widely read throughout the eighteenth century in England and France. We note, in particular, an increasing confidence in the use of independent moral reason. The so-called British moralists, culminating in David Hume (1711–76), advanced systems of moral philosophy based on 'the moral sense'—that is, on our innate (or cultivated) approvals and disapprovals. Moral

---

[5] See Gerald Cragg (ed.), *The Cambridge Platonists* (New York: Oxford University Press, 1968), 329.

criticism of Christian beliefs, especially original sin, predestination, and hell, became commonplace. Locke himself, in *The Reasonableness of Christianity*, had summarily rejected the view that men and women are born with an inclination towards evil.

In one central respect, the eighteenth-century Enlightenment drew back from the self-confidence of the Age of Reason. The great rationalist systems ceased to carry conviction. A more sceptical spirit came to prevail, and people became more aware of the limits of their rational powers. This is particularly true of Hume and Kant. But, as Ernst Cassirer has shown,[6] the typical Enlightenment attitude to religion was not one of hostility. Only in France, where more extreme forms of scepticism were embraced, and in the writings of David Hume in Britain, was there any serious opposition to religious belief. Much more typical of the eighteenth-century mind was the position known as deism, a form of natural religion, dispensing with revelation, and seeking a common framework of belief in God, freedom, and immortality behind the differences of the various creeds and confessions. Examples of deism are John Toland's *Christianity not Mysterious* (1696) and Matthew Tindal's *Christianity as Old as the Creation* (1730). Tindal argues that God must always have given us sufficient means of knowing what he requires of us. We learn from nature that rational actions carry with them their own reward and irrational actions their own punishment. 'And if our rational nature is to be the same in the next life, as it is in this, our actions must produce effects of the same kind, and that too in a much higher degree.'[7] Thus, for the deist, natural religion teaches what God requires in this life and the next. Moreover, the existence of God and the certainty of a future life are themselves truths of reason. All this yields a perfect religion. No more is required from revelation for us to be in a position to know what makes for our eternal happiness.

David Hume's scepticism about God, freedom, and immortality was, as already mentioned, somewhat exceptional in eighteenth-century philosophy. In his essay 'On the Immortality of the Soul',[8]

---

[6] Ernst Cassirer, *The Philosophy of the Enlightenment*, Eng. trans. (Princeton: Princeton University Press, 1951).

[7] Matthew Tindal, *Christianity as Old as the Creation*, with a new introduction by John Valdimir Price (London: Routledge/Thoemmes, 1995).

[8] Reprinted in Richard Wollheim (ed.), *Hume on Religion* (London and Glasgow: William Collins (Fontana Library), 1963), 263–70.

he attacks all the philosophical arguments for immortality, meta-physical arguments for an immaterial substance, moral arguments from the supposed justice of God (he pours scorn here on the idea of eternal punishment), and physical arguments from analogies in nature, which, he holds, in fact suggest the opposite—namely, that everything, the soul included, is mortal.

A serious defence of both natural and revealed religion was undertaken by the greatest Anglican divine of the eighteenth century, Joseph Butler (1692–1752), later Bishop of Durham. His *Analogy of Religion* (1736)[9] was directed chiefly against the deists. Butler attempted to show that, far from being more rationally secure than appeals to revelation, natural theology itself uses just such analogical, probabilistic reasoning as does revealed theology. In the hands of a sceptic like Hume, such an argument would undoubtedly backfire, but it has to be recognized that it is Butler's profound religious faith that provides the context within which his arguments from analogy acquire their plausibility. His point is not so much to confute the atheist as to show up the religious implausibility of the deists' pos-ition. The first chapter of Butler's *Analogy* is entitled 'Of a Future Life'. Its method illustrates that of the book as a whole. Butler does not set out, in the manner of John Smith, to prove the natural immortality of the soul. He contents himself with a careful argument to show that we have no reason to suppose that the living agent is made up of parts and thus, like the body, dissoluble at death. The importance of the subject, he goes on to say in the second chapter, lies in the supposition of our happiness or misery hereafter depending upon our actions here. The fact that we experience God's moral government of the world in this life in the consequences of our actions makes it unreasonable to suppose that there is nothing analogous to this in God's government of a future state. If we turn to Butler's sermons, preached in the Rolls Chapel, we find the same sober spelling-out of the implications of Christian faith: 'it is a manifest absurdity to suppose evil prevailing over good, under the conduct and administration of a perfect mind.'[10] And, in a sermon 'Upon the Love of God', Butler argues that, since in the present world

[9] Joseph Butler, *The Analogy of Religion Natural and Revealed to the Consti-tution and Course of Nature*, in *The Works of Bishop Butler*, ii, ed. J. H. Bernard (London: Macmillan, 1900).

[10] See W. R. Matthews (ed.), *Butler's Fifteen Sermons* (London: G. Bell, 1958), 67.

the effects of Wisdom and Power are our objects of contemplation, in the future life we may be able to contemplate the whole scheme of things, the Wisdom that contrived it, and even the Divine Nature. For it is reasonable to suppose that, as our capacities for perception improve, 'we shall have, perhaps by some faculty entirely new, a perception of God's presence with us in a nearer and stricter way'.[11] Only at the end of the sermon, having developed these tentative arguments, does Butler go on to show how consonant these suppositions are with Scripture. Butler's arguments are unlikely to be thought to carry much independent weight. They are cited here to illustrate the way in which an orthodox divine of the eighteenth century, under the influence of the style and method of Enlightenment thought, felt bound to approach the question of a future life.

The Continental Enlightenment

The greater scepticism about religion that prevailed in the French Enlightenment has already been mentioned, though many of the French *philosophes*, including Voltaire (1694–1779), were deists. Jean Jacques Rousseau (1712–78) moved through various stages of religious belief, embracing deistic belief in God and immortality, rejecting hell and original sin, yet affirming an inner personal sense of God in the soul. He opposed all forms of absolutism in religion and the State. The cases for religious tolerance and a social contract were powerfully argued in his political philosophy. Many of Rousseau's ideas were taken up in the French Revolution of 1789, which seemed to epitomize the Enlightenment's hope for political change and a better future. Its sorry outcome in terror and tyranny was one of the main causes of reaction against the Enlightenment in the nineteenth century.

It is the German Enlightenment that provides the most interesting material for our study of the Christian hope. We shall concentrate attention here on three of its strands—the historical strand, typified by Lessing's *The Education of the Human Race* (1780); the philosophical strand, culminating in Kant's *Religion within the Limits of Reason*

---

[11] Ibid. 227.

Alone (1793); and the theological strand, illustrated by the rise of biblical criticism, whose leading representative was J. S. Semler.

Gotthold Ephraim Lessing (1729–81) was a playwright and critic. But he was also interested in philosophy and theology. It may seem strange to take him as typifying the historical strand of the German Enlightenment, since he is best known for his succinct expression of the rationalists' hostility to history as the place of revelation. 'Accidental truths of history can never become the proof of necessary truths of reason.'[12] But his tract *The Education of the Human Race* popularized the notion of progressive revelation in the history of religion and illustrates both the freedom and the optimism with which the Enlightenment viewed the historical future.[13] Lessing compares God's education of the human race by gradual revelation to the way in which we educate a child. We proceed one step at a time, restricting the content of the teaching to what lies within the child's capacity to receive at each stage. Moreover, just as the child could, in time, find things out for itself, so too the human race could arrive at truth through its own rational resources. Revelation, like education, only speeds things up. It should not surprise us that the ancient Jews were unaware of the immortality of the soul or that the Bible contains morally primitive ideas. Later stages correct these childish and inadequate conceptions. In due time Christ taught both immortality and purity of heart. Lessing professes eloquent certainty that this process will continue—a new eternal gospel will complete and perfect the education of the human race. Lessing even finds some intimation of this in the medieval enthusiasts' 'three ages of the world'. He is clearly thinking of Joachim of Fiore here. Their mistake, he holds, was to suppose that final perfection could be achieved immediately. This is what made them enthusiasts. Rather, it takes thousands of years to bring the human race to maturity. It is not unreasonable to suppose that Lessing thinks of the Enlightenment and the rational recognition of the truths of revelation as the beginning of the new age.[14]

---

[12] See 'On the Proof of the Spirit and of Power', in Henry Chadwick (ed.), *Lessing's Theological Writings* (London: Adam and Charles Black, 1956), 53.

[13] Ibid. 82–98. It has been argued, with some justice, that Lessing was in fact an even more radical thinker than he allowed himself to appear in this tract, but, since our primary interest lies in the influence exerted by his published work, this question need not detain us.

[14] An indication of Lessing's radicalism and unorthodoxy comes at the end of the tract when he endorses the hypothesis of reincarnation, whereby each individual,

In philosophy, the German Enlightenment preserved more of the rationalist spirit than was the case in either England or France in the eighteenth century. The teachings of Christian Wolff (1679–1754)—a systematic version of Leibniz's philosophy—were still the basis of philosophical education when Immanuel Kant (1724–1804) was a student. But Kant himself, awakened from his 'dogmatic slumber' by reading Hume,[15] became convinced of the limits of human reason and proceeded to construct a critical philosophy on the basis of that conviction. It was Kant who, in a celebrated pamphlet, 'What is Enlightenment?', defined the Enlightenment as 'the human being's emergence from his self-incurred minority'. 'Have courage to make use of your *own* understanding! is thus the motto of enlightenment.'[16] But, in Kant's view, our understanding did not extend to metaphysical or transcendental views about God and immortality. It is true that in the *Critique of Practical Reason* (1788) Kant insists that both immortality and God are postulates of practical reason, in the sense that the absoluteness of the moral imperative imposed upon us by our own moral nature demands an endless progress towards the achievement of the highest good and a power sufficient to ensure the eventual coincidence of happiness and morality. But Kant allows no possibility of the theoretical use of these postulates, and there is much evidence from his other writings to suggest a radical reinterpretation on his part of the meaning of both immortality and God. The moral import of biblical eschatology is spelled out in thoroughly this-worldly terms in Kant's *Religion within the Boundaries of Mere Reason* (1793), where the Kingdom of God and even the millennium are interpreted as symbolizing the perfect moral community of humanity on earth, which is the object of all ethical endeavour. Kant held no easy doctrine of progress towards perfection. His treatment of radical evil is a profound moral interpretation of what

in a sequence of lives, advances towards the perfection anticipated for the human race as a whole. This may seem a long way from the teachings of the Bible and the Church, but we shall discover, in Chapter 10, how the *point* of belief in reincarnation may perhaps, after all, be incorporated into a Christian eschatology.

[15] Immanuel Kant, *Prolegomena to Any Future Metaphysics* (1783), ed. Lewis White (Beck, IN: Bobbs Merrill, 1950), 8.

[16] See Immanuel Kant, 'An Answer to the Question: What is Enlightenment?' (1784), in Immanuel Kant, *Practical Philosophy*, ed. Mary J. Gregor (The Cambridge Edition of the Works of Immanuel Kant; Cambridge: Cambridge University Press, 1996), 17.

the Christian tradition has termed 'original sin'. But, in his *Idea of Universal History* (1784) and in his *Toward Perpetual Peace* (1795), he envisages a hidden teleology in nature moving towards the realization of all human capacities in a moral commonwealth under the rule of law. Kant's insistence on our inability to speculate about eternity is repeated in *The End of All Things* (1794) and the practical import of Christian eschatology is repeatedly stressed in *Religion within the Boundaries of Mere Reason*: 'We know nothing about the future, nor ought we to look for more than what stands in rational connection with the incentives of morality and their end.'[17]

Kant's critical philosophy and his strictly moral interpretation of the Christian religion have had an enormous influence on the development of modern theology, but the prevailing view in both the nineteenth and the twentieth centuries, at least within the sphere of Church theology itself, is that that influence was bad. We shall trace, in the sequel, the many different ways in which theologians have attempted to rescue Christian eschatology both from the agnosticism entailed by Kant's conception of the limits of human reason and from his one-sided stress on the moral perfectibility of human beings. And indeed, it must be insisted, against Kant, that there is more to Christianity than purity of heart. Prayer, worship, dependence on a transcendent source of being and value, and a genuine hope for a future beyond death are among the aspects of the Christian religion that resist the Kantian translation into purely moral terms.

A more pervasive and permanent influence of the Enlightenment on modern Christian theology in all its aspects is to be found in the rise of biblical criticism. Although thinkers on the fringe of the Church, such as Reimarus, Lessing, and Kant himself, are important in this connection, we shall focus attention here on J. S. Semler, a Professor of Theology at Halle in Germany, who typifies the impact of critical thought within biblical theology itself. The importance of this subject for our topic as a whole is very great. For the first time, with the rise of disciplined biblical criticism, it became possible to appreciate the thoroughly human history and nature of the biblical witness to divine revelation. Of course the differences between the

---

[17] Immanuel Kant, *Religion within the Boundaries of Mere Reason*, in Immanuel Kant, *Religion and Rational Theology*, ed. Allen W. Wood and George di Giovanni (The Cambridge Edition of the Works of Immanuel Kant; Cambridge: Cambridge University Press, 1996), 183.

various strands and authors in the biblical canon, and the symbolic nature of much biblical imagery, had always been perceptible to profound theological minds, such as Origen, Augustine, Thomas Aquinas, and Luther. But, despite their recognition of the religious heart of the Christian gospel, there was always something arbitrary in the way in which they handled difficult texts, as in the case of Augustine's influential identification of the millennium of Revelation 20 with the age of the Church. Indeed, the inability of pre-critical theology to cope with the biblical imagery is nowhere more evident than in the case of eschatology. In other areas, such as faith in God, the salvation wrought by Christ, and the nature of the Church, it was perhaps easier to grasp the essential religious meaning. But, in eschatology, a pre-critical, oracular, understanding of Scripture often led to wild, enthusiastic 'adventist' interpretations, of which many examples have been given in this book. The wonder is not that such interpretations occurred, but that they were resisted by the mainstream churches and their theologians even in pre-critical days. A sense for the genuine religious content of the eschatological, including the apocalyptic, texts was always a possibility for Christian minds. But the rise of historical criticism in the eighteenth and nineteenth centuries provided Christian theology with a powerful tool for distinguishing the kernel from the husk, the heart of the gospel from its historically conditioned mode of expression. For scholars now became much more aware of the historical and cultural factors shaping the development of the biblical tradition. The nature of the texts, the literary genres, and the imagery used became much clearer. And the presence of decline as well as progress in the religious perceptions of the biblical authors themselves could now be both recognized and reckoned with.

Johann Salomo Semler (1725–91) was one of the first theologians to develop historical-critical methods in relation to the biblical text.[18] He is usually classified as one of the 'neologists'—a group of eighteenth-century German theologians, very much men of the Enlightenment, concerned to criticize orthodox dogma as contrary to reason, and to penetrate through to the ethical, personal, heart of

---

[18] For a brief account of Semler, see John C. O'Neill, *The Bible's Authority: A Portrait Gallery of Thinkers from Lessing to Bultmann* (Edinburgh: T. & T. Clark, 1991), 39–53.

the gospel. But Semler, unlike other more extreme neologists, did not simply reject past dogmas. He wanted to understand them historically and to see how, in their historical context, they in fact conveyed the moral essence of Christianity. This procedure came to characterize the 'liberal theology' of the nineteenth century, as we shall see. It will not surprise us to discover that the first practitioners of biblical criticism—this is less true of Semler than of many of his nineteenth-century successors—went much too far. The new methods were unrefined, and they tended to be applied indiscriminately, in the interests of theories of the 'essence of Christianity' already adopted from sources outside theology itself—most notably, of course, from the philosophers of the Enlightenment. But, for all that, Semler's insistence that Scripture *contains*, rather than *is*, the Word of God remains of lasting significance for the interpretation of the Bible.

As far as eschatology is concerned, it is interesting to note that Semler rejected Augustine's and Luther's (to say nothing of Calvin's) doctrines of predestination, both on moral grounds and as distortions of Scripture. For Semler, Scripture is about faith in Christ. The New Testament writers, he held, deliberately refuse to speak about the eternal destiny of unbelievers. In general, Semler held a Johannine eschatology, whereby eternal life is first and foremost a matter of one's relation to Christ here and now. Scriptural talk of an imminent Parousia and the end of the world was merely an accommodation to late Jewish apocalyptic and is marginal to the Bible's central concerns. The passage of history had shown it to be an error, just as Luther's expectation of an imminent end was also falsified by the passage of time. None of this prevented Semler from endorsing the ultimate Christian hope of resurrection as an essential part of scriptural faith.

Revivalism in the Eighteenth Century

Concentration on the impact of the Enlightenment on eighteenth-century Christian thought is liable to give a one-sided picture of the age. Powerful movements of thought exert influence as much by provoking reaction as by challenging traditional beliefs. As well as being the age of deism and rational theology, the eighteenth century was also the age of Pietism, Wesleyan revivalism, and the Great Awakening.

The movement known as Pietism began in Germany in the seventeenth century as a reaction against both rationalism and the dry Protestant Orthodoxy. Its emphasis lay on prayer, brotherhood, and the inner movement of the Spirit in the heart. Its religion of inwardness found expression in the hymns of Paul Gerhardt (c.1607–76) and, in the eighteenth century, in the writings and life of Count Nikolaus Ludwig von Zinzendorf (1700–60), founder of the Moravian Community of Brethren at Herrnhut in Saxony. The eschatological dimension was not lacking in Pietism—indeed it led to some revivals of millenarianism as well—but the main stress lay on present experience, felt devotion to the Redeemer. Moreover it was quite possible for Pietism, with its inner criterion of spiritual meaning, to accept a critical approach to Scripture. Semler himself was not uninfluenced by it (as well as by the Enlightenment), and in the next chapter we shall encounter a similar influence of Pietism on the young Schleiermacher (see p. 106 below).

John Wesley (1703–91) visited Herrnhut and learned much from the Moravians. His field preaching throughout the British Isles attracted enormous crowds and led to the birth of Methodism, an evangelistic movement reaching thousands untouched by the established Church.

Wesley has something of the quality of Luther in his insistence on the urgency and immediacy of God's action on the soul. But, in Wesley, the emphasis is on the possibility of love and perfection here and now. His eschatology has indeed, like that of Bucer (see p. 74 above), been called an eschatology of love. 'There is a love of God', he wrote, 'which casts out all sin.' 'I feel no sin, but all love.'[19] This perfectionism is a dangerous phenomenon in Christian preaching, but it represents a striking form of realized eschatology. It did not, of course, exclude more standard teaching on the future beyond death. The love of God that is possible for the believer now is a foretaste of heaven.

Wesley held that the kingdom of heaven is already operative here. It is, to a degree, already opened up in the soul. Nor was this anticipation of heaven restricted to the inward religion of the soul. Wesley taught that the spread of true religion would mean social

---

[19] See Hubert Cunliffe-Jones (ed.), *A History of Christian Doctrine* (Edinburgh: T. & T. Clark, 1978), 476.

transformation, the establishment of a Christian world. But there will be a day of judgement following the general resurrection and a new heaven and a new earth in which the believer's love of God will be consummated in glory. We also take note of Wesley's belief that 'the souls of all good men rest from their labours and are with Christ from death to resurrection'.[20] Although holding a conservative view of hell, Wesley refused to use the threat of it in preaching.

Another powerful religious revival took place in the United States in the 1730s and 1740s. Known as 'The Great Awakening', it is associated with the preaching of the Methodist George Whitfield (1714–70) and his fellow Calvinist Jonathan Edwards (1703–58), the most rigorous conservative theologian of the age. Edwards insisted that the inner experience of faith must be accompanied by correct doctrine; and his exposition of election and predestination is among the most uncompromising treatment that those questionable dogmas have received. His understanding of Christian eschatology is presented in parts VII to IX of his *A History of the Work of Redemption*.[21] The interesting feature of Edwards's treatment of the future course of God's providential work is that, until the coming of Christ on the clouds of heaven for the general resurrection and judgement, all the details of apocalyptic, including the usual millenarian texts from Revelation, are pressed into service to describe the future history of the Church,[22] its revival despite dark times, the overthrow of the Kingdom of Antichrist (Rome) and 'Mahomet' (Edwards had to insert something about the puzzling phenomenon of Islam), the conversion of the Jews, and then a state of peace and prosperity for the Church prior to the great apostasy and final battle, culminating in the return of Christ. When it comes to the ultimate fate of men and women after the final judgement, Edwards has no doubt whatsoever that the justice of God is as manifest in the damnation of the wicked as in the enjoyment by the elect of the 'most unspeakable and inconceivable glory and blessedness' in heaven. One can only pause in wonder at Edwards's tenacious and uncompromising theological

---

[20] John Wesley, 'The Trouble and Rest of Good Men' (http://new.gbgm-umc.org/umhistory/wesley/sermons/127).

[21] Jonathan Edwards, *A History of the Work of Redemption* (Carlisle, PA: Banner of Truth, 2003).

[22] Edwards interprets Isaiah's prophecy about the crooked being made straight and the rough places plain as referring to 'a wonderful unravelling of the difficulties in the doctrines of religion'!

mind, untouched by the critical spirit of the Enlightenment and unaware of the moral enormity of some aspects of his interpretation of Christian doctrine.

Millenarian Revivals

The revivalist movements mentioned in the previous section were for the most part too concerned with inward religion to allow enthusiasm to be diverted in the direction of millenarian speculation. Resistance to the contemporary Enlightenment did occasionally take millenarian form in German Pietism and indeed in the Church of England. But the most striking eighteenth-century example of millenarianism is to be found in the writings of Emanuel Swedenborg (1688–1772) and in the sect that bears his name.

Swedenborg was a Swedish scientific writer drawn to mystical and visionary states. His teaching, set out in a number of books, including *The Apocalypse Revealed* and *The True Christian Religion*, became the basis of the New Jerusalem Church, which still claims a world membership of over 40,000. Swedenborg's 'adventism' has some novel features. He applied the four sections of the great image of Nebuchadnezzar's dream in Daniel 2 not to four kingdoms but to four 'churches' in the history of God's dealings with the world. The fourth church was the Christian Church, which had itself divided into pieces—the Greek, the Roman Catholic, and the Reformed. The Last Judgement, Swedenborg claimed, had already occurred in the world of the spirit. He himself had seen it with his own eyes in the year 1757, and Christ had come again in the word of revelation that he had given to his servant, Swedenborg. His followers went on to found the 'New Jerusalem Church', in which Revelation 21's prophecy of a new heaven and a new earth was to be fulfilled. We have here an intriguing example of millenarian fantasy— the claim to special revelation, arbitrary identifications of details in Daniel and Revelation, and a spiritual elite embodying the new vision. At this late stage in the history of the Christian Church, Swedenborg made no concrete prediction about the historical future. In claiming that the last things had already happened in the spiritual plane, he avoided the inevitable disappointments of earlier millenarian prophecies.

Conclusion

The two poles of eighteenth century religion—Enlightenment theology and revivalist piety—are indicative of the tensions that the birth of the modern age brought about for Christianity. Where eschatology is concerned, there is no doubt that much was lost from classical Christian faith when its hope for God's ultimate future was turned into a philosophically grounded belief in immortality. Moreover, as we see from Hume and Kant, the philosophical arguments themselves were pretty shaky. The confidence of John Smith on this question was premature, and the tentativeness of Joseph Butler could easily backfire. As for the historical future, the Enlightenment did indeed open up the way for a much more positive attitude to what could be done by way of improving the conditions and the quality of life on earth. There was permanent gain here, even if Enlightenment ideas of progress and perfectibility were greatly exaggerated, in view of humanity's inveterate tendency towards the abuse of power. The aftermath of the French Revolution was a bitter blow to Enlightenment hopes.

It has to be admitted that, in both religion and theology, the Enlightenment led to superficiality. The pietist and revivalist reactions are not surprising. But, for all their religious vigour, these movements too tended to be theologically weak. Even the partial exceptions to this generalization, such as Wesley's eschatology of love and Edwards's rigid predestinarianism, failed to take the measure of the new attitude to Scripture that was becoming possible with the rise of biblical criticism. Again this is not surprising; for the critics were, for the most part, using their new methods in the interests of just such superficial rational or natural theologies against which revivalists were reacting. But biblical criticism, for all its initial exaggerations and indiscipline, was one of the permanent achievements of the Enlightenment in the sphere of Christian theology, and nowhere more so than in respect of eschatology. In the long run it enabled Christian eschatology to recover its rightful place as one of the chief dimensions of the Christian religion. This recovery, as we shall see, is a major aspect of twentieth-century theology. For it was over a hundred years before the effects of the Enlightenment were properly assimilated and a balanced theological perspective on tradition and modernity achieved.

7

The Nineteenth Century

Introduction

The nineteenth century was a time of turmoil for the Christian religion. Not only had the assaults and encroachments of Enlightenment philosophy to be reckoned with, but also the Industrial Revolution and the rise of modern science (especially in the area of biological evolution) were creating grave problems for the practical and theoretical credibility of Christianity. Radical secular alternatives to the traditional Christian hope appeared on the scene and were embraced by many. Not surprisingly, within the Christian churches, strong reactions took place against the world of post-Enlightenment thought. We shall consider briefly here the Evangelical Revival, the Oxford Movement, and Roman Catholic ultramontanism,[1] culminating in Vatican I (1870), as well as the numerous 'adventist' sects that sprang up in the course of the century. But our main concerns in this chapter will be the more positive responses to Enlightenment and post-Enlightenment thought, which are to be found in the development of liberal Protestantism and in the beginnings of Christian social theology. We shall note how, in these strands of nineteenth-century Christianity, the focus of Christian hope tended more and more to be the historical rather than the ultimate future.

---

[1] 'Ultramontanism' is the tendency to centralize authority in the Roman Catholic Church 'beyond the mountains' in Rome.

Hegel and German Idealism

Before turning to these theological developments, however, we must pause to consider a powerful philosophical movement in Germany at the turn of the century, which took up certain Enlightenment motifs, in some ways reacted against the Enlightenment, but also went beyond it in highly positive though ultimately dangerous ways, as far as religion was concerned. German Idealism was perhaps a surprising sequel to Kant's critical philosophy. Far from being deterred by the strict limits to the scope of reason asserted, in their different ways, by Hume and Kant, the Idealists took first the human subject, then mind or spirit in general, as the key to the interpretation of reality, and worked out all-embracing metaphysical systems in which nature, history, art, the State, religion, and philosophy were seen as cumulative ways in which Absolute Spirit objectivized itself in the history of the world. This kind of synthesis was most fully developed in the writings of Georg Wilhelm Friedrich Hegel (1770–1831). Hegel thought of himself as a Christian philosopher and of his work as showing how the traditional doctrines of God and creation, incarnation, redemption, and the Spirit could be interpreted and validated philosophically. His philosophy is still an important influence on Christian theology. Admittedly he has been accused of pantheism, but it would be more accurate to describe Hegel's position as panentheism;[2] for, in his view, the world exists in God and is to be understood as the objectification and self-expression of the immanent and Absolute Spirit. Above all, Hegel is significant for his philosophy of universal history—that is, of history as a whole as the purposeful realization of ever more adequate forms of political, cultural, and religious life, each taking up and transcending something of all the less adequate forms that had gone before.

It will readily be seen that such a dynamic philosophy of Spirit has distinct possibilities for an interpretation of Christian eschatology. Hegel has sometimes been mocked for supposedly teaching that the self-unfolding of Spirit in the course of human history had reached its

---

[2] See John Macquarrie, *In Search of Deity: An Essay in Dialectical Theism* (London: SCM Press, 1984), ch. X.

climax in his own philosophy. But in fact Hegel taught no such thing. Rather, his philosophy was intended to bring the inner teleology of history to expression and to reflect the movement of Spirit towards ideal forms of freedom, social organization, and religion. In this sense we must see in Hegel a powerful advocate of belief in progress.[3] However, it is difficult to see the basis in Hegel's thought for belief in any ultimate, transcendent future goal to human history. This is because his conception of the relation between finite and infinite, time and eternity, is vertical rather than linear. Human history as a whole participates in the divine life just by being its self-unfolding in time. Consequently personal immortality has no place in his system. It is spirit as such—the infinite—that is eternal. 'The immortality of the soul must not be represented as first entering the sphere of reality only at a later stage; it is the actual present quality of Spirit.'[4] This kind of 'realized' eschatology bears out the common criticism of Hegel from a Christian theological point of view, that he allows the individual and, for that matter, the State, ultimately speaking, to be subsumed into the Absolute.

Hegel is mentioned here, not because his Absolute Idealism could ever be regarded as an adequate interpretation of the essence of Christianity, but because his influence on the history of Christian thought in the modern period has been so great. It was, after all, a monumental attempt to fuse together the heart of the Christian tradition and post-Enlightenment thought in all its aspects. We shall need to ask ourselves to what extent nineteenth- and twentieth-century theology has been distorted, not least in the sphere of eschatology, by the influence of Hegelianism.

Schleiermacher and Nineteenth-Century Liberal Protestantism

Friedrich Daniel Ernst Schleiermacher (1768–1834) was the greatest theologian of the nineteenth century and has been called the 'father of modern theology'. Concerned to rescue religion and theology both

[3] Hegel was less utopian than some, in that he believed that states would always resort to war, when their interests clashed.

[4] Georg Wilhelm Friedrich Hegel, *Lectures on the Philosophy of Religion*, iii (London: Routledge & Kegan Paul, 1974), 57.

from Enlightenment rationalism and from Kantian moralism, Schleiermacher attempted to secure an independent basis for religion and the Christian faith in people's immediate awareness or feeling of absolute dependence. In expounding Christianity as the highest historical embodiment and transmitter of this God-consciousness, Schleiermacher used to great effect the skills of biblical criticism and the new science of hermeneutics (the interpretation of texts). He thus illustrates the possibility of critical theology in a relatively conservative religious context.[5]

The fact that, for Schleiermacher, the key to the interpretation of every Christian doctrine lies in what he calls its 'redeeming efficacy'— that is, its place in a religious system that fosters the highest form of God-consciousness—means that traditional eschatology was bound to play a relatively minor role in his understanding of the Christian faith. Christ the Redeemer is experienced now as the Christian submits to his lordship, and as those conscious of redemption come together in an active fellowship animated by the Holy Spirit. Hope for the historical future is hope for the growth of the Church as the focus of this highest form of God-consciousness that has appeared in the history of religions. Certainly Schleiermacher, like Irenaeus (see pp. 42–3 above), sees creation as a process in which humanity grows in consciousness of God, and he looks for an eventual consummation of the Church—an expansion of Christianity over the whole world. But he realizes that this is not in fact a likely outcome in the actual course of human history. 'We cannot forget that during all that time the propagation of the species goes on, and that sin develops anew in each generation.'[6] So in the end he is unwilling to dispense with the doctrines of the persistence of human personality and the consummation of all things beyond death.

Schleiermacher's main argument for immortality is not a philosophical one, nor is it a general religious argument, as though immortality were bound up with God-consciousness as such. It is, rather, bound up with faith in the Redeemer. Schleiermacher holds that it is not possible to experience redemption and the

---

[5] The influence of Pietism on Schleiermacher has already been mentioned.

[6] Friedrich Daniel Ernst Schleiermacher, *The Christian Faith* (1830), Eng. trans., ed. H. R. MacIntosh and J. S. Stewart (Edinburgh: T. & T. Clark, 1928). All the quotations in this and the following paragraphs may be found in the section entitled 'The Consummation of the Church', pp. 696–722.

God-consciousness that Christ makes possible, without accepting Christ's own conviction, against the Sadducees, that we survive bodily death. The Church was right to develop, however figuratively, 'prophetic doctrines' concerning the last things.

Schleiermacher's tentative treatment of these prophetic doctrines is very interesting. The doctrine of the return of Christ, he holds, symbolizes the perfection of the Church beyond the conditions of mortality and continuing procreation. The doctrine of the resurrection of the flesh affirms the continuity between the present and the future life. But Schleiermacher admits to wavering between the idea of a single general resurrection (preceded by an intermediate state, itself the object of uncertainty on Schleiermacher's part) and the idea of 'the consummated Church only growing little by little out of the earthly life which goes on alongside of it'. The doctrine of the Last Judgement is held to constitute the final exclusion from the common consciousness of the consummated Church of every wrong and evil; and the doctrine of eternal blessedness is held to consist in either the possession of, or else the ascent towards, unimaginable perfection. The latter can be represented only as 'an unimpeded knowledge of God in all and along with all'. Despite Schleiermacher's extreme diffidence over saying anything categorical about the last things, of one matter he was sure: the idea of eternal damnation cannot bear close scrutiny. Ignorance cannot be part of the perfected state and knowledge of others' misery would be bound to excite sympathy in the blessed. So, although there are traces of the idea of eternal damnation in Scripture, it is better to develop the universalistic traces that Scripture also contains—namely the view 'that through the power of redemption there will one day be a universal restoration of all souls'.

To turn from Schleiermacher to the leading proponents of the new discipline of historical criticism of the Bible is to encounter much more radical figures. It is easy to understand the opposition that they aroused and the consequent suspicion of biblical criticism as such. As a matter of fact, the historian Ferdinand Christian Bauer (1792–1860), founder of the Tübingen School of New Testament criticism, and the theologian David Friedrich Strauss (1808–74), author of *The Life of Jesus Critically Examined* (1835/6), introduced and applied methods of study of the Bible that, in the long run, were to prevail and become indispensable for Christian theology. But their early use of these methods was often crude and ill-judged, and they were constrained by philosophical perspectives that gravely distorted not only Christian doctrine but also the historical facts themselves. Bauer's school was responsible for the influential but erroneous thesis of a major division between early Jewish Christianity and Paul, resolved in an unhistorical, gnostic, way by the Johannine writings of the second century. Bauer himself went through a long Hegelian phase before reverting to a purely ethical interpretation of the significance of Christianity. Strauss, too, was a follower of Hegel. His conviction of the mythical nature of all the supernatural elements in the gospel led him to treat the resurrection and ascension stories as symbolizing the progress of humanity towards perfection. In late writings, he moved away from Christianity altogether, and explicitly denied belief in immortality.

The anti-supernatural and anti-transcendentalist approach of these writers contributed towards the marked shifting of the focus of the Christian hope towards a this-worldly liberal theology of human progress. But the phrase 'Liberal Protestantism' is most properly applied to the school of highly influential (and somewhat less radical) theologians from Ritschl to Harnack, whose inspiration was Kant rather than Hegel.

Albrecht Ritschl (1822–89) shares something of Schleiermacher's insistence on keeping religion apart from philosophy, although his Kantianism and his difference from Schleiermacher come out in his view that it is the ethical significance of Christianity that makes it the highest form of religion. Ritschl's hostility to mysticism, Pietism, and all theologies of feeling and experience is well known. Yet his understanding of religion, and of Christianity in particular, was certainly theistic. Jesus reveals the forgiving love of God that makes reconciliation and human community possible. It is that love that takes effect and evokes response in love of the neighbour. 'The association of mankind . . . through the reciprocal moral action of its members' is how Ritschl characterizes the Kingdom of God, towards which, under God, humanity is moving.[7] This conception of the Kingdom of God as the moral community of the future does not entirely replace a transcendent eschatology in Ritschl's thought, but the weight of his

---

[7] Albrecht Ritschl, *The Christian Doctrine of Justification and Reconciliation*, Eng. trans. (Edinburgh: T. & T. Clark, 1900), 284.

concern lies here, and it was this conception of the progressive realization of the ethical Kingdom of God on earth that came to constitute the heart of liberal Protestant eschatology.

Ritschl's pupil Johann Wilhelm Herrmann (1846–1922) showed himself to be even more committed to an ethical interpretation of the Christian gospel. The significance of Christianity, as of the preaching of Jesus, lay in 'the Lordship of God in human beings themselves'.[8] The Kingdom of God is no longer seen as a future goal but as a present power of energetic action in the world, and eternal life as the power that God gives the Christian to bear his cross and live freely, joyfully, and hopefully for others.

Liberal Protestantism reached its climax in the thought of Adolf von Harnack (1851–1930), for whom the essence of Christianity[9] consisted in the fatherhood of God and the infinite value of the human soul. Just because humanity is rooted in the eternal, it is love of God and love of the neighbour that constitute the heart of religion and morality. God's Kingdom is God's spiritual power, understood only from within, as individuals experience and realize this love in brotherly fellowship. Harnack's ethic, like Herrmann's, has a strong individualistic flavour, but he is closer to Ritschl in allowing, without emphasizing, a transcendent future aspect to Christianity's gospel. Indeed, the following quotation from Harnack may serve to illustrate the nature and the extent of Liberal Protestantism's residual faith in the Christian hope of heaven:

It is not by any speculative ideas of philosophy but by the vision of Jesus' life and death and by the feeling of his imperishable union with God that mankind, so far as it believes in these things, has attained to that certainty of eternal life for which it was meant, and which it dimly discerns—eternal life in time and beyond time.[10]

For all that, the stress remained on the realization of eternal life in time.

The liberal temper was not so strong in England as in Germany. We find it in figures such as Renn Dickson Hampden (1793–1868) against

---

[8] See Wilhelm Herrmann, *The Communion of the Christian with God*, Eng. trans. (London: SCM Press, 1972).

[9] Harnack's book, *Das Wesen des Christentums*, came out in 1900. In English translation, it was given the title *What is Christianity?* (London: Williams and Norgate, 1901; 5th edn., London: Ernest Benn, 1958).

[10] Harnack, *What is Christianity?*, 121.

whom Newman and the Tractarians reacted with such vigour. For Hampden, Christianity is a matter of will and feeling rather than of doctrine. Most strikingly, we find the liberal temper in Thomas Arnold (1795–1842), Headmaster of Rugby School, whose methods in education were highly influential in the nineteenth century. Arnold's sermons sought to penetrate beneath the surface of biblical prophecies in order to draw out the moral and spiritual truths embedded in them. A similar concern, later in the century, may be found in the influential collection *Essays and Reviews* (1860).[11] Benjamin Jowett (1817–93), later to be Master of Balliol College, Oxford, contributed an essay to this volume 'On the Interpretation of Holy Scripture'. This was a fine example of the assimilation of biblical criticism by a much more moderate mind than that of the German radicals. Jowett saw the absurdity of taking the things 'that must shortly come to pass' (in the book of Revelation) as referring to the events of modern history. None of these English liberals denied the ultimate future dimension of the Christian hope. But their interest lay in the present and in the immediate future. Christianity, for them, was a moral force, indeed the moral force, behind education and progress. Belief in the life of the world to come remained part of the Christian framework, but critical study of the Bible showed that detailed knowledge of that future was not revealed to us. Nevertheless, there was one point over which the English liberals challenged the accepted framework and that was again the question of everlasting punishment. Another contributor to *Essays and Reviews*, Henry Bristow Wilson (1803–88), writing on the national Church, advanced the hope that the morally and spiritually immature would be given conditions in the future life where they might grow and be restored, so that 'all, both small and great, shall find a refuge in the bosom of the Universal Parent, to repose, or be quickened into higher life, in the ages to come, according to His Will'.[12] Wilson's views became the object of a celebrated lawsuit, but, as we shall see, such questioning of eternal punishment was not confined to liberal Christian opinion.

---

[11] Frederick Temple et al., *Essays and Reviews* (London: John W. Parker, 1860).
[12] Ibid. 762.

Conservative Eschatology in the Nineteenth Century

The main religious movements in nineteenth-century England may be regarded, in part at least, as reactions against modernity. The Enlightenment and all that it stood for were seen by many as a threat to the traditional faith. Both the Evangelical Revival and the Oxford Movement were attempts to recapture the living heart respectively of the biblical Protestant and of the Catholic traditions. In both cases Christian eschatology in its traditional forms was reaffirmed. The evangelicals, the followers of Charles Simeon (1759–1836) in Cambridge and the Clapham Sect, including William Wilberforce (1759–1833), in London, were active in philanthropy and in the promotion of Christian mission abroad. But a strong element in the motivation of their actions was hope of heaven and fear of hell. Thus Isaac Milner (1750–1820), President of Queens' College, Cambridge, and Dean of Carlisle, who converted Wilberforce in the course of a coach ride to Paris, wrote in a sermon: 'To be happy in another life, to square all our conduct by that object steadily and primarily kept in view; to attend to the things of this life only as necessary, not as objects of choice... these are the grand objects in the religion of Jesus.'[13] Most evangelicals, insisting that this life alone offers us the chance of redemption, encouraged a didactic use of the deathbed, entered into protracted debates on the afterlife, especially on the theme of heavenly reunion with loved ones, and continued to preach the threat of everlasting punishment.

The Tractarians of the Oxford Movement may have been less individualistic, with their eschatology centred on the communion of saints, and their reaffirmation of purgatory and prayers for the dead may have somewhat mitigated the stark alternatives of evangelical preaching. But the ultimate and awesome choice between heaven and hell continued to provide the context of their piety and their striving after holiness. Edward Bouverie Pusey (1800–82), one of the leading Tractarians for nearly fifty years, became increasingly

[13] Quoted from Bernard M. G. Reardon, *From Coleridge to Gore: A Century of Religious Thought in Britain* (London: Longman, 1971), 30.

conservative in his views on hell, reacting sharply against the growth of Victorian universalism. In 1880, in *What is of Faith as to Everlasting Punishment?*, he defended the eternity of hell against the views of Frederick William Farrar (1831–1903), Dean of Canterbury and author of *Eric, or Little by Little*. But already, in 1839, in *The Day of Judgement*, Pusey had written:

be our first thought morning by morning to think of the morning of the resurrection; be our last night by night, the sleep of death, after which cometh the judgement ... remember the parching flame, the never-dying worm, the everlasting fire, the gnashing of teeth, 'the smoke of torment' which goeth up for ever and ever; and where they have no rest day nor night. Set heaven and hell before your eyes, so you may escape hell and by God's mercy attain heaven.[14]

John Henry Newman (1801–90) remarks in his *Apologia Pro Vita Sua* that from the age of 15 he had 'held with a full inward assent and belief to the doctrine of eternal punishment, as delivered by our Lord Himself, in as true a sense as I hold that of eternal happiness; though I have tried in various ways to make that truth less terrible to the imagination.[15] Examples of such attempts may be found in his insistence on holiness as a necessary condition for the attainment of heaven, so that sin creates its own hell, and in the curious speculations that, much later, as a Roman Catholic, he permitted himself on whether the lost remain perpetually conscious of the eternity of their punishment. But the full nature and the powerful spiritual force of Newman's eschatology may best be appreciated from *The Dream of Gerontius*, the poem that he wrote in 1865. Later set to music by another Roman Catholic, Edward Elgar, *The Dream of Gerontius* conveys the inwardness of Catholic eschatological piety better than any other work. In the poem the soul of Gerontius, speeded on its way by the prayers of the Church, wakes, refreshed, to find itself borne by an angel 'with extremest speed' to the 'Just and Holy Judge'. The voices of demons are heard on the one hand and those of the angelic host on the other. The soul asks 'Shall I see My dearest Master,

---

[14] Quoted from Geoffrey Rowell, *Hell and the Victorians: A Study of the Nineteenth-Century Theological Controversies Concerning Eternal Punishment and the Future Life* (Oxford: Clarendon Press, 1974).

[15] John Henry Newman, *Apologia Pro Vita Sua* (1864), ed. Ian Ker (Penguin Classics; Harmondsworth: Penguin Books, 1994), 27.

when I reach His throne?', and the angel replies, 'Yes for one moment thou shalt see thy Lord ... One moment, but thou knowest not, my child, What thou dost ask: that sight of the Most Fair Will gladden thee, but it will pierce thee too.' The prayers of those left on earth, together with the intercession of the Angel of the Agony, are again heard as the soul is brought 'Into the veilèd presence of our God'. 'O happy, suffering soul!' sings the angel; 'for it is safe, Consumed, yet quickened by the glance of God'. The soul in this moment of judgement cries:

Take me away, and in the lowest deep there let me be, And there in hope the long night watches keep ... There will I sing, and soothe my stricken breast, Which ne'er can cease To throb, and pine, and languish, till possest Of its Sole Peace. There will I sing my absent Lord and Love: Take me away, that sooner I may rise, and go above, And see Him in the truth of everlasting day.

The angel now enfolds the soul, poising it over the penal waters and singing: 'Farewell, but not for ever! brother dear, Be brave and patient on thy bed of sorrow, Swiftly shall pass the night of trial here, And I will come and wake thee on the morrow.' We notice how the whole weight of this picture of the soul's destiny lies on the particular judgement and purgatory, through which the soul will pass and rise to be with the Lord. There is little room in this picture for the general judgement, the general resurrection, or indeed the resurrection of the body.

Despite the resistance of the Evangelicals and the Tractarians to liberal theology and the spirit of the age, it must also be acknowledged that many relatively conservative minds in the nineteenth century found the traditional doctrine of everlasting punishment morally incredible. One of these was Frederick Denison Maurice (1805–72). Maurice was not himself a universalist, but his deeply moral sensibility made him unwilling to think of God's purpose for men and women in terms of rewards and punishments. He came to the conviction that in talk of 'eternal death' as of 'eternal life' the word 'eternal' referred not so much to temporal duration as to the quality of life with or without God. Eternal life was the state of fellowship with God, eternal death that of being cut off from God. Maurice did not deny the ever-present and awful possibility of such loss. There were times when the possibilities of resistance in a human will to the loving will of God seemed almost infinite to him. 'But I am obliged to believe in an abyss of love which is deeper than the abyss of death: I dare not lose faith in that love.' The furore over the publication of these views in *Theological Essays* in 1853[16] led to Maurice's resignation from his professorship at King's College, London. But the views themselves gained wide support in the later nineteenth century.

A striking further example of this trend is that of Thomas Rawson Birks (1810–83), a prominent Evangelical, whose *Victory of Divine Goodness* appeared in 1867. Birks did not, any more than Maurice, affirm universalism categorically, but he qualifies the doctrine of hell, in the light of Christ's universal atonement, by suggesting that, in the end, the lost would come to recognize, albeit with shame and humiliation, the goodness and the love of God. This halfway house between the doctrine of everlasting punishment and Christian universalism may not seem very plausible, but it illustrates how even a leading Evangelical found difficulty in the traditional belief.

A third example of the Victorian decline in the old belief in everlasting damnation is that of F. W. Farrar, against whom, as noted above, Pusey directed his late tract. Farrar, at the time Archdeacon of Westminster, published his *Eternal Hope* in 1878. Again without affirming universalism, Farrar denounced the preaching of hellfire as incompatible not only with the love but also with the justice of God. An important break with tradition, which we have already noted in respect of H. B. Wilson's contribution to *Essays and Reviews* and which we shall be taking up and examining in subsequent chapters, was Farrar's insistence that a person's destiny was not 'finally and irrevocably sealed at death'.

Our picture of conservative religion in England in the nineteenth century, then, cannot be solely one of Evangelical and Tractarian reaction. Relatively conservative churchmen as well as liberal educationists were more and more prepared to let their conviction of the moral force of Christianity modify the way in which the Christian hope had previously been conceived.

It could also be argued that the nineteenth-century liberal belief in progress also had its effect on conservative religion precisely in the unbounded optimism with which the Evangelicals and the Tractarians embraced the causes of education and mission. In a later

---

[16] Frederick Denison Maurice, *Theological Essays*, with an Introduction by Edward F. Carpenter (London: James Clarke & Co., 1957), 323.

section we shall see how Christian social theology too was far from being just a liberal affair.

To turn briefly to the world of continental Roman Catholicism is to encounter very rigid forms of conservatism culminating doctrinally in Vatican I of 1870. We shall not look for developments in eschatology here, though Newman's correspondence affords interesting evidence of contemporary debate among Catholics in England on eschatological matters. As far as this-worldly hope was concerned, six years before Vatican I, Pope Pius IX, in his *Syllabus of Errors*, had denounced rationalism, liberalism, socialism, communism, and the view that the 'Roman Pontiff can and ought to reconcile and adjust himself with progress, liberalism and modern civilization'.[17] Yet there were other voices in the Roman Catholic world, as we shall see.

A lone Protestant voice in Denmark, that of Søren Kierkegaard (1813–55), went unheard until the twentieth century. Kierkegaard reacted against the philosophy of Hegel as passionately as he did against the Church of his day. In many ways a precursor of existentialism, he affirmed the faith and experience of the individual as the point at which the eternal breaks into time. In this he prefigured also much twentieth-century eschatology, with its refusal to identify God's rule with any phenomenon in the world, whether Church, State, or history.

The Theory of Evolution

The opposition between science and religion that developed during the nineteenth century and that still affects the credibility of Christianity in many people's minds, reached a climax of notoriety in the clashes over the theory of evolution as expounded by Charles Darwin (1809–82) in his *The Origin of Species* (1859). The confrontation between Bishop Samuel Wilberforce (son of William Wilberforce) and the Darwinian, Thomas Henry Huxley, at the meeting of the British Association in Oxford in 1860 is too well known to require

[17] Denzinger-Schönmetzer, *Enchiridion Symbolorum Definitionum et Declarationum de rebus fidei et morum*, 38th edn. (Freiburg in Breisgau: Herder, 1999), no. 2980.

retelling. These clashes were inevitable, given that a critical approach to the Bible had not yet been properly assimilated by the churches' theologians. For the Bible's treatment of 'the first things' can no more be taken literally than can its treatment of 'the last things'. But in many ways these clashes were a pity. An evolutionary view of life—and indeed of the cosmos—is quite easily reconciled with the doctrines of creation and providence, and indeed with a Christian eschatology, as we shall see in Chapter 9 in connection with the thought of Teilhard de Chardin. But already in the nineteenth century a number of thinkers, both religious and non-religious, were quick to see the possibilities of evolution for a theory of human progress, improvement, and indeed perfection. Henry Drummond (1851–97), in his *The Ascent of Man* (1897), saw evolution as the manner of God's working and self-revelation in a natural world that culminates in altruism and love. Henri Bergson (1859–1941), in his *Creative Evolution* (1906), argued that the theory of evolution required the postulation of an *élan vital*, a vital impetus, pervading the whole process and giving it its direction. Later, in *Morality and Religion* (1932), he was to suggest that evolution is 'God's undertaking to create creators'.[18] Having evolved, human beings now have the power to create a better world.

But one of the most intriguing applications of evolutionary thinking—this time to the problems of ultimate eschatology—was the view known as 'conditionalism'. Conditionalism is the view that human beings, although created mortal, acquire the capacity to receive immortal life, as and in so far as they acquire faith in Christ. Clearly, the theory of evolution could be regarded as dealing a heavy blow to the view that we are by nature immortal. But a religious evolutionism could equally well interpret our emergence as the emergence of creatures capable of receiving immortality. Moreover 'conditional immortality'—conditional, that is, upon the acquisition of faith—provided an answer to the difficulty of eternal punishment. The wicked or faithless are not raised to punishment; they simply cannot be raised. Faith, in other words, is a necessary condition of immortality. In the nineteenth century, we find conditionalism being advanced by a number of writers, including liberal evangelicals, to

---

[18] Henri Bergson, *The Two Sources of Morality and Religion*, Eng. trans. (London: Macmillan and Co., 1935), 218.

whom the text of 2 Timothy 1: 10 ('Christ...who abolished death and brought life and immortality to light through the gospel') implied this doctrine. Its most prominent advocate was the Congregationalist Edward White (1819–98), whose *Life in Christ* (rev. edn, 1875) was widely read and discussed. White argued that the New Testament taught the survival of the fittest, in the sense of those who embrace righteousness and take hold of the Redeeming Love.

The Radical Opposition

Christian eschatology also came under strong attack in post-Hegelian philosophy. In order to achieve a just appreciation of the Christian hope in the modern twentieth-century world, we need to be aware of this hostility, as it came to expression in certain intellectual and political circles in the course of the nineteenth century.

One of the first exponents of this sharp criticism of the Christian hope was Ludwig Andreas Feuerbach (1804–72). Feuerbach sought 'to turn Hegel on his head', to convert theology into anthropology, and to focus our concern solely on ourselves and our potentialities in this world. God, for Feuerbach, was an illusory projection of the ideal essence of humanity, and immortality a selfish belief, deflecting us from our proper concern with the here and now. The strength of this position lay in the fact that the Christian hope of heaven had indeed been advanced all too often at the expense of concern for this world. But whether such hope was bound to have that effect was not so clear. Moreover, the illusory nature of the hope of heaven was more a matter of assertion than of argument in Feuerbach's writings.

The same may be said of Karl Marx (1818–83), who greatly sharpened Feuerbach's criticism by showing the social and economic basis of the alienation of men and women from their true selves, which, like Feuerbach, he held to lie behind the phenomenon of religion. Religion 'is the fantastic realization of the human essence since the human essence has not acquired any true reality'.[19] It is the opium of the people precisely because it diverts attention from

[19] Karl Marx, *A Contribution to the Critique of Hegel's Philosophy of Right* (1844). See Karl Marx, *Early Writings* (Harmondsworth: Penguin Books, 1975), 244.

the changes necessary on earth by its illusory hope of the hereafter. Marx substituted for Christian eschatology what may be called a thoroughly secular, this-worldly, eschatology—namely, an allegedly scientific analysis of the way in which the economic and social relations of human life could and would be decisively and irreversibly transformed. Marx was not concerned to paint a picture of some ideal future utopia. He was sharply critical of all utopianism. Marx's optimism concerning the post-revolutionary classless society, in which people's real interests and needs would be universally satisfied, was based on his detailed analysis of the structures that, he held, prevented such forms of social life in the present, capitalist, phase of human history.

Marxist appreciation of the apocalyptic tradition has already been mentioned. Marx's collaborator Friedrich Engels (1820–95) wrote an essay in praise of *The Book of Revelation* (1883), precisely because it seemed to him to reflect a revolutionary movement against the ruling powers. Similarly, many Marxists saw in Thomas Münzer and the Anabaptists (see pp. 80–1 above) precursors of their own revolutionary programme.

The optimistic, secular, eschatology of Marxism came to be widely criticized on a number of grounds: for its false analysis of capitalism, for its unfulfilled predictions of the course of history, for its neglect of the ever-present possibility of the abuse of power, for its willingness to sacrifice innumerable lives for the sake of an uncertain future, and for its inability to cope with our mortality. But, for all these criticisms, it remained for a long time the most powerful secular alternative to Christian eschatology, and many Christians in the twentieth century adopted elements of Marxist theory into their own understanding of Christian hope for the future of humanity on earth.[20]

Only in the late twentieth century, with the collapse of the Soviet Union and the freeing of Eastern Europe from Soviet domination, was Marxism largely deprived of its power and attraction, at least in Western eyes.

Another nineteenth-century enemy of other-worldly Christian eschatology was Friedrich Wilhelm Nietzsche (1844–1900), although he was equally opposed to socialism and the idea of inevitable

[20] See Nicholas Lash, *A Matter of Hope: A Theologian's Reflections on the Thought of Karl Marx* (London: Darton, Longman and Todd, 1981).

progress. Against all eschatologies, religious and secular, he affirmed the notion of 'eternal recurrence', the extraordinary view that the whole history of the universe is endlessly repeated.[21] Nietzsche is mentioned here only because he expressed so vividly the sense that Christianity's beliefs in God and immortality—and indeed Christian morality—had come to constitute a monumental revolt against reality, a reproach, one might think, more plausibly directed against his own philosophy.

In more sober terms, however, the conviction that the Christian hope of heaven turns people's attention away from the immediate problems and needs of the present has become pervasive in the modern world. It represents a challenge to Christianity that cannot be brushed aside.

Social Theology

For all the sharp dichotomies between the worlds of Wilberforce and Huxley and between the worlds of Pius IX and Karl Marx, in the long run Christianity was to prove its ability to assimilate and profit by both scientific and social criticism. Indeed, as our survey of Christian eschatology down the centuries will have shown, the Christian hope has seldom been purely other-worldly, to the neglect of the present and the historical future. Quite apart from the millenarian sects, the sense of humankind's eternal destiny has inspired Christians of all times to charitable action, missionary endeavour, and the creation of forms of communal life under God. We have only to think back to theories of the Christian empire, the two kingdoms, the divine ordinances, and the godly commonwealth, to realize that political and social life on earth was constantly being brought within the sphere of Christian concern and hope. And we have just seen how eighteenth- and nineteenth-century optimism about the education and progress of humanity found not only Christian expression but also Christian reinforcement, especially at the hands of the liberal

---

[21] See Friedrich Wilhelm Nietzsche, *Thus Spoke Zarathustra*, ed. Adrian Del Capo and Robert Pippin (Cambridge: Cambridge University Press, 2006), 177–8, 184–5.

Protestants in the powerful use made of the notion of the Kingdom of God. Christian eschatology, far from diverting attention to the hereafter, has again and again inspired, on the one hand, a theology of secular power and, on the other, an ethic of work for the realization of God's Kingdom in the historical future.

It has to be admitted, however, that by the eighteenth century most Christian theologies of secular power were for the most part static, authoritarian, and hierarchical, and that, in the nineteenth century, the Kingdom of God tended to be conceived only in terms of the ethical community of benevolent individuals. A few radicals apart, the churches were slow to appreciate the social implications of hope for God's Kingdom here on earth. Nevertheless, there were voices and movements in the nineteenth century that did begin to see and to stress the social consequences of the gospel in a new way.

One such movement was that of the Christian Socialists in England, of whom the leaders were J. M. F. Ludlow (1821–1911), Charles Kingsley (1819–75), and F. D. Maurice, whose views on eternal punishment have already been mentioned. It was a short-lived movement, at least as far as these men were concerned, for Kingsley had little staying power and Maurice, suspicious of political commitment, turned his attention to the education of working men. But all three recognized that the state of the poor required more than just charitable relief and that social justice could never be the fruit of benevolence alone. Ludlow was the most radical of the three. More committed to democracy and socialism than the others, he realized that organized action was necessary if social conditions were to be transformed. But he also realized, as indeed did Kingsley and Maurice, that social cooperation and unity required a religious base, a faith in One Father. This was what differentiated Christian socialism from the secular socialism of the day. Later movements, such as Stewart Headlam's Guild of St Matthew (1877) and Henry Scott Holland's Christian Social Union (1889) addressed themselves to the same problem and sought to 'study how to apply the truths and principles of Christianity to the social and economic difficulties of the present time'.[22] But none of these movements succeeded in working out an interpretation of Christian hope

[22] See Peter d'A. Jones, *The Christian Socialist Revival 1877–1914: Religion, Class, and Social Conscience in Late-Victorian England* (Princeton: Princeton University Press, 1968), 173.

for society strong enough to challenge and transcend the secular ideologies of the day.[23]

As was pointed out above, ultramontanist Roman Catholicism set its face against the socialist and progressive strands of nineteenth-century political thought. But at an earlier stage the writing of Félicité Robert de Lamennais (1782–1854) had already suggested another way in Catholic France. Even more radical than Ludlow, he had pleaded eloquently for the separation of Church and State and for a democratic socialist form of human community. But Lamennais's views were condemned, and he left the Church. Even when the tone of papal pronouncements was modified, as it was in Leo XIII's *Rerum Novarum* (1891), to express concern for the condition of labour, socialism was still condemned.

The nineteenth century, then, can be said to have seen only the beginnings of social theology.

The 'Adventist' Sects

Our survey of nineteenth-century Christian eschatology cannot omit the 'adventist' sects that, quite against the spirit of the age, sprang up during the course of the century. Millenarianism was by now almost entirely a sectarian phenomenon, and what purported to rest on the literal acceptance of apocalyptic texts can in fact be seen to involve more and more bizarre interpretations.

It would not be accurate to describe the Plymouth Brethren as purely an adventist sect. They began in 1831 as a group of undenominational evangelical Christians, concerned to recapture the spirit of the primitive Church. But John Nelson Darby (1800–82), whose followers formed the Exclusive Brethren, is particularly notable for his teaching on biblical 'prophecy'. He claimed that the second coming would take place in two stages: first, the secret 'Rapture', that is, the taking-up of the faithful and the resurrected saints to meet the Lord in the air (1 Thess. 4: 14–15), after which a long period of disaster on earth would culminate in the battle of Armageddon.

[23] Much the same can be said of the *Evangelischer Sozial Kongress* in late-nineteenth-century Germany.

Then Christ would return together with the saints to defeat his enemies and reign for a thousand years. This is only part of the scheme of divine preordained 'dispensations' that Darby taught as underlying human history, past, present, and future. This 'dispensationalism' became widely influential outside the sphere of the Brethren, especially in the United States.

Another example of millenarian teaching from the same period is that of Edward Irving (1792–1834), to whom the Catholic Apostolic Church looked for inspiration. Irving worked out from scriptural texts that the second coming would take place in 1868. His followers appointed twelve 'apostles', and allocated to each an area of the world in which to carry out missionary work. Despite the passage of the date announced and despite the death of the last 'apostle' in 1911 (so that no more ministers could be ordained), the sect still exists in expectancy of Christ's second coming.

A much greater influence may be traced back to the preaching of the former American Baptist William Miller (1782–1849), who set the date of Christ's advent first for 1843 and then for 1844. Despite the disappointments of the passage of these years, the Millerite movement gave birth to several adventist sects, of which the largest are the Seventh Day Adventists, numbering over two million people today. Although they ceased to set a precise date for the second coming, the imminent return of Christ continues to form one of their main doctrines. They also expect a millennial rule and a final resurrection (the dead remaining unconscious until then) at which the wicked will be annihilated by fire and the righteous given immortality in a new earth fashioned from the ruins of the old.

We may also mention the Christadelphians, founded in 1848 in the United States by John Thomas (1805–71), who taught that Christ would return to rule over a restored Israel in Jerusalem, and the Jehovah's Witnesses, another American sect, which is highly active at the present day. Its adventist teaching goes back to its founder, Charles Taze Russell (1852–1916) and was developed by Joseph Franklin Rutherford (1869–1941). Various dates have been set for Christ's secret second coming and for the end of the world. A striking feature of Russell's teaching was that all who have ever lived would rise from the dead at the beginning of the millennium. Those who failed to respond to Christ's rule during this final time of trial would die the second death—meaning extinction. It is to be noted that both the

Seventh Day Adventists and the Jehovah's Witnesses adopt forms of 'conditionalism' (see p. 116 above).

Modern millenarianism might well be considered even more implausible than medieval or Reformation millenarianism in that, unlike the earlier movements, praised by Marx and Engels, the modern sects can hardly be described as symbolizing radical social protest. It is worth repeating, therefore, that Christian theology can only describe these various and mutually incompatible adventist beliefs as resting on a complete failure to discern the nature of biblical prophecy, let alone the nature of the apocalyptic literature of late Judaism and the early Church. As was indicated in Chapter 1, the great prophets of the Hebrew Bible were not concerned to predict the future hundreds or even thousands of years ahead. They did not regard the future as predetermined but rather as subject to the providence of God, as nations and individuals responded or failed to respond to God's law. Their prophecies reflected spiritual insight into the will of God and into what happens when people flout it. Late Jewish and early Christian apocalyptic to some extent fell away from the heights of biblical prophecy precisely in adopting a deterministic picture of history in the divine plan. But even there the authors had no thought of the distant future, as though its detailed course could be symbolically predicted.

Conclusion

To conclude this chapter, we return to the dominant strands of nineteenth-century Christian theology, those of Liberal Protestantism, the more or less conservative reactions, and the beginnings of social theology. In summarizing the implications of these movements for the articulation of the Christian hope, we need to stress that none of them succeeded in achieving a balanced understanding of Christian eschatology. The tendency of Liberal Protestantism was to play down the ultimate Christian hope and to equate the Kingdom of God with the perfect ethical community towards which humanity, under God, was progressing. And even here they failed to recognize that changing structures, as well as changing peoples' attitudes, was necessary for the realization of the Kingdom of God on earth. The Evangelical

Revival, the Oxford Movement, and ultramontanist Roman Catholicism were, for the most part, very suspicious of any attempt to politicize the gospel and reacted as sharply against the ideas of progress and socialism as they did against the idea of evolution. The deeply felt personal faith of the converted individual or of the committed churchman in the nineteenth century certainly yielded much in the way of philanthropy and good works, and it inspired a worldwide missionary thrust whose goal was expressed at the World Missionary Conference at Edinburgh in 1910 as 'the evangelization of the world in this generation'. But the eschatology of these movements was largely traditional and other-worldly. Only in two respects did these conservative groups reflect the influence of modernity. Where the ultimate future was concerned, belief in everlasting punishment was beginning to be eroded, and, where the historical future was concerned, the need to work out the social implications of the gospel was beginning to be felt.

One way of summarizing the problem of nineteenth-century Christianity would be to bring out its failure to integrate eschatology and ethics. The Liberal Protestants and indeed the early Christian socialists were too bland about human progress. Not only did they fail to reckon sufficiently with the forces of evil in human life, both individual and collective. They neglected the intractable problem of death and of the undeniable hopelessness of many particular lives, however bright the future of humanity might be. The conservatives were more alive to these aspects of the human predicament and to the power of the Christian hope to enter into and transform the darkest situations of sin and despair. What neither strand succeeded in achieving was the recognition, still less the realization, of an eschatological faith in the ultimate triumph of God's grace already effective here and now, in the transformation not only of individual lives but of the structures of society too.

8

The Twentieth
Century I:
The Reaction against
Liberal Theology

The History of Religions School

Liberal Protestantism, with its conviction that the essence of Christianity consisted in the gradual realization of an ethical Kingdom of God on earth, was already being challenged before the turn of the century by the work of a loosely associated group of German scholars, known as the 'history of religions school'. Their chief concern was to study the Old and New Testaments and the history of Christianity in their full historical and religious contexts, the Old Testament in the light of the ancient near-eastern religions, the New Testament in the light of Jewish and Hellenistic modes of thought and expression, and Christianity in the light of the whole history of religions. Two writers associated with this group will be mentioned here as making important contributions to our theme of eschatology, the New Testament scholar Johannes Weiss (1863–1914) and the systematic theologian and sociologist Ernst Troeltsch (1865–1923).

Weiss's short book *Jesus' Proclamation of the Kingdom of God* (1892) set out to show that, far from having preached 'the fatherhood of God and the brotherhood of man', Jesus had proclaimed an out-and-out eschatological message of God's imminent in-breaking from beyond to destroy the old world and create a new, where he, Jesus, the Messiah, would be king. Weiss held that Jesus gradually became certain that he must first die and then return on the clouds of heaven to reign with his disciples over the new Jerusalem. Two points need to be made about Weiss's startling reconstruction. The first is that it was very crude and only partially true. Weiss made no distinction between eschatology and apocalyptic and did not get very far towards understanding the framework of ideas within which Jesus's eschatological preaching took place. But, as will be clear from our treatment of these issues in Chapter 2, for all these deficiencies in Weiss's reconstruction, it is impossible to ignore the eschatological, or even the apocalyptic, dimension to Jesus's preaching. The other point to be made about Weiss is that he did not himself know what to do with his discovery. At the end of his book he somewhat disarmingly says:

The real difference between our modern Protestant world-view and that of primitive Christianity is ... that we do not share the eschatological attitude ... We do not await a Kingdom of God which is to come down from heaven to earth and abolish this world, but we do hope to be gathered with the church of Jesus Christ into the heavenly 'Kingdom'. ...[1]

The work of Ernst Troeltsch, the systematic theologian of the history of religions school, was much more constructive and suggestive. Despite the attempts of Karl Barth and others to treat his thought as the climax of Liberal Protestantism, Troeltsch was in fact just as convinced as Barth that the liberal ethical version of the Kingdom of God, especially as put forward by Hermann, would not do. He accepted Weiss's rediscovery of the eschatological nature of Jesus's preaching, but went on to offer a theological interpretation of that eschatology that attempted to do justice to its lasting significance in the history of religions. For Troeltsch, the eschatology of Jesus and the early Church was mythical language, but language that expressed two essential and irreplaceable religious truths, first that absolute value was objectively rooted and based in God, in the beyond and not in our own subjective power, and secondly that absolute truth and value were essentially future realities and goals never to be identified with any actual historical, social, or religious accomplishment. Thus, at the

---

[1] Johannes Weiss, *Jesus' Proclamation of the Kingdom of God*, Eng. trans. (London: SCM Press, 1971), 135–6.

same time, Christian eschatology inspires us both to work for the Kingdom of God and also to look for a transcendent future in which their work will be taken up and transformed. These perspectives enable us to differentiate Troeltsch from the liberals, and to find lasting value in his work. It has to be admitted, however, that Troeltsch's conception of the future absolute goal was rather vague. Indeed, it became even more vague in Troeltsch's last writings, as he succumbed more and more to a sense of the historical relativity of all the world's religions. It has been pointed out that it was Troeltsch's failure to discern the presence, by anticipation, of the absolute future of God's Kingdom in the coming of Jesus that accounts for this relativism and this vagueness.[2] But the overall framework of Troeltsch's interpretation of New Testament eschatology still has much to offer.

Albert Schweitzer

The same can hardly be said of the remarkable figure of Albert Schweitzer (1875–1965). In his famous book *The Quest of the Historical Jesus* (first German edition 1906), Schweitzer traced the story of research into the life of Jesus from Reimarus in the eighteenth century to his own older contemporary William Wrede (1859–1906). He showed how nineteenth-century liberal lives of Jesus had painted pictures modelled on their authors' own ideas of ethics, progress, and the Kingdom of God. Only Weiss (anticipated at the beginning of the story by Reimarus) had recognized the unhistorical nature of such pictures of Jesus and recovered the eschatological character of his preaching. Schweitzer's thoroughgoing eschatological conception of the preaching and life of Jesus was even more radical than that of Weiss. According to Schweitzer, not only had Jesus prophesied an imminent end, teaching, in the Sermon on the Mount, an 'interim ethic' suited to the short interval before the end, but had then resolved to suffer and to die, precisely to take the messianic woes upon himself, so that the end might come and the messianic reign begin.

[2] See 'The Basis of Ethics in the Thought of Ernst Troeltsch', in Wolfhart Pannenberg, *Ethics*, Eng. trans. (Philadelphia: Westminster Press, 1981), 87–111.

Schweitzer held that Christianity could never depend on going back to this strange, enigmatic figure of the historical Jesus. Rather, Jesus's world-renouncing stance, expressed in the apocalyptic language of his time, had released a spiritual force in the world that required no historical backing. It is precisely this ability to reject the world and its claims that continues, so Schweitzer thought, to make the spirit of Jesus such a powerful force in world history. For our own time this would not, of course, be a matter of apocalyptic preaching. As is well known, Schweitzer renounced his music and his professorship and went to Africa as a medical missionary. But the gap between the eschatological figure of Jesus as Schweitzer saw him and the religious energy for our own time that he still found in the Christian tradition is too great for Schweitzer's position to carry conviction.

Karl Barth and Dialectical Theology

The attacks of Weiss and Schweitzer were not the only problem for Liberal Protestant ways of understanding progress towards an ethical Kingdom of God. The First World War dealt a shattering blow to the optimism that had characterized both secular and religious views of history in the nineteenth century. The breakdown of European civilization and the terrible slaughter of the trenches in France precipitated a loss of confidence in the whole idea of progress and provoked sharp reactions in Christian theology as in other areas of thought and culture. In 1918 Barth's book on the *Epistle to the Romans* appeared.[3] It marked the beginning of a new phase and a new movement in Protestant theology. In this book, Karl Barth (1886–1968), who was to become undoubtedly the greatest twentieth-century Protestant theologian, issued a sharp challenge to those who thought in terms of the gradual realization of the Kingdom of God on earth. For Barth, the Bible spoke rather of the infinite, eternal, and 'wholly other' God, breaking into time and history from beyond, and laying claim to people's faith and action here and now. Every moment

---

[3] Barth's *Römerbrief* was thoroughly revised for a second edition in 1921. For the English translation of the sixth edition, see Karl Barth, *The Epistle to the Romans* (London: Oxford University Press, 1933).

is the eschatological moment, where eternity breaks into time in a Word of judgement and grace that creates faith and a life centred on God.

The movement initiated by Barth became known as 'dialectical theology' or sometimes 'the theology of crisis'. The former title reflects the paradoxical language of both 'yes' and 'no' that Barth felt driven to use in order to bring out the 'infinite qualitative distinction' between God and humankind (the influence of Kierkegaard being strong at this point). The latter title reflects the theme of judgement (*krisis* in Greek), the crisis brought upon human affairs when confronted by the transcendent God. Associated with Barth in this movement were Eduard Thurneysen, Friedrich Gogarten, Rudolf Bultmann, and Emil Brunner, and even Paul Tillich and Paul Althaus, some of whom will be considered later in this chapter. The journal of the movement was called *Zwischen den Zeiten*, 'Between the Times', its title indicating the eschatological thrust of dialectical theology. Admittedly, the idea of standing 'between the times'—that is, between the time of Christ's resurrection and the time of Christ's final revelation—might appear to reintroduce the future dimension, pointing forward to that final revelation. But, in fact, for the early Barth, every time stood equally 'between the times', and it was the vertical dimension, God's Word from above, that carried the weight of Christian eschatology.

It is worth pausing to compare and contrast the ways in which Barth and Troeltsch tried to interpret and apply the eschatology of the Gospels as rediscovered by Weiss and Schweitzer. It could be said that Troeltsch was more successful than Barth in retaining and emphasizing the future reference of Christian eschatology. But the vagueness and ambivalence that we found in Troeltsch's conception of the absolute are completely absent from Barth's theology. For Barth, the eternal breaks into time with a concrete and specific Word, challenging us here and now to repentance and faith.

This feature of Barth's theology became even stronger as it developed, away from its early more 'existentialist' phase, into the great christocentric *Church Dogmatics* of Barth's mature years. The Word from beyond was now understood, more and more in traditional incarnational terms, as God's gift of himself in his Son, Jesus Christ. This presence and self-revelation of God incarnate in Jesus Christ were made by Barth to carry the whole weight of Christian theology. Everything, it seems, has already been done. Each generation is challenged to let that great act of God take effect in individual, communal, and social life, until the final universal revelation, at the end of time, of what God in Christ has already done. Jesus Christ is himself 'the last thing', the eternal, decisive, act of God in history, and the pivot on which all human destiny turns.

Such is the christocentric emphasis of Barth's theology that many commentators have questioned whether he retained any future eschatology at all. He may, unlike Troeltsch, have discerned the *presence* in Jesus of God's absolute future Kingdom in the world, but the balance appears to have swung to the opposite extreme, nothing being left for the actual future but the final revelation of what has already been accomplished. Against this it has been protested that the Christian hope cannot just be for a final *revelation* of all human history in relation to God's act in Christ.

In order to understand this protest, we must examine what Barth said about the future a little more closely. He certainly wrote at length and with enthusiasm of the Christian hope for the direct vision of Jesus Christ, at the end of time, when his Lordship over all creation will be unveiled. This is what Barth understood by the Parousia. Moreover such is the christological concentration in Barth's thought that, for him, that final revelation will constitute a 'Last Judgement' only in the sense that the judgement and redemption already effected by Christ will then finally be recognized in all its universal scope.

The implications of all this for the individual's hope of heaven are striking. Barth, we discover, was deeply suspicious of the idea of eternal life as a continuing temporal process 'after' bodily death. 'Resurrection', he wrote, 'means not the continuation of life, but life's completion.'[4] There is bestowed upon us 'unconditional participation in the glory of God.'[5] This is certainly something for which we now hope. In time, we look forward to eternity. But eternity is not more time; it is rather a matter of being caught up into God's time, where we shall see our whole life, and God's whole creation, in relation to what God has done in Christ. This conception was spelled out in a most interesting way in a letter in which Barth explained his

---

[4] Karl Barth, *Dogmatics in Outline*, Eng. trans. (London: SCM Press, 1949), 154.
[5] Ibid. 153.

view of 'eternal life' in contradistinction to ideas of survival such as spiritualists toy with. Eternal life, wrote Barth,

is not another and second life, beyond the present one. It is this life, but the reverse side which God sees although it is as yet hidden from us—this life in its relation to what he has done for the whole world, and therefore for us too, in Jesus Christ. We thus wait and hope, even in view of our death, for our manifestation with Him, with Jesus Christ who was raised again from the dead, in the glory of not only the judgement but also the grace of God.[6]

This is the first example that we have come across of a view that will recur in twentieth-century eschatology—a kind of 'non-temporal' conception of our participation beyond death, in God's glory. It is, in part, an attempt to do justice to the significance of earthly life: it is *this* life that we shall see from God's eternal standpoint. But we can look forward to seeing it judged and redeemed, freed by what Christ has done from all sorrow and pain. The matter is complicated by Barth's obscure conception of eternity as God's time, in which past, present, and future are held together as a whole. But we can perhaps appreciate the protest often made against Barth's idea of Christian hope being only for a *revelation* of the ultimate and lasting truth about the past. Indeed it is to be doubted whether Barth's view of time and eternity and their relation makes much sense. It is difficult to see how this world with all its failures and its stunted and thwarted lives can participate in God's glory without being changed and renewed in a much more substantial sense than can be captured by talk of future revelation. Powerful as Barth's christocentric eschatology undoubtedly was, with its insistence that eternity has already broken decisively into time, it lacked that central feature of Christian hope for a new creation and a new *world* beyond death.

We cannot leave the subject of Barth's eschatology without noting three further positive aspects of his reflections on this theme. The first concerns the troublesome doctrine of predestination that we somewhat summarily rejected in Chapter 5 (see p. 74 above). On this topic, Barth, from within the Calvinist tradition, achieved a remarkable *tour de force*. Since for him the whole relation between eternity and time is focused in Christ, it is true in all eternity that the destiny of all men and women is fulfilled in him. Christ takes upon himself

---

[6] Karl Barth, *Letters 1961–1968*, Eng. trans. (Edinburgh: T. & T. Clark, 1981), 9.

their damnation and their election to salvation. Thus in the end Christ is the only rejected one, yet at the same time he is eternally God's chosen one, and through him the way to reconciliation with God is opened up to all. This is a striking reinterpretation of predestination and much to be preferred to Calvin's or even to Augustine's version. But it may be doubted whether we really need this complicated apparatus. As we shall see, an understanding of creation as open to the future and of God's intention, in and through his saving acts in Christ, to embrace everyone is sufficient to dispel the notion that all is fixed in advance. The idea of predestination goes with the idea that eternity already enfolds past, present, and future. If the latter idea is rejected, the former can readily be discarded as well.

Barth's doctrine of predestination does, however, imply a second feature of his eschatology worthy of special comment—namely its tendency towards universalism. If in God's eternal decree all men and women are saved in Christ, then no rejection of God on anyone's part can be final. However terrible the effects of sin, and Barth never minimized the judgement people bring upon themselves by their acts and omissions, they are nevertheless, because of Christ, forgiven, and must, in the end, come to see themselves in the light of the divine grace. Barth was wary of drawing this conclusion explicitly. In a lecture entitled *The Humanity of God*, in which he redressed the balance from his earlier insistence of the otherness of God, Barth meditated upon the affirmation of humanity to be discerned in God's gift of himself to us in Jesus Christ. He did not go so far as to say that this definitely means universalism. But he did ask those alarmed by the notion to agree 'that we have no theological right to set any sort of limits to the loving-kindness of God which has appeared in Jesus Christ'.[7]

The third feature of Barth's treatment of the Christian hope that calls for comment is his ethics and especially his social ethics. For, despite the controlling emphasis on what God has done and on our own powerlessness to bring about the Kingdom of God on earth, Barth drew quite radical conclusions from his understanding of the gospel for the ordering of human life on earth. As we shall see in the final section of this chapter, Barth must be counted amongst the twentieth-century advocates of Christian socialism. Indeed it may be thought to be a definite implication of his eschatology, with its

[7] Karl Barth, *The Humanity of God*, Eng. trans. (London: Collins, 1961), 62.

emphasis on this life seen from the perspective of eternity, that our task in response to the gospel is to obey God's will for society as well as for our own individual lives here and now. Fellow-humanity (*Mitmenschlichkeit*) is of the essence of humanity made in the image of the Trinity. If Christian hope is based on what God has done in Christ, it will inevitably work itself out on earth in terms of individual and social ethics: 'thy will be done.'

Realized Eschatology

The theologians who supported dialectical theology in the 1920s soon went their own distinctive ways, and of no one is this more true than Rudolf Bultmann (1884–1976). Bultmann was the most uncompromising of modern theologians in his recognition of the strangeness of the world of the Bible and of the mythological nature of the world view of its authors. His programme of 'demythologization' was intended, very positively, as a means of extracting the inner meaning of the biblical message from its clothing in myth, and interpreting it, existentially, for today. Existentialism is a twentieth-century philosophy of life that concentrates everything on what it is to choose and to live authentically. Christian existentialism, as Bultmann expounded it, involves an understanding of human existence as enabled to find authenticity by a Word from God that transforms my self-understanding and creates faith.

The eschatology of the Bible, especially that of the apocalyptic writings, according to Bultmann, was thoroughly mythological in form. Parousia, resurrection, the end of the world, heaven, and hell were all mythological ideas in the sense of being ways of representing the eternal and the beyond in vivid this-worldly picture language. Their existential meaning was not some future series of events but rather the ever-present possibility of an end to my worldly, inauthentic, existence, and a beginning to the authentic life of faith. For Bultmann, the Christ-event and the preaching of the Christ-event constitute the eschatological moment in which, as I hear the Word, my existence is put in question. Two quotations will serve to illustrate this interpretation: 'Where this Word resounds, the end of the world becomes present to the hearer, in that it confronts him with the decision whether he will belong to the old or to the new world.'[8] 'Every instant has the possibility of being an eschatological instant and in Christian faith this possibility is realised.'[9]

We may be pardoned for thinking that, for Bultmann, the word 'eschatological' had come to mean little more than 'existential', at least where my existence is thought of as determined here and now by the Word of God. And it seems as if Bultmann too had transferred the reference point of eschatological language entirely from the future to the present. He even took the notion of living 'between the times' to refer not to chronological time but to the believer's constant openness to the future. This means, of course, that the future did not disappear entirely from Bultmann's theology, since the authentic life of faith, made possible by this Word, is a matter of facing the future with confidence and faith. Men and women of faith are unafraid of the future, including death. They cannot picture a future beyond death, but their trust in God's Word has the character of unshakeable hope, even in the face of death.

Many criticisms have been made of Bultmann's existentialist interpretation. It has been accused of excessive individualism, of having nothing to say about God's purpose in creation and providence, of failing to do justice to Christian hope for the future realization of the Kingdom of God, whether on earth or in heaven. A Christianity pared down to the moment of encounter between the Word of God and the faith of the individual, however religiously powerful in its existential force, is an impoverished Christianity.

Meanwhile, in England, a milder, but also influential form of 'realized eschatology' was being put forward by the New Testament scholar Charles Harold Dodd (1884–1973). It was Dodd who popularized the phrase 'realized eschatology' in order to bring out its predominantly present character, contrasted with the future emphasis of Weiss's and Schweitzer's thoroughgoing (or 'consequent') eschatology. With consummate skill, Dodd showed that the parables of Jesus in their original setting had conveyed the challenging message of Jesus that the Kingdom of God had come upon his hearers and was in their midst and that *now* was the

---

[8] Rudolf Bultmann, *Glauben und Verstehen*, iii (Tübingen: J. C. B. Mohr, 1960), 129.
[9] Rudolf Bultmann, *History and Eschatology*, Eng. trans. (Edinburgh: University Press, 1957), 154.

time of judgement and salvation. 'Unless we have interpreted the Gospels quite wrongly, the thought of Jesus passed directly from the immediate situation to the eternal order lying beyond all history, of which He spoke in the language of apocalyptic symbolism.'[10] According to Dodd, the preaching of Jesus and the preaching of the Church confront both individual and society with the final challenge of the presence of eternity in time. Those who believe *have* eternal life. From the moment one comes to be in Christ, one *is* already immortal, a new creation. Dodd thus claims both John and Paul for realized eschatology. In his commentary on *The Epistle of Paul to the Romans*, Dodd says: 'The life after death is not a new life: it is the life he has been living all the time in Christ, only lived under different conditions. This sense of a sort of interpenetration of two worlds, the deathless order being already present in moral experience, is a distinctively Christian contribution to the problem of a future life.'[11] If this reminds us of Barth, the words 'lived under different conditions' show that Dodd's is the less radical interpretation. Dodd knows that, for Jesus and for Paul, the blessedness of our present experience of the Kingdom is not exhausted by what falls within the bounds of time and space. 'Our destiny lies in the eternal order.'[12] And indeed Dodd came to admit that 'inaugurated eschatology' was probably a better way of putting his position than 'realized eschatology' had been. But the fact remains that Dodd's conception of eternity was very much a timeless, Platonic, one, and the relation between time and eternity a vertical rather than a horizontal one.

Together, the views of Barth, Bultmann, and Dodd make out a powerful case for placing the emphasis on the present rather than on the future, where Christian eschatology is concerned, and for taking the 'last things' to mean the things of ultimate significance that God has done and does already. But, as we shall see, this emphasis on 'now' and 'already' has come under increasing attack in subsequent Christian theology.

[10] C. H. Dodd, *The Parables of the Kingdom* (London: Nisbet, 1935; Fontana edn., London and Glasgow: Collins, 1961), 154.
[11] C. H. Dodd, *The Epistle of Paul to the Romans* (London: Hodder & Stoughton, 1932; Fontana edn., London and Glasgow: Collins, 1959), 142.
[12] Dodd, *The Parables of the Kingdom*, 156.

Some Other German Theologians

Of those associated with Barth in the early days of dialectical theology, it will be sufficient to consider here, in addition to Bultmann, three leading German theologians, each of whom went on to develop a distinctive theological position in contradistinction to that of Barth: Emil Brunner, Paul Althaus, and Paul Tillich.

The theology of Emil Brunner (1889–1966) was for a long time appreciated in the English-speaking world as more balanced than that of his great contemporaries, Barth and Bultmann. He certainly taught the centrality of Christ and the newness of 'eschatological existence' in response to God's 'final' acts in the gifts of Christ and the Spirit. But he refused to rule out all other knowledge of God and he refused to treat the biblical hope for the future as largely mythological in nature. In his book *Eternal Hope* and in the last part of his three-volume *Dogmatics*, Brunner argued that, although historical time takes on a new character through the coming of Christ, which opens up eternity to the believer, we still live in a state of 'eschatological tension', looking forward in hope to the consummation of history at the Parousia. Against Bultmann, he asserted that the New Testament hope for an eternal future is not inextricably bound to apocalyptic mythology. 'There is no need of an apocalyptic mythology on which to establish an Eschatology. It *is* established in Jesus, the Christ.'[13] Brunner insisted on the paradox of the 'now already' and 'not yet' that pervades the New Testament. The meaning of life and of history is given from beyond, by anticipation in the Christ-event, and finally in the consummation of history, at the Parousia. Eternal life and the Kingdom of God both have this dual character of present availability and future promise. The tension must be maintained. Similarly the tension, often noted in earlier chapters of this book, between the idea of 'departing and being with Christ' and that of Christ's appearing in glory at the end of history must also be maintained. According to Brunner, the apparent gap between these two events—the death of the individual and the end of history—is a

---

[13] Emil Brunner, *The Christian Doctrine of the Church, Faith, and the Consummation: Dogmatics*, iii, Eng. trans. (London: Lutterworth Press, 1962), 344.

feature of our temporality that we must suppose to be transcended in God's eternity. We shall later question the intelligibility of this solution.

But what did Brunner understand by the Parousia? He affirmed the *presence* of Christ in all three dimensions of time. He has come, he comes, he will come. The latter cannot be regarded solely as mythology. 'Faith in Christ without the expectation of Parousia is like a flight of stairs that leads nowhere, but ends in the void.'[14] But the New Testament pictures of the Parousia *are* mythological. The final event is literally unimaginable. Nevertheless, the truth at its heart must be affirmed: that history will be brought to an end and Christ fully revealed in the final consummation. The imminence or non-imminence of the end is of no importance for faith.

Brunner also affirmed the importance of the doctrine of the resurrection of the body in bringing out the necessity, in God's new creation as in the old, for a principle of distinction between Creator and creature and a principle of individuation for each human being. But clearly the resurrection body will not be flesh and blood. On the themes of judgement and the final consummation, Brunner, having categorically rejected the Calvinist doctrine of double predestination, expressed a strong sense of the ever-present possibility of our bringing hell upon ourselves. But, at the same time, he expressed confidence and hope in the universal saving efficacy of God's grace. These two affirmations cannot be separated or asserted independently. Brunner remained a dialectical theologian! As for the final consummation, this can be expressed only in symbols and myths, whose underlying truths can be only barely stated: we shall see God face to face; we shall experience, in fellowship, the fulfilment of our destiny; and it is in and through Christ that we shall be brought to the Father.

Another German theologian who made significant contributions to the subject of eschatology was Paul Althaus (1888–1966). In the first edition of his book *The Last Things* (*Die Letzte Dinge*, 1922) Althaus taught what he called an 'axiological' eschatology. ('Axiology' means the theory of value.) That is to say, he interpreted the Christian doctrine of the last things as symbolizing the eternal value that God's acts in Christ give to every moment in life and in history. This is particularly interesting in that it translated the liberal's theme

[14] Ibid. 396.

of a future ethical Kingdom of God into the 'vertical' relation of present 'realized' eschatology. However, Althaus realized that God's will for us can never be expected to find perfect consummation within history, any more than within an individual life. Parabolic language about the Parousia and the future Kingdom of God must be taken to refer to a consummation beyond history. Consequently, millenarianism must be decisively rejected as a doctrine of the end-time. On the other hand, 'as an expression of the relationship between concrete historical service and the world to come, or of the responsibility of orientating everything here and now upon earth towards the Kingdom that is to come, it has a real and obvious value as a parable'.[15]

In later editions of his book and in the revised article on 'Eschatology' that he contributed to the third edition of the German encyclopaedia *Religion in Geschichte und Gegenwart*, Althaus made it quite clear that an ethical, existentialist, understanding of eschatology is inadequate by itself. Although based on experience of what God has done already, Christian eschatology is primarily concerned with the consummation of God's saving purpose for individuals, for history, and for the cosmos. Althaus was well aware of the factors that make this-worldly hope for a perfected Kingdom of God unrealistic. In face of death, recurrent evil, and cosmic waste, Christianity looks beyond time and history for a new world, as prefigured in the risen Christ. Since the location of ultimate Christian hope lies in the beyond, it is as much a mistake to look for signs of the end within history as it is to look for progressive realization of the Kingdom within history. 'Antichrist' remains a potent symbol for the ever-present possibility of an increase of radical evil on the human scene, and the Church of Christ remains an indication of the ever-present possibility of the greater effectiveness of God's grace within history. But the future is open, the end of history is not fixed in advance, and it in the light of his transcendent hope that the Christian works for a better world. Hope for a new world does not lead Christians to forsake this world. Rather, it inspires them and empowers them to ethical action in the present.

---

[15] This is taken from the English translation of Althaus's article on 'Eschatology' in the second edition of *Religion in Geschichte und Gegenwart*. It may be found in Jaroslav Pelikan (ed.), *Twentieth Century Theology in the Making*, i (London: Collins, 1969), 291–2.

The eschatology of Paul Althaus may be regarded as a fairly balanced exposition of the Christian hope. Its main weaknesses lie in its relative pessimism regarding God's providence within the historical process and its sharp disjunction between this world and the new world to come. As we shall see, later Protestant theology has had much more positive things to say both about the historical future and about its relation to the transcendent consummation. Althaus himself renounced all speculation concerning the ultimate future. In his view, the only way of speaking of the consummation of all things is in parables, drawn from whatever fullness of life is given in present experience. Althaus mentions in particular the I–Thou relation of personal existence and love, and, of course, present experience of life together in Christ, as authentic sources for such parables.

Paul Tillich (1886–1965) is included here as a German theologian, despite the fact that he left Germany in 1933 and taught and wrote for the rest of his life in the United States. Tillich combined a broad metaphysical conception of the 'ultimate reality' at the heart of human history with an existentialist interpretation of salvation as the 'new being' that overcomes people's estrangement from themselves and from the 'ground of their being'. He dealt with eschatology in the last part of his *Systematic Theology* under the heading of 'History and the Kingdom of God'. Tillich tried to steer a middle path between utopian ideas of progress, on the one hand, and purely transcendental forms of eschatology, on the other. As far as the Kingdom of God within history is concerned, Tillich was prepared to speak of elements of progress and of divine providence in the sense of creativity working through the spontaneity of creatures and human freedom. But he was equally aware of the ambiguities of power and of the ever-present possibility of the 'demonic', where some finite aspiration is absolutized and pursued unconditionally. The guiding concept in Tillich's analysis of history was that of the *kairos*: the significant moment, when something new and creative becomes possible in human history, the opportunity is given for prophetic vision, and the Kingdom of God manifests itself in a particular breakthrough.

As far as the Kingdom of God as the end of history is concerned, Tillich regarded the eschatological symbolism of the Christian tradition as referring to the elevation of the temporal into eternity. As with most of the theologians considered in this chapter, it was his

conception of eternity that made Tillich wary of traditional eschatology's talk of the future. In Tillich's case, however, we can hardly speak
of a 'vertical' relation between time and eternity, since the dimension
of 'height' was constantly rejected by him as a metaphor for talk of
God. Rather, Tillich employed his own technical vocabulary of
'existence' and 'essence', and spoke of the 'essentialization' of all
things temporal as they participate in, and find fulfilment in, the
eternal. Only the negative elements of temporal existence are
excluded. In Tillich's own words, 'nothing which has been created
in history is lost but it is liberated from the negative element with
which it is entangled within existence'.[16] He was prepared to use the
bold metaphor of the temporal becoming 'eternal memory' but
glosses this as 'living retention' of the remembered thing in which
the positive potentialities of history are fulfilled. Since this is a matter
of universal participation, Christian theology, he claimed, cannot
retain the notion of 'eternal damnation', however seriously it takes
the condemnatory side of the divine judgement. Tillich insisted that
the self-conscious self cannot be excluded from eternal life, but, since
eternity transcends temporality, such self-consciousness cannot validly
be pictured on the analogy of our present experience.

Like Brunner and Althaus, Tillich moved beyond 'realized eschatology' and tried to do justice to the ultimate nature of the Christian
hope. Moreover, it might be thought that he succeeded in avoiding
the sharp disjunction between this world and the beyond, which
characterizes the thought of the other two theologians considered
in this section. But reasons will be given in subsequent chapters for
questioning the intelligibility of any such conception of our non-
temporal participation in God's eternity.

Nicolas Berdyaev

There has not been space in this book to deal with the treatment of
the Christian hope in Eastern Orthodox theology. Only a bare reference was made above (p. 49) to the notion of 'divinization', which the
Eastern churches took over from the Greek Fathers for the ultimate

---

[16] Paul Tillich, *Systematic Theology*, iii (London: SCM Press, 1964), 424.

destiny of humankind in relation to God. But it is worth pausing at this point to mention a remarkable Russian philosopher, Nicolas Berdyaev (1874–1948), who lived in Paris as an émigré from 1922. His book *The Destiny of Man* may be deemed a classic of Christian existentialism. It is first and foremost a book on ethics. Berdyaev shows how the gospel ethics of redemption transcends the ethics of law and leads to an ethics of creativeness and freedom. The Kingdom of God cannot be equated with any social or economic programme. It is a spiritual principle, challenging natural men and women, not only in their sinful nature, but in their ideas of goodness too. It puts both capitalism and socialism in question, although the will to bring about social justice is certainly implied by its concern with the moral and personal freedom of everyone. But the freedom of men and women, as envisaged in the gospel message of the Kingdom, is a spiritual category. Ethics must deal too with the problems of eschatology, with the overcoming of death and hell. In the last part of his book, entitled 'Eschatological Ethics', Berdyaev wrote very powerfully of the problem of death and of the hell that people can undoubtedly bring upon themselves. The possibility of hell, at least subjectively speaking, is the measure of our spiritual freedom. On the other hand, there cannot be an objective hell. An objective hell would make nonsense of faith in the eternal Kingdom of God. On the contrary, God in Christ defeated death and hell, and an ethics based on the gospel sets itself to overcome not only injustice and unfreedom but death and hell as well. The final victory is the victory of the spiritual and the eternal over all these negative things.

Berdyaev's writing on the theme of eternity is more than a little ambiguous. At times he seems to suggest a purely existentialist interpretation: 'Eternal life is not a future life but life in the present, life in the depths of an instant of time.'[17] There is no denying, however, his conviction of the reality of the eternal Kingdom. We have a foretaste of it in moments of ecstasy. But in itself it is 'the attainment of perfection, deification, beauty and spiritual wholeness' beyond time.[18]

Here, then, is another voice, this time out of the Eastern tradition, struggling with the paradoxical relation between time and eternity.

[17] Nicolas Berdyaev, *The Destiny of Man* (London: Geoffrey Bles, 1937), 261–2.
[18] Ibid. 291.

But there is one further point to be derived from Berdyaev. Despite his sense of eternity over against all times, he was prepared to hint at the possibility of other times, other 'aeons', between our own time and the attainment of eternity. For the conquest of death and hell is not fully accomplished in the course of our earthly span. Despite a critical reference to the theory of reincarnation, Berdyaev wrote: 'it is essential to recognize that man's final fate can only be settled after an infinitely greater experience in spiritual worlds than is possible in our short earthly life.'[19] Although a moment may lead us from time to eternity, nevertheless, if cosmic regeneration be not attained in our world-aeon, 'there will be other aeons in which the work of salvation and transfiguration will be continued. That work is not limited to our earthly life.'[20] This is an idea to which we shall be returning in Chapters 10 and 11 below.

The Development of Social Theology

It remains, in this survey of non-Roman Catholic eschatology in the first half of the twentieth century, to consider how social theology was developed during this period. In the light of the reaction against Liberal Protestant conflation of the Kingdom of God with a perfected ethical society on earth, we shall not now expect a straight translation of Christian eschatology into some form of social utopianism. The examples of Barth, Tillich, and Berdyaev will already have suggested that the relation between the Kingdom of God and its social-ethical implications for the historical future was now being thought of much more dialectically. Yet, somewhat paradoxically, this distancing from an identification of the Kingdom of God with any historical future form of social life on earth led to much more specific and realistic social-ethical commitments on the part of Christian theologians. Divorced from utopianism and within the framework of a more transcendent eschatology, Christian hope for the historical future took on much more concrete forms.

This is most clearly seen in the social ethics of Karl Barth. Barth had been influenced in his thinking on these matters by the younger

---

[19] Berdyaev, *The Destiny of Man*, 275.   [20] Ibid. 294.

Blumhardt (Christoph Friedrich Blumhardt (1842–1919)), a German pastor who had actively taken part in Social Democratic politics in the early years of the twentieth century. More radical influences still were the Swiss theologians Leonard Ragaz (1868–1945) and Hermann Kutter (1869–1931), who endorsed contemporary talk of social revolution as reflecting the will of God. The young Barth associated himself with these religious socialists, joined the Social Democratic Party, and, as a pastor in Safenwil in Switzerland, was active on behalf of the working classes. But Barth's disillusionment with liberal theology and his development of the theology of crisis, described above, led him to withdraw his earlier claim that socialism is a predicate of the gospel, and to develop a much more critical attitude to the relationship between theology and politics. Nevertheless, Barth remained a radical in politics. He disliked the actual developments of socialism in post-war Europe, but he never abandoned the view that the gospel had radical implications for society as well as for the individual. This sympathetic, yet critical, stance made him refuse to join the chorus of Western anti-communism after the Second World War; and his correspondence with the Czech Protestant theologian Josef Hromadka (1889–1969),[21] who tried to make a positive Christian contribution to the building of the new socialist state in Czechoslovakia, reveals Barth's enduring desire that the gospel should be interpreted concretely for the current historical situation, both East and West.

A similar development may be seen in the religious socialism of Paul Tillich. In Germany in the 1920s Tillich's commitment to the struggle for social justice led him at first to support the cause of revolution. The revolutionary situation of Germany after the First World War might well be thought to exemplify his conception of a *kairos*—a critical moment when 'the eternal judges and transforms the temporal'.[22] But in fact the alleged *kairos* passed, and, in Russia, the revolution took on a 'demonic' character. Tillich continued, in his early writings after moving to America, to defend Christian socialism, in contradistinction to Marxist utopianism, and he continued, despite warning against premature solutions, to advocate the prophetic

---

[21] See Barth, *Letters 1961–1968*, *passim*.
[22] See Paul Tillich, *The Protestant Era* (Chicago: University of Chicago Press, 1948), ch. 3.

spirit, looking for 'the signs of the times', and bringing the judgement of the gospel to bear upon political conservatism.

Earlier, in America, Liberal Protestantism had taken a less individualistic form than in Germany. The influence of Walter Rauschenbusch (1861–1918), who drew Christian socialist implications from Ritschl's theology of the ethical Kingdom of God, was considerable. In his *Christianity and the Social Crisis* (1907), Rauschenbusch argued that Christianity had more in common with communism than with individualistic competition, and that Jesus had lived in the hope of a great transformation of the social life about him. This 'Social Gospel' movement in America persisted well into the 1930s. It was challenged by Reinhold Niebuhr (1892–1971) on grounds of its naive utopianism. Niebuhr set against such liberal perfectionism what he called 'Christian realism'—a prophetic stance, similar to Tillich's, in which the vertical dimension of the gospel love ethic reveals the ambiguities of human achievement in the social sphere and yet at the same time inspires the struggle for social justice. In the second volume of his Gifford lectures on *The Nature and Destiny of Man* (1943), Niebuhr argued that 'grace' is related to 'nature' partly as fulfilment and partly as negation. There is a progressive dynamism in human history. New tasks and possibilities arise, but at the same time new ambiguities arise. 'There is no escape from the paradoxical relation of history to the Kingdom of God. History moves towards the realization of the kingdom, but yet the judgement of God is upon every new realization.'[23] Niebuhr set this dialectical conception of history and the Kingdom of God in the context of the 'end' of history. He argued that the New Testament hope of the Parousia cannot be taken literally, but must be taken seriously. If taken literally, it fosters an unrealistic utopian millenarianism. If ignored, it can only be in favour of a notion of eternity that annuls rather than fulfils the historical process. The Parousia, then, is a symbol for 'the sufficiency of God's sovereignty over the world and history and in the final supremacy of love over all the forces of self-love...'.[24] Christian hope is for the fulfilment, not the negation, of the historical process, but it is for a fulfilment that lies beyond the temporal process itself.

---

[23] Reinhold Niebuhr, *The Nature and Destiny of Man: A Christian Interpretation*, ii (London: Nisbet, 1943), 296.

[24] Ibid. 300.

The symbols of the Last Judgement and the resurrection point to the same transcendent consummation of history. Yet such a hope at the same time affirms the eternal significance of our historical existence and prompts our involvement in historical tasks and obligations.

Among the successors to the Victorian Christian Socialists in England was R. H. Tawney (1880–1962),[25] whose attacks on capitalism, largely on Christian grounds, did much to shape the reports of the Conference on Christian Politics, Economics and Citizenship (COPEC) at Birmingham in 1924, at which the leading figure was William Temple (1881–1944). Temple, later to become Archbishop of Canterbury, was by far the most significant advocate, in English Christianity during the 1930s and early 1940s, of more or less radical Christian social thought. His *Christianity and Social Order* (1942) may still be seen as a perceptive statement of the basic principles by which human society should be ordered, but it lacks a developed theological framework such as Temple's German and American contemporaries were providing. If one turns to Temple's earlier theological works, one finds, admittedly, a recognition of the dual aspects of 'immanence' and 'transcendence' —on the one hand, the divine Spirit working immanently in the human world through the Christian Church and its concern for persons and for social order; on the other hand, the transcendent consummation of the Kingdom of God freed from the limitations of earthly existence. But Temple's somewhat 'idealist' conception of the relation between immanence and transcendence may well be thought to lack the power of dialectical theology or of the prophetic realism of Niebuhr and Tillich.

Conclusion

Protestant theology, in the first half of the twentieth century, reacted sharply against the nineteenth-century liberal equation of the Kingdom of God with a perfected human world on earth. It reintroduced the dimension of eternity in religiously powerful ways. If, at first, these took the form of 'realized' or 'existentialist' eschatology, soon a more balanced perspective was achieved. While Christianity bore

---

[25] See, e.g., R. H. Tawney, *The Acquisitive Society* (London: George Bell, 1921).

witness to a Word from beyond that both challenged and inspired all human progress in the spheres of love and justice, it also recognized that the 'end' of history lay in the eternal order above the conditions of mortality. Such theologies maintained a strong emphasis on divine judgement in both individual and social life, but, for the most part, resisted any permanent objectification of the idea of hell. The Parousia was seen to symbolize the final manifestation, beyond history, of Christ's eternal reign. But, as we have seen, the greatest problem area for all the theologians considered in this chapter was the relation between time and eternity.

9

The Twentieth Century II: Roman Catholic Theology

Catholic Modernism

The last decade of the nineteenth century and the early years of the twentieth saw a short-lived movement within Roman Catholicism, which, in the milder climate of Leo XIII's pontificate, reacted sharply against the dogmatic intransigence of Vatican I. Catholic Modernism shared something of the spirit of Liberal Protestantism, especially in its respect for critical study of the Bible, but differed from Liberal Protestantism in its recognition of the necessity of the development of doctrine. Whereas Harnack (see p. 109 above) had tried to get back to the pure teaching of Jesus about God and humanity, Alfred Loisy (1857–1940), in his *The Gospel and the Church* (1902), sought to show how Christianity was bound to change and develop as the social and intellectual context changed from age to age. Moreover, Loisy rightly discerned that the original teaching of Jesus was far from what Harnack supposed. Jesus's eschatological message of the Kingdom, determined as it was by first-century apocalyptic modes of thought, could not possibly be appropriated, just as it was, for the modern world. The Christian Church was rather a form of life and worship that had simply as a matter of historical fact emerged from those beginnings. Jesus had preached the Kingdom, but it was the Church that had come, and the Church would naturally adapt and develop its teaching and practice in order to be the vehicle of faith in each succeeding age.

On this view, the doctrines of the Church could no longer be regarded as fixed and unalterable. Belief in the fires of hell, for example, was only one of the traditional beliefs challenged in the writings of the modernists. But Catholic Modernism was condemned by Pope Pius X in 1907, and the movement was suppressed. It cannot be regarded as a major element in modern Roman Catholic eschatology. It is mentioned here only because one of the figures associated with the movement largely escaped censure and continued to exercise considerable influence in the non-Catholic world as well as the Catholic world. This was the lay theologian and philosopher Baron Friedrich von Hügel (1852–1925), who wrote extensively on eschatology and whose book *Eternal Life* (1912) remains a classic in this field. The author was very much aware of the problematic nature, to the modern mind, of the apocalyptic element in the teaching of Jesus. But his moderation, compared with other Catholic Modernists, is shown by the way in which he indicated the lasting significance of apocalyptic. According to von Hügel, Jesus cannot be thought of as only an apocalyptic visionary. His parables show an astonishing appreciation and affirmation of our earthly life and its context in nature. His taking on himself the role of the suffering servant shows a profound insight into the nature of self-sacrificing love. But the apocalyptic element reveals how closely and immediately God was present to Jesus and in him. Here we come to the heart of von Hügel's own interpretation. Although his lifelong preoccupation with mysticism led him to affirm the reality of human experience of infinite, eternal Spirit, and indeed to see in mystical experience and ecstasy a foretaste of the life of heaven, he nevertheless remained aware that we are creatures of time and cannot escape succession. Consequently, the eternal comes to men and women, not as a sense of timeless absorption, but as a sense of imminent divine in-breaking. This is the true significance of the apocalyptic element in the teaching of Jesus. It captures the immediacy of divine presence and action without succumbing to mystical monism. Moreover, as in Jesus's own case, this awareness of the eternal does not deflect people's attention from the earth or from human concerns and needs. Rather, it enhances them and energises human progress—but without fanaticism, since it does not identify the absolute with any finite human project.

There is much of interest in von Hügel's writing on the topics of heaven, purgatory, and hell. He points out that Christian theology of the afterlife is not concerned with simple unending existence. The specifically religious desire for immortality begins with God, rests on God, and ends in God. Its character is determined by the ultimate Beauty, Truth, and Goodness on which it depends. But our only indication of the nature of the supernatural destiny to which our relation to God points is our present experience of that relation now. Since grace operates gradually in the sanctification of the redeemed here on earth, it is reasonable to suppose a time of gradual purgation hereafter before the final consummation of heaven is reached. We note that von Hügel was also prepared to defend something like the medieval doctrine of limbo, on the ground that many human beings, often in infancy, pass into the beyond without knowing 'the solicitations of the supernatural'.[1] It is a mark of his relative conservatism that he was not prepared to speculate about further possibilities of growth and of experience of the supernatural beyond the grave for such truncated natural lives. As far as hell is concerned, von Hügel found himself unable to reject its permanence, since Scripture and tradition both bear witness to the seriousness of human choice and the abiding consequences of human action. As with heaven, intimations of the nature of hell may be gleaned from present experience. Rejection of God brings its own hell here and now, and we may imagine an enhancement of this state hereafter. It is curious how insensitive this sensitive writer was to the problematic nature of a final consummation that would include permanent experience of the loss of heaven for some.

Teilhard de Chardin

The most interesting twentieth-century Roman Catholic writer on the topic of the Christian hope—though, again, his works failed to find official favour—is the Jesuit palaeontologist Pierre Teilhard de Chardin (1881–1955). On the basis of his study of fossils and of the evolution of

---

[1] Friedrich von Hügel, *Essays and Addresses on the Philosophy of Religion. First Series* (London: J. M. Dent, 1921), 205.

life, Teilhard developed a most impressive vision of the universe as a process of 'cosmogenesis', evolving ever new and more complex levels of being, each manifesting the creativity of the divine Spirit, which draws the whole process onwards in the direction of a final consummation, which Teilhard called 'point Omega'. In *The Phenomenon of Man* (1955), Teilhard concentrates on the emergence of the 'biosphere'—the world of life—and from it the 'noosphere'—the world of thought—and points out that the inner dynamism of the whole process must be assessed from the standpoint of what has in fact emerged—namely, humanity, with all our powers of intellect and communication. Teilhard is perfectly well aware that, from one point of view, the fundamental stuff or energy of the universe, under the law of entropy, is relapsing into simple, basic, less-organized forms, but, from another point of view, we recognize the presence of something making for greater complexification and greater unity. Teilhard calls this 'radial energy' and the law of cosmogenesis 'the Law of Complexity-Consciousness', under which, as complexity increases, the 'within' of things, the network of conscious communication, increases too. The universe, in other words, has given birth to a world of spirit, which must itself develop more and more in the direction of ever-more complex unification. The noosphere, through greater knowledge and communication, inevitably tends towards social solidarity and love.

Teilhard deftly marries this evolutionary vision of the universe with Christian theology by speaking of the incarnation of the principle behind the whole process in Jesus Christ. The process of convergence within the noosphere may now be called 'Christification', and the Church may be seen as a sign of the spiritual community gradually being fashioned out of the basic energies of creation. But Teilhard does not restrict his attention to the Church. The pressure towards socialization and unity is a universal pressure, built into the nature of things.

Teilhard's work is a remarkable attempt to overcome the dichotomies between matter and spirit, profane and sacred, science and religion. Teilhard attempts, too, to overcome the dichotomy between teleology—the discernment of the inbuilt direction of things—and eschatology, the belief in decisive divine intervention at the end. This is the aspect of Teilhard's thought on which we must concentrate here. What was his vision of the future of humanity? What did he mean by the Omega point? How did he envisage its realization?

On the one hand, Teilhard's whole picture of cosmogenesis was of a single, continuous process, marked, certainly, by critical thresholds and qualitative novelty, as first life and then mind (and then Christ) appear on the scene. But we are encouraged not to think of radical breaks or discontinuities in the process. In *The Future of Man*, Teilhard draws attention to the way in which humanity has already achieved global species consciousness. He expects more and more universal socialization, but not only in a collectivist sense. The human world will become ever more personal, recognizing ahead of it the personal focus of Christ, who already incarnates the creative logos and love at the heart of evolution, and who will, in the end, be seen to be the ultimate centre of universal convergence. Thus out of the human world will emerge the 'ultra-human',[2] where the energies of creation reach their climax in a spiritual community, centred on Christ. This sketch of Teilhard's vision of the historical future may not in fact have gone far enough. For the increased socialization and unification that he envisaged are apparently to be characterized by a concentration or compression of psychic energy in a 'collective super-consciousness'. This conception of the ultra-human is certainly not easy to grasp.

On the other hand, not even Teilhard could deny the discontinuities that mark, not only the story of cosmic evolution, but also the life of every human being. At times, one feels that he has forgotten the death of individuals, but in fact, as his reflections on his own death make clear—he died, as he had wished, on Easter Day—he looked for the participation of all centres of thought and spirit in the ultimate point of convergence:

The universe is a collector and conservator, not of a mechanical energy, as we supposed, but of persons. All round us, one by one, like a continual exhalation, 'souls' break away, carrying upwards their incommunicable load of consciousness. One by one, yet not in isolation. Since, for each of them, by the very nature of Omega, there can only be one possible point of definitive emersion—that point at which, under the synthesising action of personalising union, the noosphere...will reach collectively its points of convergence—at the 'end of the world'.[3]

---

[2] Pierre Teilhard de Chardin, *The Future of Man*, Eng. trans. (London: Collins, 1964; Fontana edn., 1969), ch. XXI.

[3] Pierre Teilhard de Chardin, *The Phenomenon of Man*, Eng. trans. (London: Collins, 1959; Fontana edn., 1965), 299.

Moreover, Teilhard recognized that the final achievement of the 'trans-human' at point Omega will involve a critical transition to a state 'transcending the dimensions and the framework of the visible universe'.[4] It will be 'the passage, by translation or dematerialisation, to another sphere of the Universe: not an ending of the Ultra-Human but its accession to some sort of Trans-Human at the ultimate heart of things'.[5]

So, clearly, Teilhard did envisage discontinuity. The Omega point transcends the conditions of physical evolution. But equally it is the whole temporal process that gives birth to this new spiritual climax. It is out of the noosphere and its convergence towards socialization and unification that the ecstasy of transcendence will be achieved. It is certainly not true, for Teilhard, that 'each generation is equidistant from eternity'. On the contrary, 'the Parousia will be realised in a creation that has been taken to the climax of its capacity of union'.[6] We should note that Teilhard's optimism did not lead him to affirm universalism at this point. He was aware of the resistance of spirit to its destiny and the possibility of a refusal by some of the final ecstasy. But the reader may well wonder whether talk of 'the conscious torment of an endless decomposition' makes much sense in the context of Teilhard's total vision.

What then did Teilhard really mean by 'the Omega point'? It is the divine centre of convergence that lies 'ahead of, or rather in the heart of, a universe prolonged along its axis of complexity'.[7] It is that which draws humanity beyond the climax of 'hominization' into a supreme unification with Christ and with God. This central focus, at once universal and personal, is, in Teilhard's writings, a way of referring both to the final state of union with Christ and with God of which Paul speaks when he says that God will be 'all in all' (1 Cor. 15: 28), and also to the divine reality at the heart of things, already operative in the process leading to that consummation.

[4] Teilhard de Chardin, *The Phenomenon of Man*, 318.
[5] Teilhard de Chardin, *The Future of Man*, 311.
[6] Ibid. 322.   [7] Ibid. 127.

More Recent Roman Catholic Eschatology

For all his visionary genius, Teilhard de Chardin remains an isolated figure, and his posthumously published writings cannot be taken to typify the Roman Catholic Church's formulation of the Christian hope. In order to obtain a more characteristic and official picture of Catholic eschatology in the latter part of the twentieth century, we turn to a recognized teacher, Michael Schmaus (1897–1993), whose six-volume *Dogma* was composed in the light of the great changes in the Roman Catholic Church initiated by Vatican II (1962–5).[8]

The second half of volume six of *Dogma* is devoted to the last things. Schmaus begins by pointing out the eschatological character of every Christian doctrine, for the absolute future and final end of creation are what all things are made for. He then contrasts secular and biblical eschatology. Although the latter is rightly understood to demand a 'political theology', involving the critique of society and the struggle against injustice, it can never absolutize any social or political order, nor identify the Kingdom of God with any future this-worldly utopia. That would leave the transcendence of God's Kingdom out of account. Christian hope is for a transformed world beyond the end of history. 'The future form of the Kingdom will be more than simply the revelation of what is now at work.'[9] It will rather be the fulfilment and completion of what is only now begun— the community of unconditional and unreserved love as humanity and the whole creation are transfigured and taken into full and visible relation to the God who is Love. The Church, as the eschatological community, is the 'trail-blazer' and mediator of this absolute future.

Turning to the last things themselves, Schmaus deals next with the coming of Christ. The second coming, he insists, is not a spatial event, but the removal of the veil that hides Christ's glorified mode of existence. It presumes that humankind 'has undergone a transformation into a condition wherein it is able to recognize the glorified

[8] Unlike Vatican I, Vatican II was specifically intended by its instigator, Pope John XXIII, to rethink the teaching, organization, worship, and practice of the Church in the context of the modern world.

[9] Michael Schmaus, *Dogma 6: Justification and the Last Things* (Kansas City and London: Sheed & Ward, 1977), 162.

Christ'.[10] We should not speculate about the time of this transformation or the end of history. Even the biblical signs of the end 'are not presented as a chronology of events, but simply point to the expiration of historical time'.[11] This means resurrection. It is an indication of the breadth of modern Catholic teaching that Schmaus refused to restrict the scope of this to the baptized: 'owing to the Christocentricity of the world, the unbaptized also live within the effective sphere of the risen Lord and this relationship calls for a final maturing'.[12] Resurrection, Schmaus goes on to say, means resurrection of the person. That is the element of continuity. We may well suppose that God will give men and women a new spiritual body, but it is implausible to think in terms of a transformation of our present physical body. It is the person who is transformed and given a new resurrection body.

Schmaus was also prepared to consider the possibility that the resurrection of individuals takes place immediately upon their death. Similarly, as far as the responsibility of individuals is concerned, judgement will take place immediately. This view would still require an interval before the final gathering of all the redeemed into the glorified body of Christ, and the final objective manifestation of God's valuation of all human lives (and indeed of their 'cultural, scientific, artistic and philosophical creations'). There will indeed be a final consummation, but there is no need to postpone resurrection and judgement till then.

In dealing with the final consummation, Schmaus speaks in trinitarian terms. It is through his Holy Spirit that God will gather men and women into 'the unity of a personal Whole which is Jesus Christ'.[13] This almost Teilhardian language is supplemented by the further Pauline teaching that in Christ humankind and all creation will be drawn into union and dialogue with God the Father. And Schmaus insists on the never-ending dynamism of this culmination. 'God can reveal himself to man at ever new depths, and since he is infinite this process will never come to an end. Because of his infinity God's mystery is inexhaustible.'[14]

On death, purgatory, and hell, Schmaus writes in careful, but rather traditional terms. Death is not to be feared. It is the moment in which a human being is called into the life of God. Moreover, it is

[10] Schmaus, *Dogma 6*, 177.   [11] Ibid. 184.   [12] Ibid. 192.
[13] Ibid. 207.   [14] Ibid. 208.

not unreasonable to maintain that one is given a last chance at death to accept God's love. But 'death creates a condition of finality'.[15] Schmaus here endorses the Church's repudiation of Origen's teaching on further opportunities for repentance and growth beyond the grave. The majority of those who have turned to God, whether soon or late, will still require a process of purification, in which, as part of the communion of saints, they benefit from the prayers of the faithful on earth. But the doctrine of the finality of death means the real possibility of everlasting hell for those who reject God to the end. It is a state that they bring upon themselves, and its possibility manifests 'the ultimate, incalculable seriousness of human responsibility'. Schmaus recognizes that this doctrine is a scandal, but he affirms it none the less, and indeed expands on the nature of this condition of absolute loss. A person's 'unqualified revolt against God is a revolt against love itself, which means that he is enclosed in himself, incapable of dialogue with any other being. There is no community of the damned; every lost soul exists in such frigid isolation that he is not even aware of whether there are other souls in hell."[16]

Schmaus's conception of heaven has already been indicated in what has been said about the final consummation. It is 'an exchange of love between God and man', best captured in the traditional language of 'the vision of God'. It is again spelled out in trinitarian terms: 'Our conversation with God is a participation in that dynamic wherein the eternal Word engages with God the Father, in the Holy Spirit, in the inner trinitarian exchange of knowledge and love.'[17] This will include communion with friends and others in the body of Christ and an ever-deepening insight into the mysteries of the universe. Again, Schmaus stresses the dynamism of this final consummation. It is never-ending growth into joy and knowledge and love.

The trinitarian character of Catholic teaching on the future of humanity in relation to the God who made us was brought out with great profundity by another major theologian, Hans Urs von Balthasar (1905–88). In his *Man in History* (1963), in an article on 'Trinity and future' in *Elucidations* (1971), and in his *Love Alone: The Way of Revelation* (1963), Balthasar argued that only a triune God who does not stand over against us as the wholly transcendent but

[15] Ibid. 222.   [16] Ibid. 255.   [17] Ibid. 267.

comes to draw us to God from within can both allow us freedom to make or mar our world and at the same time enter into our self-made hell and gather us up into God. Uniquely among the world's religions, Christianity teaches the perfectibility of humanity beyond history, as men and women are gathered up, not by force, but by self-emptying love into the Love that is God. The entering of the eternal into time in the passion and cross of Christ (including the descent into hell) gives us a hope that is neither a flight from time nor a utopian vision of the future. We now can face the future including death, in the confidence of the trinitarian love 'in which God gave his Son into lostness in order not to allow man to remain alone in the lostness of his being'.[18] Balthasar refuses to try 'to bring hell and the love of God into logical and systematic harmony'.[19] The abyss is there, and the love of God shows up the abyss. But God incarnate, by his descent into hell on Holy Saturday, enters into it himself, and, if we hold fast to God's love and take our part in the redemptive suffering, we find that we can hope for the salvation of all.

All this received much fuller treatment in the final volume of Balthasar's *Theo-Drama* (German edition 1983), in which he reflects at length on how the triune God embraces the whole world story from beginning to end, without abrogating our finite freedom. Just because God in Christ enters into, shares, and absorbs the worst the world can do, we are able to hope and trust that, in the end, for all its horrors, hell will be empty, and the triune God will be all in all.[20]

I now turn to consider two Roman Catholic theologians, each of whom has made striking, if rather more controversial, contributions to the topic of the Christian hope: Edward Schillebeeckx (b. 1914) and Hans Küng (b. 1928). Schillebeeckx maintained a certain reserve regarding the 'last things' in the sense of human destiny after death.[21] He certainly held that the death and resurrection of Jesus are the ground of hope for a general resurrection for all men and

[18] Hans Urs von Balthasar, *Elucidations*, Eng. trans. (London: SPCK, 1975), 56.
[19] Hans Urs von Balthasar, *Love Alone the Way of Revelation: A Theological Perspective*, Eng. trans. (London: Burns & Oates, 1968), 78.
[20] Hans Urs von Balthasar, *Theo-Drama: Theological Dramatics*, v. *The Last Act*, Eng. trans. (San Francisco: Ignatius Press, 1998). For commentary, see Aidan Nichols, *No Bloodless Myth: A Guide through Balthasar's Dramatics* (Edinburgh: T. & T. Clark, 2000), chs. 14–17.
[21] See, e.g., Eduard Schillebeeckx, *Christ: The Christian Experience in the Modern World*, Eng. trans. (London: SCM Press, 1980), 790.

women. But what God has in store for his creation cannot be defined. He quotes 1 Corinthians 2: 9: 'no eye has seen, nor ear heard, nor the human heart conceived, what God has prepared for those who love him.' The ultimate future can be expressed only in parables and visions, drawn from partial experiences of meaning already undergone. Moreover, that final salvation, Schillebeeckx insists, will not be detached from, and regardless of, what people actually make of their future, under God, within history. The Bible speaks of the inheritance of the Kingdom by those who have fed the hungry, welcomed strangers, clothed the naked, and visited the prisoners. Consequently, Christian confidence in face of death is not a matter of turning away from present tasks, but rather of being freed for work in the world without anxiety, in true communion with God. For it is the religious depth of the present that alone gives hope for the future. This means that Christian eschatology is primarily concerned with those decisive acts of God that liberate us, both inwardly and outwardly, for building a better world, despite human limitations and despite the fact of death. In the next section we shall see how this emphasis on the historical future as the focus of concern in genuinely eschatological hope has been worked out in twentieth-century Roman Catholic 'liberation theology'.

Hans Küng, of the University of Tübingen in Germany, fell into some disfavour with Rome; but the fact remains that his book *On Being a Christian* is one of the most successful works of apologetic ever published. It is chiefly concerned with what is special to Christianity in today's world, including the world of religion. Küng endeavours to bring out the special significance of Jesus's message and of his life and death in terms of being, and being enabled to be, radically human. He spells out the personal, communal, and social aspects of the liberation that being a Christian involves. The emphasis, then, is on Christian life and action in this world. But Küng does not neglect the eschatological dimension that characterizes both the preaching of Jesus and the faith of the Church. On the contrary, it was precisely the conviction of God's absolute future Kingdom breaking into and transforming the present that animated Jesus's message. While some demythologizing of the apocalyptic form of that message is necessary, the tension between the 'not yet' and the 'but even now' must be sustained. God's absolute future throws us back on the present, but also the present directs us to God's absolute future. Life now is to be shaped in the light of the absolute future, but equally our present time must not be made absolute at the expense of the future. It is because the future belongs to God that we must shape the present, both of the individual and of society, in its light.

What Küng understands by 'resurrection' can be gleaned from his treatment of the resurrection of Jesus.[22] It was not in the strict sense a historical event, but rather 'a transcendental happening out of human death into the all-embracing dimension of God'. Resurrection 'involves a completely new mode of existence in God's wholly different mode of existence'. It is 'a radical transformation into a wholly different state'. It cannot be imagined by us, only hinted at in symbols. It cannot involve bodily continuity in the sense of the persistence of molecules, but it must involve the same living person. In the case of Jesus, what this means is that 'the crucified lives forever with God, as obligation and hope for us'. We too will share in God's victory over death. Despite the use of the future tense here, Küng in fact rejects temporal language of life 'after' death as misleading. Eternity is not characterized by 'before' and 'after'. It means a new life that 'escapes the dimensions of space and time'.

One can see why Küng, like Barth, adopts this point of view, and there is no denying his intention to speak of a real and new life in God beyond death, an assumption into ultimate reality. And there is no denying Küng's conviction that such a resurrection faith does constitute the hope and inspiration of Christian life and action here and now. But whether the language of time can thus be removed from our talk of the ultimate relation between humanity and the eternal is not at all clear. In the sequel we shall find grounds for thinking that both Barth and Küng are in error at this point.

On hell, Küng writes as follows:

The New Testament statements about hell are not meant to provide information to satisfy curiosity and fantasy about the hereafter. They are intended to put before us here and now the absolute seriousness of God's claim, and the urgency of man's repentance. The 'eternity' of the pains of hell ('fire') affirmed in a number of New Testament metaphors remains subordinated to God and his will. There are some New Testament texts, not balanced by

---

[22] The quotations in this paragraph come from Hans Küng, *On Being a Christian*, Eng. trans. (London: Collins, 1977), 348–61.

others, which suggest that the consummation will bring about a reconciliation of all and mercy for everyone.[23]

We begin to realize that the more creative modern Catholic eschatology, while refusing to affirm universalism outright, has become very wary of affirming the permanent objective reality of hell.

In a later book, *Eternal Life?* (1982), Küng develops these points in much greater detail, and sums up the Christian hope in these words:

I can rely on the hope that in the eschaton, in the final end-time, in God's Kingdom, the alienation of Creator and creature, man and nature, logos and cosmos, and the divide between this side and the beyond, above and below, subject and object, will be abolished. God then will not merely be in everything, as he is now, but truly all in all—taking everything, transformed, into himself—because he gives to all a share in his eternal life in unrestricted, endless fullness.[24]

Finally, in this section, must be mentioned another more traditional Roman Catholic theologian, Joseph Ratzinger (b. 1927), who, in 2005, was to become Pope Benedict XVI. In 1977, Ratzinger published a major work on eschatology that appeared in English in 1988 under the title *Eschatology: Death and Eternal Life*. This thorough study of the principal eschatological themes in the Bible, in Church history and in modern systematic theology, led Ratzinger to insist that Christianity requires an, albeit non-dualistic, conception of the human soul, whose immortality consists in being drawn by God into the Body of Christ, both here and beyond death, eventually to partake, with all the redeemed, in the final resurrection and consummation of all things. Ratzinger's reluctance to speak of resurrection at death stemmed from his recognition that we are not taken out of time into eternity, but are rather part of a Christ-centred process, yet to be perfected in the ultimate future. This allowed him to give full significance to the need for purification in purgatory and also to the Parousia: 'Faith in Christ's return is . . . the certainty that the world will, indeed, come to its perfection . . . through that indestructible love which triumphed in the risen Christ.'[25]

---

[23] Ibid. 369–70.
[24] Hans Küng, *Eternal Life?*, Eng. trans. (London: Collins, 1984), 283 (translation much emended).
[25] Joseph Ratzinger, *Eschatology: Death and Eternal Life* (Washington: Catholic University of America Press, 1988), 213.

We may also note here, as a mark of continuing, if gradual, development of Christian doctrine even in more conservative Catholic minds, that it was Pope Benedict himself who, in 2007, was to announce the decision by the Vatican's Theological Commission to drop the idea of 'limbo' as the place for unbaptized infants in the hereafter (see p. 58 above). The Commission's argument, presumably accepted by the Pope, was that the traditional concept of limbo seemed to reflect an 'unduly restrictive view of salvation'. It went on to say that there is greater theological awareness today that God is merciful and wants all human beings to be saved. Grace has priority over sin, and the exclusion of innocent babies from heaven does not seem to reflect Christ's special love for 'the little ones'.[26]

Liberation Theology

The Roman Catholic theologians discussed in the previous section were all anxious to bring out the bearing of Christian eschatological hope on the immediate historical future. In this they reflect and express one of the chief concerns of the Church since Vatican II. Vatican II itself, as can be seen from the document *Gaudium et Spes*, and from the papal encyclical *Populorum Progressio* that followed shortly on its heels, represented considerable advances in Roman Catholic social ethics since the days of *Rerum Novarum* (see p. 121 above). But, despite their detailed denunciation of many contemporary social evils, it is clear that Vatican II, *Populorum Progressio*, and the aforementioned theologians were still thinking in terms of development and reform rather than of social revolution. Nor did they identify the eschatological kingdom with a transformed social order on earth. Liberation theology, by contrast, has tended both towards endorsement of revolution and towards the translation of Christian eschatology into this-worldly political terms. This comment will have to be qualified, as we shall see, but that these very radical tendencies were to be found in Latin American liberation theology is undeniable.

[26] For the full text of the Commission's statement, see www.vatican.va/ roman_curia/congregations/cfaith/cti_documents/rc_con_cfaith_doc_20070419_ un-baptised-infants_en.html.

Most of the Roman Catholic Latin American exponents of liberation theology did part of their training in Europe. Among the influences on their thought are not only Marxist writers such as Ernst Bloch, whose *Das Prinzip Hoffnung* (1954–9) was such a seminal book for Christian–Marxist dialogue in the 1960s and for the Protestant 'theologians of hope' whom we shall be considering in the next chapter, but also for the 'political theology' of European Catholics such as Johannes Baptist Metz (b. 1928), Professor of Fundamental Theology at the University of Münster (where the radical millenarians once held sway). In his book *Theology of the World* (1968), Metz argued that political theology has a twofold function, the negative, critical, function of showing up the utter inadequacy of the privatization of the gospel in post-Enlightenment, especially existentialist, theology, and the positive function of determining anew 'the relation between religion and society... between eschatological faith and societal life'.[27] Since the main target of Metz's criticism was privatized religion, the emphasis naturally fell on the political, social, aspects of the Christian gospel. Metz, however, did not identify Christian eschatology with the social gospel. He spoke of the 'eschatological proviso' that prevents the simple identification of the biblical promises with any actual socio-political form. His theology remained critical at this point too, and that is why Schmaus was able to endorse his approach within the wider framework of his own transcendent eschatology.

The Latin American theologians of liberation, however, were reluctant to hold back at this point for fear of justifying a refusal of complete political commitment. Gustavo Gutierrez (b. 1928), for example, while commending Metz's political theology as being a breath of fresh air on the European scene, went on to criticize its abstractness and the weakness of its actual political analysis. In the context of poverty and institutionalized violence in South America, the starting point of Christian theology, according to Gutierrez, had to be commitment to the revolutionary process. He equated this with 'conversion to the neighbour, the oppressed person, the exploited social class, the despised race, the dominated country'.[28] From this perspective he interpreted the eschatological promises of

[27] Johannes Baptist Metz, *Theology of the World*, Eng. trans. (London: Burns & Oates, 1969), 111.

[28] Gustavo Gutierrez, *A Theology of Liberation: History, Politics and Salvation*, Eng. trans. (London: SCM Press, 1974), 204–5.

salvation—the Exodus tradition and the great prophets in the Old Testament, the subversive Gospel message of the Magnificat in the New. Christian eschatology has inescapable implications at the level of social and political 'praxis'. 'The life and preaching of Jesus postulate the unceasing search for a new kind of man in a qualitatively different society.'[29] Yet even Gutierrez refused to identify the Kingdom with a just society on earth. Every realization of brotherhood and justice, under the inspiration of the announcement of the Kingdom, opens up the promise and hope of complete communion of all men and women with God. The political is grafted into the eternal.

It was the Mexican theologian José Porfirio Miranda (b. 1924) who expressed most clearly the fear that an eschatology oriented on the ultimate future will betray an unwillingness to work for radical change here and now. In *Being and the Messiah* (1973) he developed a form of realized eschatology, interpreting the Gospels as announcing the arrival of the eschaton. The eschaton is not beyond history. We are already in the final and definitive stage of history. We must look and work for liberation and justice in the present.[30]

Whatever the merits of liberation theology as a form of Christian social ethics—and even here its prior endorsement of Marxist analyses of the situation in Latin America and in the world generally is open to trenchant criticism—its reading of Christian theology, and especially eschatology, must surely be deemed unbalanced. Certainly there is something to be said for its treatment of sin and salvation. Sin is not merely a private affair. It affects all human relations, political relations among them. Consequently salvation must include liberation from oppression and from inhuman social structures as well as personal spiritual liberation. But Christian hope itself extends beyond the boundaries of social and political liberation as it extends beyond the bounds of personal liberation during a particular lifetime on earth. Reflection on the fact of death prevents the Christian theologian from resting content with any form of purely realized eschatology. Only a hope that transcends death can meet the religious needs of people, whether as individuals or as members of society.

---

[29] Gutierrez, *A Theology of Liberation*, 231.
[30] Other Roman Catholic Latin American liberation theologians include Leonard Boff (b. 1938), Hugo Assmann (b. 1933), Juan Luis Segundo (1925–96), and José Severino Croatto (b. 1930).

In January 1979, Pope John Paul II addressed the Third Conference of Latin American bishops at Puebla, Mexico. While reaffirming the teaching of Vatican II and of Pope Paul VI on justice and human rights, he explicitly rejected any view that emptied the Kingdom of God of its full content and interpreted it as being reached by the mere changing of structures. He quoted his immediate predecessor, John Paul I, who warned that 'it is wrong to state that political, economic and social liberation coincides with salvation in Jesus Christ, that the Regnum Dei is identified with the Regnum hominis'. The Church's task is rather to proclaim the whole truth about our condition. 'The complete truth about the human being constitutes the foundation of the Church's social teaching and basis also of true liberation.'[31] This critical stance towards liberation theology has been maintained by Benedict XVI, and the movement has in any case lost much of its cutting edge with the disillusionment with Marxism that has followed the collapse of the Soviet Union.

Karl Rahner

I have reserved a separate section of this chapter for the thinker regarded by many as the Roman Catholic Church's leading twentieth-century theologian, Karl Rahner (1904–84). Rahner's views on eschatology are best gathered from the short last chapter of his *Foundations of Christian Faith* (1976), from the articles on 'Beatific Vision', 'Death', 'Eschatology', 'Hell', 'Last Things', and 'Parousia' that he contributed to the encyclopaedia *Sacramentum Mundi*, and from a number of articles in his multi-volume *Theological Investigations*.

Rahner insisted that of all theological assertions eschatological assertions must be controlled by certain fundamental hermeneutical principles (that is, basic principles of interpretation). This goes for the assertions of Scripture and tradition just as much as for those of theology. The two most important principles are these: (1) we must distinguish between 'the conceptual mode and the real content of an eschatological assertion'[32]—in other words, we have to try to see what

[31] *John Paul II in Mexico: His Collected Speeches*, Eng. trans. (London: Collins, 1979), 74–5.
[32] Karl Rahner, *Foundations of Christian Faith: An Introduction to the Idea of Christianity*, Eng. trans. (London: Darton, Longman & Todd, 1978), 433.

a given mode of speech or traditional conceptuality is really getting at; and (2) we must always interpret eschatological assertions on the basis of present experience of salvation. We do not have access, independently, to the future as a topic of speculation. We make inferences about the future on the basis of present experience. These two principles were very important for Rahner. The first introduces considerable flexibility in his handling of eschatological topics, since many traditional ideas can be put down to the conceptual mode rather than to the real content. The second exercises considerable control over eschatological speculation. It made Rahner very suspicious of apocalyptic, for example. At one point he wrote: 'To extrapolate from the present into the future is eschatology, to interpolate from the future into the present is apocalyptic.'[33] And the latter he considered not to be a proper mode of religious or theological activity. Actually he did concede that apocalyptic can perform, rather more crudely, the same tasks as eschatology, provided it is subjected to the second fundamental hermeneutical principle of eschatological assertions.

Rahner, therefore, tended to reject apocalyptic; but he also rejected purely existentialist or realized eschatologies that translate the Christian hope into present terms alone. Despite being controlled by present experience—indeed because of present experience of salvation—Christian eschatology must attend to the future and to the ultimate fulfilment of God's intention for humanity and for the world. And, despite the above-mentioned restrictions on speculations about the future, Rahner was in fact a very speculative theologian, offering profound meditations on what can be extrapolated about the future from present experience of salvation.

The first topic on which Rahner offered such meditations is that of death. Like many moderns, he was deeply suspicious of traditional conceptions of the immortality of the soul. Human beings are too much bound up with nature and the world. Death is too final and absolute a phenomenon for the conception of the release of the soul from its body at death to carry conviction even for Christian thought today. Rather the death of individuals is the consummation of embodied life, in and through which a human being is given that final fulfilment in relation to God for which one was created and

---

[33] Karl Rahner, *Theological Investigations, Volume IV*, Eng. trans. (London: Darton, Longman & Todd, 1966), 337.

one's whole life was a preparation. At an earlier stage, Rahner was prepared to speculate that the transition at death might be thought of as a transition to a cosmic relation between the finite human being and the whole world of which it had been a particular embodied part.[34] Rahner later abandoned this notion in favour of that of the perfected spirit 'informing' a glorified body quite unrelated to present material substance, though still related to a glorified environment in God's eternity.

The most notable feature of Rahner's view of eternal life was his attempt to characterize it in terms of the fulfilment or validation of a finite human life by the eternal God beyond time altogether. This transposition to another mode of existence cannot be thought of as taking place in temporal continuity with the time span of earthly life. Both for the individual at death and for the world at its 'end', the transition will be out of time into eternity. Only so, Rahner thought, could eternal life be final and definitive and not an endless repetition of what had gone before. So once again, as with Barth and Küng, we find a resolute attempt to retain the notion of a 'future' final fulfilment beyond death and the end of the world in terms other than those of temporal continuity. The factors making for this conception are particularly clear in Rahner's case. Not only is it a question of the classical restriction of temporality to this world in its present state; it is also one of a conviction of the lasting significance of this life, the finality of death, and the impossibility of further cycles of failure, repentance, or renewal in the consummated beyond. 'The achieved final validity of human existence which has grown to maturity in freedom comes to be *through* death, not *after* it. What has come to be is the liberated, final validity of something which was once temporal, and which therefore formed time in order to be, and not really to continue on in time.'[35]

There is no denying that this attempt to find the real content of eschatological assertions in a fulfilment or validation of this life and this world beyond time makes for very interesting treatment of the problems that have plagued traditional eschatology concerning the relation between death and resurrection, particular and general

[34] This is the aspect of Rahner's treatment of death on which John Hick concentrates his criticism in the pages devoted to Rahner in John Hick, *Death and Eternal Life* (London: Collins, 1976), 228–35.
[35] Rahner, *Foundations*, 437.

judgement, the intermediate state and the Parousia. Rahner was even prepared to allow that these difficulties belong only to 'the conceptual mode' in which eschatological assertions are made and that, if we try to think through to the real timeless content, they do not arise. In reality, the transformation or validation of the individual is but one element in the transformation of world history and the cosmos in general. The Parousia was placed by Rahner firmly beyond the transition from history to eternity. It is 'the fulness and the ending of the history of man and the world with the glorified humanity of Christ—now directly manifest in glory—in God'.[36] He was even prepared to gloss the 'return' of Christ as 'the arrival of all things at their destination in Christ'.

The balance between individual and collective eschatology was carefully maintained by Rahner. Just as it is my life and decisions here that are 'validated' and taken up into God's eternity, so it is this world's history and that of the human collectivity that find eternal consummation in the beyond. Just as in the former case this eschatological hope imposes ethical demands on my own life, so in the latter case does it impose political demands on man in society. Thus far did Rahner too endorse political theology.

Rahner's insistence on the finality of death and the non-temporal nature of the eternal consummation into which we and the world are eventually to be taken might lead us to suppose that there is no place in his eschatology for purgatory, still less for universalism. But on both these issues there is evidence suggesting that Rahner was prepared to think again. In a curious short article, composed in dialogue form, on 'Purgatory',[37] he at least toys with the idea of 'a postmortal history of freedom', not only for those already committed to God, but also for those who never had the chance to make such a decision. He suggests that this might be thought of, not as a further phase of time as we know it here on earth, but as something 'analogous' to our time. Moreover, Rahner's much discussed notion of 'anonymous Christians'[38] (see p. 218 below) appears to open the door to the idea

[36] Karl Rahner (ed.), *Encyclopedia of Theology: A Concise Sacramentum Mundi* (London: Burns & Oates, 1975), 1158.
[37] Karl Rahner, *Theological Investigations, Volume XIX*, Eng trans. (London, Darton, Longman & Todd, 1984), 181–93.
[38] Karl Rahner, *Theological Investigations, Volume VI*, Eng trans. (London: Darton, Longman & Todd, 1969), 390–8. See also *Foundations*, 306. The idea of

of universal salvation. As with Balthasar, Schillebeeckx, and Küng, Rahner was reluctant to speak of hell in objective terms parallel to talk of heaven. Recognition of the possibility of eternal loss, he says in *Foundations of Faith*, must not be made a matter of objectivizing speculation. It is a permanent warning and an indication of our freedom and responsibility, but it is not to be thought of in strict parallel with Christian faith that the human race will find a blessed and positive fulfilment in Jesus Christ. 'The existence of the possibility that freedom will end in eternal loss stands alongside the doctrine that the world and the history of the world as a whole will *in fact* enter into eternal life with God.'[39]

This eternal life beyond our time is the beatific vision granted to redeemed humanity—to individuals, that is, as members of the communion of saints. It consists in the vision and enjoyment of God himself in his triune being.

There are many questions that this profound treatment of Christian eschatology raises for the reflective mind. As with Barth and Küng, it is not at all clear that the conception of a timeless eternity, or indeed the conception of something 'analogous' to our time, makes much sense. We have already noted some ambiguity in Rahner's writings over these issues. Nor can we avoid some suspicion of a residual clash in Rahner's thinking between the notion of the validation of *this* whole life and the idea of the beatific vision as a new transformed experience of God. All this means that we are going to have to question the traditional conception, supposedly endorsed by Rahner, of the finality of death.[40]

Conclusion

Much can be learned about the Christian hope from the study of Roman Catholic eschatology in the twentieth century. Wise things were said about the basis in present experience of salvation for

anonymous Christianity is discussed by Jacques Dupois in his *Christianity and the Religions: From Confrontation to Dialogue*, Eng. trans. (London: Darton, Longman & Todd, 2002), 53–5.

[39] Rahner, *Foundations*, 444.

[40] A full treatment of Rahner's eschatology may be found in Morwenna Ludlow, *Universal Salvation: Eschatology in the Thought of Gregory of Nyssa and Karl Rahner* (Oxford: Oxford University Press, 2000).

assertions concerning the future, about the distinction between pictorial modes of thought and the real content of doctrine, about the creative purpose of God leading to a fulfilment and completion in a perfected creation beyond death, and about the relation between this ultimate hope and both individual and social life in the historical future. Many of the earlier problems that beset Christian eschatology—the gap between death and resurrection, the intermediate state, the relation between Particular and Last Judgement, and the meaning of the Parousia doctrine—have all found partial resolution in the writings of the Roman Catholic theologians discussed in this chapter.

Some disagreement has been shown over the necessity of conceiving both God's eternity and the eternal life to which creatures are called in non-temporal terms, and some differences have emerged over the objective reality of hell as more than a dreadful possibility implied by human freedom. Further uncertainties have arisen over the degree to which we can postulate new and higher experience for humankind beyond the grave. A strong tendency to maintain the finality of death has been observed. Of course the notions of a non-temporal consummation and of the finality of death tend to go together. Both notions, it may be observed, accentuate the problem of evil—the fate of those untold numbers of human beings who, whether through no one's fault or through their own fault, fail to realize worthwhile lives and discover the resources of the spirit for creative human existence, both as individuals and as members of society. No understanding of the Christian hope that fails to meet this problem can ever be judged entirely satisfactory.

10

The Twentieth Century III: Later Protestant Theology

The Scientific Context

In turning to Protestant theology in the latter part of the twentieth century, it seems sensible to pause a little in order to examine the scientific, philosophical, and religious contexts in which the topic of the Christian hope now came to be considered.

We have already encountered the scientific context in our treatment of the effect of evolutionary theory on nineteenth-century eschatology and in our discussion of Teilhard de Chardin. Indeed it is probably the case that, of all scientific notions, evolutionary theory has had the most pervasive effect in making Christian theology rethink its fundamental conception of God's world. As indicated earlier, the doctrines of creation and providence can quite easily be reconciled with an evolutionary picture of the cosmos. But the picture of an evolving world, under the creative Spirit of God, gradually attaining higher levels of created being, and of human beings emerging from nature and from pre-human forms of life into history and culture and the world of the spirit, is very different from the mythical picture of a perfected creation in the beginning. It is true that the theory of evolution had come under some strain in the biological sciences themselves, but the problems in that connection concerned the mechanics of certain key transitions in the process; and, whatever the outcome of these scientific debates, mainstream

Christian theology was not going to go back on the overall evolutionary picture or on the conception of humanity emerging from very primitive conditions. It might well be that the story of the evolution of life, consciousness, and personality are not fully explicable without the postulation of a hidden creative persuasion behind and immanent within the whole process. But that Christian theology had now to think in terms of a more or less gradual process from small beginnings right up to a perfected consummation in the future is beyond question or doubt. Similarly, of course, the Christian doctrine of the Fall had now to be reinterpreted as expressing the gap between human beings and their creator and the state of alienation from God that must first be overcome before we can enter into the relationship with God and our neighbour for which we were made. For the most part, Christian theology had come to accept these changes, and indeed it is precisely in the light of such an evolutionary picture that the future rather than the past or even the present had come to dominate the world of theological ideas.

It is not only in respect of the theory of evolution, however, that modern science has had a profound effect on Christian theology of creation and the future. Twentieth-century cosmology and elementary particle physics also compelled theologians to re-examine what they said about the basic material creation and its potentialities for future transformation. Again, many of the discoveries in these areas were quite easy to reconcile with a religious point of view. Some cosmological discoveries were widely held to favour the notion of a mind and a purpose behind the emergence of life and personality here (or elsewhere) in the universe. It was not just the general, though remarkable, fact that the basic energies of material substance, under the fundamental laws of nature, have it in them so to combine as to produce, eventually, the conditions for life and life itself, but also the much more specific fact that the range of initial conditions whereby the chemical basis of life can appear at all—just so much total mass and just such a speed of expansion—is so extraordinarily narrow. Be that as it may, one thing was for certain: the universe, notwithstanding the vastness of inter-galactic space, is a person-producing process, and it was not unreasonable, in the manner of Teilhard de Chardin, both to assess the whole story and also to extrapolate its future on the basis of what has in fact emerged here. Nor is this just a biased preference by living persons in favour of life and mind. When we consider the fundamental particles and forces out of which all this has come, the levels of organization and the capacities acquired in and through the evolution of humanity are, quite objectively, of an order of magnitude more significant than any other phenomena in the universe. The fact that matter can so order itself as to become conscious of itself and of its world, in all the widely ramifying complexity of modern science itself, must surely say something about the nature of the whole creative process in the midst of which we find ourselves. In particular, we have to reckon with the openness of the world to producing free, creative, beings, who themselves greatly increase that openness and make the future of the world, at least within certain broad parameters, strictly unpredictable.

On the other hand, the actual nature of the physical and chemical basis of life and its environment does not really encourage long-term hope for the future of humanity and of creation. As is well known, the span of time during which a star such as the sun will sustain a planetary system such as ours, capable of producing and maintaining life, is finite. Eventually, although we are talking here of thousands of millions of years, every star will either burn itself out, or explode, or, perhaps, implode into a black hole. Moreover, according to the second law of thermodynamics, the whole physical universe is gradually thinning out into less-ordered and more-random states, leading to the eventual heat-death of the universe. Admittedly, the universal applicability of the second law of thermodynamics is a controversial matter, and there has been interesting recent work on the way in which, despite the general tendency towards disorder, the universe has in fact shown itself capable of producing much more ordered states, such as life on earth. But the overall point remains that such ordered sequences are temporary, not permanent, states in a physical universe such as this.

Moreover, modern knowledge of the deep embeddedness of consciousness, character, and mind in the physico-chemical structure of living organisms has made it much more difficult to think of human beings as composite creatures, made up of body and soul, the latter being fundamentally unaffected by the long-term destiny of material substance.[1]

---

[1] John Hick discusses this problem in his Eddington Memorial Lecture, *Biology and the Soul* (Cambridge: Cambridge University Press, 1972).

The consequence for theology of this recognition both of the remarkable properties of material substance in the production of persons through cosmic and biological evolution and also of the dependence of personal life on what, in the long run, are undoubtedly temporary states of physico-chemical organization is the absolute necessity of postulating further creative acts of God, if we are to have a future not only beyond the death of individuals, but also beyond the heat-death of the universe.

Quite apart from reflection on the bearing of scientific knowledge on the ultimate future of humanity, modern attitudes to the more immediate historical future have also been greatly affected by science. There was—and is—a tendency for wild swings between optimism and pessimism here. On the one hand, technological developments raised the hope of the eventual conquest of poverty and disease and the creation of a well-ordered 'global village' through mass communication and rational planning, in which humanity will learn to live in peace and prosperity, using greatly increased opportunities of leisure in creative and fulfilling ways. On the other hand, the pressure of limited natural resources, the possibility of ecological disaster through the very growth of technology and industry, and the persisting nuclear threat combined to induce a widespread pessimism over our ability to survive the twenty-first century without the collapse of our hard-won civilization. Indeed, the threat of nuclear disaster gave greater vividness than ever before to the biblical symbol of Armageddon.

These uncertainties gravely affect the usefulness of any attempt to predict, in a disciplined, scientific, manner, the short-term, middle-term, and long-term future. 'Futurology', as this discipline is called, attempts to extrapolate forwards into the future from present trends and tendencies. At its best, it offers a range of possible scenarios, more plausible in the shorter than in the longer term. It is never easy to be sure that all the relevant factors have been taken into account, but the longer the forecast, the greater the number of variables, and the greater the uncertainty. Unlike Christian eschatology, futurology lacks the single interpretative key—God's saving action in the death and resurrection of Jesus Christ—that gives the Christian hope its sure foundation.[2]

---

[2] On the scientific context, see further Arthur Peacocke, *Creation and the World of Science* (Oxford: Clarendon Press, 1979), and John Polkinghorne, *Science and Theology: An Introduction* (London: SPCK, 1998).

The Philosophical Context

The twentieth-century philosophical context of Christian eschatology was predominantly negative. The main mid-century currents of analytical philosophy—logical positivism and linguistic analysis—were hostile to religion and metaphysics, and often involved denial of the coherence of the notion of life after death. Continental existentialism, for the most part, also affirmed the finality of death (in the sense here of nothing at all beyond death) as a necessary boundary to authentic human life.

The main philosophical problems that are raised over the question of life after death concern continuity and individuation. What would make a purported post-mortem individual the same person as the person who lived on earth, and what would enable a post-mortem individual to be a particular person in relation to other persons? For it is the physical body, despite its gradual changes over time, that fulfils both these functions in respect of our present existence. The problem of individuation is exacerbated if one is thinking of the immortality of the soul rather than of the resurrection of the body. But if, in the interests of a means of individuation, the notion of resurrection is preferred to that of immortality, then further difficulties are encountered over the relation between the resurrection body and the earthly body. As we have already seen, modern knowledge of what matter is makes talk of bodily resurrection very difficult. Talk of a new 'spiritual body' only reinforces the problem of continuity.

Broadly speaking, philosophers of religion attempted to defend the coherence of the notion of life after death by suggesting that, while rooted in the body and in its physical environment, the human being becomes a person, endowed with mental and spiritual capacities not essentially tied to its physical base. It is possible to suppose that God might sustain in being, in another mode, the person whose memories, character traits, and developing history of interpersonal relations have been freed from their particular bodily base on earth.

H. H. Price (1899–1984) developed such speculations in purely mentalistic terms.[3] He supposed that, over a lifetime on earth, a human being

[3] See H. H. Price, *Essays in the Philosophy of Religion* (Oxford: Clarendon Press, 1972), ch. 6.

acquires a store of mental images that can become the basis of an 'image world' beyond death, in which the disembodied mind can exist with all its memories and (now 'telepathic') relationships intact. Price made the intriguing suggestion that each individual's 'image world' will depend on the quality of his or her memories and desires on earth. This would allow for some reinterpretation of talk of heaven, purgatory, and hell. But the disadvantages of this view lie in the somewhat thin and 'unreal' character of such image worlds, and particularly in their lack of a common, stable, environment for further growth and experience.

John Hick (b. 1922) preferred to postulate the divine creation of a 'replica' person in another space, unrelated to the spatial system of the present universe. This replica would be endowed with just the memories and character traits that were to be found associated with the previous earthly body.[4] This was Hick's version of the resurrection of the body. Some of the difficulties raised against this view, such as the possibility of two or more such replicas, may be far-fetched, given that we are speaking of God's acts of new creation. But the problem of continuity on Hick's view is very great. It is very hard to see that a replica could really be the same person as the person who lived on earth before.

This discussion shows that, once the resurrection of the body is taken to mean the provision of a new, glorified, and perhaps non-material 'body' and environment, we require something like the immortality of the soul to guarantee continuity, so that it is the same person who lives in two such different modes of existence. H. D. Lewis (1910–92) and Richard Swinburne (b. 1934) have been the most determined defenders, in recent philosophy, of the mind–body dualism that allows the survival of the very same person across the boundary of death into a new resurrection 'body' and a new resurrection 'world'.[5]

Of one thing we may be sure. Few modern philosophers of religion would now argue, on philosophical grounds alone, for the natural

[4] The 'replica' theory is discussed in John Hick, *Death and Eternal Life* (London: Collins, 1976), ch. 15.

[5] See Hywel D. Lewis, *The Self and Immortality* (London: Macmillan, 1973), and Richard Swinburne, *The Evolution of the Soul* (Oxford: Clarendon Press, 1986). By contrast, the German theologian Oscar Cullmann (1902–99) was the strongest advocate of the resurrection of the dead as opposed to the immortality of the soul. See his *Immortality of the Soul; or Resurrection of the Dead? The Witness of the New Testament* (London: Epworth, 1958). But he does not take the measure of the seriousness of the problem of continuity, once the essentially perishable nature of the body is fully appreciated.

immortality of the soul. The philosophical arguments concern, rather, the coherence of what is recognized to be a basic postulate of theism. Belief in life after death is a consequence of belief in God.

Not surprisingly, where theism is philosophically eroded, belief in life after death is eroded too. An interesting example of this connection is to be found in the work of D. Z. Phillips (1934–2006). On Phillips's 'non-cognitive' analysis of religious language, to participate in the reality of God means no more than to acquire, through contemplation and religious practice, certain moral and religious modes of thought.[6] This remains a minority view among philosophers of religion, certainly among philosophical theologians.

Returning, then, to philosophical theism, we may note one further feature of late-twentieth-century philosophy of religion—namely, the increasing conviction among analytical philosophers sympathetic to theism that the concept of God can no longer be spelled out in non-temporal terms. Of all aspects of the traditional Augustinian and Thomist concept of God, the attribute of timelessness in the characterization of God's eternity is found more and more difficult to defend.[7] If this is so, and if we must rethink the concept of God in essentially temporal terms (although, of course, without beginning or end or the losses of the past that characterize perishable things), then clearly our understanding of the ultimate future of humanity and of creation cannot possibly take non-temporal forms. This philosophical context encourages us to continue to speak of life *after* death and to analyse its meaning.

The Religious Context

This book, by reason both of its particular subject matter and also of limitations of space, has restricted itself to hope for the future as it has found expression in the Judaeo-Christian tradition. Very little has

---

[6] D. Z. Phillips, *Death and Immortality* (London: Macmillan, 1970), 49.

[7] See Nelson Pike, *God and Timelessness* (London: Routledge & Kegan Paul, 1970); John Lucas, *The Future: An Essay on God, Temporality and Truth* (Oxford: Basil Blackwell, 1989); Richard Swinburne, *The Coherence of Theism* (Oxford: Clarendon Press, 1977); Anthony Kenny, *The God of the Philosophers* (Oxford: Clarendon Press, 1979); Keith Ward, *Rational Theology and the Creativity of God* (Oxford: Basil Blackwell, 1982).

been said about other religions. This isolationist approach cannot be maintained in modern theology. Increasing contact with men and women of other faiths has led the Christian theologian to reckon with the experience, spirituality, and beliefs of the other great religions. Our own Christian recognition of the way in which divine revelation is mediated through human, culturally and historically conditioned, forms of thought and experience has made us look much more favourably on the idea of divine revelation mediated to other people through other traditions. Even where Christ is seen as final, and uniquely determinative, in the salvation that he brings, other ways to God and other conceptions of human blessedness in relation to the transcendent must be seriously pondered in the modern disciplines of comparative religion and theology.

The comparative study of different conceptions of salvation and of the ultimate destiny of humankind is a fascinating and essential task.[8] Regrettably, it cannot be attempted here. But one pervasive notion, to be found in the religions of the Indian subcontinent, must be mentioned as having an important bearing on our present concern with twentieth-century eschatology. That is the Indian belief in reincarnation. The reason why this has an immediate bearing on our treatment of the Christian hope is that Indian belief in reincarnation is closely bound up with a way of dealing with the whole problem of evil that presents such a stumbling block to traditional Christian faith. It rests on the profound religious conviction that a single human life on earth, liable to being thwarted or cut short at any moment, cannot be the one and only opportunity for a human being to find salvation and eternal blessedness.

Now the way in which this consideration is developed in Indian reincarnation belief is hardly likely to commend itself to Western minds. The problems of identity and continuity are even greater than in the case of life after death. Occasional fragmentary 'memories' can hardly carry the weight of the criteria for being the same person as one who lived on earth in different circumstance and a different history of interpersonal relationships before. Moreover, our scientific

---

[8] See S. G. F. Brandon, *Man and his Destiny in the Great Religions* (Manchester: Manchester University Press, 1962), and *The Judgment of the Dead: An Historical and Comparative Study of the Idea of a Post-Mortem Judgment in the Major Religions* (London: Weidenfeld & Nicolson, 1967). See also Keith Ward, *Religion and Human Nature* (Oxford: Clarendon Press, 1998), chs. 11–14.

knowledge of the basis of personality and character in certain specific biological configurations hardly permits transfer across different but similarly structured organisms. But the idea that the present distribution of evil and suffering is totally incommensurate with the value of human lives, if a single life span is all there is, is a very powerful religious idea. And it has led some Christian theologians, notably John Hick, in *Death and Eternal Life*, to suggest that belief in reincarnation represents a mythical recognition of the necessity of postulating further opportunities of growth and development beyond death. We have already come across the sense that a single life span on earth cannot possess the absolute significance that the mainstream Christian tradition has accorded it. Origen and Gregory of Nyssa in patristic times, Schleiermacher, H. B. Wilson, and F. W. Farrar in the nineteenth century, and Nicolas Berdyaev in the twentieth have all supposed that God gives further opportunities beyond the grave for repentance and maturing in the fulfilment of potentialities. Hick now calls attention to the further evidence from other faiths supporting this view.

Interestingly enough, Karl Rahner called attention to Indian belief in reincarnation as perhaps having some bearing on the Christian doctrine of purgatory.[9] But, as we saw, Rahner, in most of his work, was committed to the idea of the finality of death. Purgatory was, for him, principally a matter of the maturing of spirits whose wills are already directed towards God. Consequently Rahner was unable to make unequivocal use of the main insight coming from Indian religion in this connection—namely, the religious necessity of thinking in terms of further opportunities beyond a single lifespan for all.

Process Theology

Turning to particular movements in Protestant theology in the second half of the twentieth century, we consider first a school of thought that draws its inspiration from the philosopher Alfred North Whitehead (1861–1947), a school known as 'process theology'. This has been chiefly an American phenomenon, although it made a

---

[9] Rahner, *Foundations of Christian Faith*, 442.

modest, if increasing, impact on European theology, and indeed to some extent on Roman Catholic thought as well. The main feature of process theology is a new metaphysic of 'event' or 'process' rather than 'substance' that includes both God and the world—God being, in his so-called consequent nature, the all-inclusive process, creatively making possible, and receiving into himself, all finite, achieved, values from the world of nature and the human. This means that God himself, at least in his relation to the world, is thought of in temporal terms as active love.

Clearly, this makes for an evolutionary, open-ended, view of the creative process, not too dissimilar from that of Teilhard de Chardin. Whitehead himself was less optimistic than Teilhard. The future is always open to new creative possibilities, and Whitehead believed in human progress and divine providence. But there is no consummation to the process. Civilizations rise and fall, and one day life on earth will cease. And, while all achieved value is taken into God and indeed in part comes to constitute God's own future, the divine creative process is never ending, and it is far from clear that Whitehead saw the retention of value in God as including personal immortality.

The most notable thinker to draw on Whitehead's philosophy for the articulation of a Christian theology and eschatology was Charles Hartshorne (1897–2000), for whom immortality consists in God's remembering all we have been in our lives on earth. We are preserved beyond death in the divine omniscience. To do justice to Hartshorne, we must recognize that a very strong and positive sense of 'memory' seems to be implied here. For God's past is not lost as ours is. God, who is ever open to new experience, retains his past experience as well. Our lives contribute to God's life and are retained as moments in the developing divine consciousness. Even so, it is hard not to agree with John Hick that this is hardly a doctrine of *our* new life beyond death.[10]

Other process theologians differ in the degree to which they try to interpret the notion of divine memory more positively, so as to include some conception of lived experience for us after death. Norman Pittenger (1905–97) came to think that the retention of all the achieved values of a person's life in the divine memory was sufficient to do justice to the Christian hope. All the language of biblical

[10] See Hick, *Death and Eternal Life*, 220.

eschatology is, for Pittenger, a mythological way of expressing confidence in God as the cosmic 'lover' of all there has been and will be.[11] But John Cobb (b. 1925) has attempted to give more specific content to the idea of *our* being preserved in the divine future: 'In such a future all that matters about our selfhood is preserved, but it is continued, developed, transformed, and purified, passing from the compartmentalized and protected psyche that we now know into myriads of free and open selves unconcerned with their peculiar lines of inheritance'.[12]

In itself, the notion of retention in the divine memory must surely be judged to be inadequate. Reflection on the problem of evil—the mass of unfulfilled and thwarted lives—together with reflection on the arbitrariness of the restriction of significance to this earthly life alone, leads us to postulate further growth and further opportunity beyond the grave. It might have been thought that process theology, with its firm conviction of the temporality of God, would be less tempted to 'freeze' the finite lives of creatures in the creator's memory. But certain features of the process metaphysic, as developed by Whitehead and Hartshorne, appear to have prevented many members of this school from taking advantage of the notion of divine temporality in the interests of a more substantial doctrine of life after death. As Keith Ward points out in *Rational Theology and the Creativity of God*, there is no need to follow Whitehead in reducing substances to processes. One can accept temporality in God without supposing that finite, created, processes are destined only to be received into the divine process as modes of *God's* future. We may conclude that John Cobb is on firmer ground in his speculations concerning the real future fulfilment of creatures themselves.

The notion of the retention of past values in the divine memory, as it has been developed in process theology, is certainly not to be rejected in its entirety. It may well play a part in our eventual sketch of a contemporary eschatology, both in respect of the past values of particular human lives and in respect of the many temporary values of natural beauty, including animal life, and cultural artefacts, which we can hardly suppose to be transferable, in their present form, to a

[11] Pittenger's small book *After Death, Life in God* (London: SCM Press, 1980) expounds this view.
[12] John B. Cobb, Jr., 'What is the Future? A Process Perspective', in Ewert H. Cousins (ed.), *Hope and the Future of Man* (Philadelphia: Fortress Press, 1972), 14.

resurrection world. These things may indeed be held in the divine memory and perhaps made available to perfected creatures for their contemplation. But persons themselves, if they are to find future fulfilment and consummation, must be thought of as destined for more than this. Christian hope is for an actual participation, by persons themselves, in however transformed conditions, in God's ultimate future.

Theologies of Hope

The most notable feature of post-Barthian theology in Germany was the recovery of the significance of the future in the Christian scheme of things. We shall restrict ourselves in this section to the two best-known representatives of this trend, Jürgen Moltmann (b. 1926) and Wolfhart Pannenberg (b. 1928).

The phrase 'theology of hope' is associated, in the first instance, with Moltmann, who published a book of that title in 1964. Subtitled 'On the Ground and the Implications of Christian Eschatology', it set out to re-establish the eschatological character of all Christian doctrine and to make the future and hope for the future the dominant and guiding motifs of Christian theology. It stressed the centrality of 'promise' in Old Testament religion, the cosmic scope of apocalyptic, as taken over by New Testament writers, the way in which the resurrection of Jesus Christ anticipates the future of creation, and finally the historical mission of the 'Exodus Church' in working for the liberation and transformation of human life, in the light of the coming lordship of the risen Christ. If Moltmann's first book seemed unduly optimistic, his second, *The Crucified God*, went out of its way to show that the specifically Christian hope is centred not on points of progress, value, and achievement in human life, but rather on the liberation of the poor and oppressed with whom God identified himself in the cross of Christ. It is the anticipation of God's future in the resurrection of the *crucified* one that inspires and enables Christian hope for a liberated world. Two further books, *The Church in the Power of the Spirit* and *The Trinity and the Kingdom of God*, spelt out the Church's task in relation to the coming Kingdom and provided a vigorous theological exposition of the trinitarian history of God's dealings with the world in the creation of a world open to the future, in the liberating lordship of the crucified one, and in the new creation of a free community, energized by the Holy Spirit. It is in this connection that Moltmann expressed a preference for Joachim of Fiore's conception of a threefold Kingdom of Father, Son, and Spirit over that of orthodox Protestantism's twofold Kingdom of nature and grace. Admittedly, Moltmann did not take Joachim's divisions as demarcating different chronological phases. They are different moments in a single divine action. But the point is that, according to Moltmann, orthodox Protestantism left out the work of the Spirit in the history of human freedom, and thus gravely under-estimated Christianity's significance as a liberating force in the world.

Indeed it becomes clear that Moltmann's predominant concern is with hope for the historical future and with a theology of liberation, although by no means just political liberation.[13] Something will be said in the next section about his more recent work's concern with ecology and the whole future of the planet. But it would be a great mistake to think that this concern displaces the ultimate Christian hope in Moltmann's theology. On the contrary, it is precisely the ultimate hope of resurrection, anticipated in Jesus Christ, that opens up, empowers, and demands Christian hope for this-worldly liber-ation in all its aspects. It is quite clear from his major eschatology book, *The Coming of God*,[14] that, for Moltmann, it is this future consummation, when God will be all in all, that constitutes the ultimate basis for Christian hope.

A passage in his earlier work, *The Crucified God*, might easily have misled us on this point.[15] There Moltmann expressly rejected the idea that resurrection life is a further life after death, in the sense of the immortality of the soul or spirit. But he was certainly not denying the new life and the new creation in which death is overcome, and the power of which is already active in the midst of this world's strife. We might think that a denial of resurrection life as life 'after' death is an echo of Barth or Rahner. If so, it was an inappropriate echo; for

[13] See Jürgen Moltmann, *The Future of Creation*, Eng. trans. (London: SCM Press, 1979), 97–114.
[14] See Jürgen Moltmann, *The Coming of God: Christian Eschatology*, Eng. trans. (London: SCM Press, 1996).
[15] Jürgen Moltmann, *The Crucified God: The Cross of Christ as the Foundation and Criticism of Christian Theology*, Eng. trans. (London: SCM Press, 1974), 169–71.

Moltmann is very far from being in captivity to a non-temporal conception of the eternal. In his essay 'Creation as an Open System', in *The Future of Creation*,[16] he writes, of the consummation of creation, that glorified humanity's participation in the life and glory of God cannot possibly be thought of in terms of the abolition of time. 'If the process of creation is to be completed through God's indwelling, then the unlimited fulness of divine potentiality dwells in the new creation.' Life systems remain open, even when glorified: 'there will be time and history, future and possibility in the Kingdom of glory as well . . . they will be present in unimpeded measure and in a way that is no longer ambivalent.' 'We must think of change without transience, time without the past, and life without death.' Moltmann has no reservations about drawing the consequences of this for the doctrine of God: 'the being of God must no longer be thought of as the highest reality for all realized potentialities, but as the transcendent making possible of all possible realities.'

In another essay in *The Future of Creation*, entitled 'Trends in Eschatology',[17] Moltmann makes much of the difference between those for whose understanding of eschatology 'the present determines the future' and those for whom 'the future determines the present'. It is clear that Moltmann himself belongs in the latter category. Certainly he makes a strong case for thinking in terms of hope for God's future Kingdom breaking into the sin, poverty, and oppression of the human world. But, if the cross and resurrection of Jesus Christ and the gift of the Spirit are an anticipation of that future kingdom, present and active already in creation, then it is not unreasonable to make present experience of salvation and liberation a key to hope for God's future. In other words, Moltmann appears to have exaggerated the difference between taking the future or the present as one's starting point in eschatology.

It is worth noting, however—and this confirms what has been said about the futurist, post-mortem, emphasis in his eschatology—that Moltmann is now to be included among upholders of belief, rather than just hope, in universal salvation in the ultimate restoration of all things. With reference to Balthasar's discussion of Christ's descent into hell, he places his final emphasis on God's all-reconciling love.[18]

---

[16] Moltmann, *The Future of Creation*, 115–30.   [17] Ibid. 18–40.
[18] Moltmann, *The Coming of God*, 254.

When we turn to Pannenberg's theology, we certainly encounter a more systematic and philosophical mind. Admittedly there is much the same emphasis in his writings as in Moltmann's on human beings as open to the future, on the eschatological nature of all Christian theology, and on the future consummation of God's Kingdom as determining both present significance and present tasks. But Pannenberg operates with a much more telling and all-embracing conception of the significance of apocalyptic for the understanding of reality, and a much more radical, if difficult, conception of God as the 'power of the future'.

For Pannenberg, the chief significance of inter-testamental and Christian apocalyptic, for all its bizarre imagery, was the conviction that came to expression there of universal history reaching its God-given culmination in the resurrection of the dead and the realization of God's kingdom. Naturally, with his insistence on human beings' openness to the future, Pannenberg does not endorse the deterministic tendencies of biblical apocalyptic. As we shall see, he criticizes any conception of God that implies that all is fixed in advance. But the great achievement of apocalyptic was its conception of reality as history, and of history as a totality moving towards a consummation in which all will take part. This understanding of reality was a necessary precondition for the reception by the first Christians of Jesus's resurrection. Only because of the apocalyptic framework were they able to understand Jesus's resurrection as an anticipation of the end and thus a revelation within history of the significance of history as a whole. Pannenberg has a very interesting comment on the Parousia expectation in this connection. In fact, like most modern theologians, Pannenberg locates the Parousia beyond history in the end, but he remarks that, just because the end was uniquely anticipated in Jesus's resurrection, 'the eschatological future was nearer then than at any other time'.[19] This yields considerable insight into the puzzling phenomenon of the imminent Parousia expectation that required so much adjustment in later Christian thought.

Pannenberg's conception of God as the power of the future is a much more problematic affair. He develops in this connection a whole ontology of the future, which is very hard to grasp. He had

---

[19] Wolfhart Pannenberg, *Jesus—God and Man*, Eng. trans. (London: SCM Press, 1968), 108.

come to hold that the essence of any reality is fully achieved only in the end, in its ultimate future, which then, by a kind of retroactive force, establishes its nature all along. This goes for human beings, history, Christ, and God, whose ultimate reality becomes apparent and effective only in the future consummation. The purpose of this strange ontology apparently stemmed from the need to counter certain prominent objections to the idea of God in modern atheism. Only on such a view of God, according to Pannenberg, could our freedom and openness to the future be reconciled with faith in God. Only the God of hope provides the condition of a meaningful freedom—'the freedom through which men transform their traditions and renew their historical world'.[20] Such an ontology does not, however, seem to be a necessary step for Christian theology to take. Maybe if it can be read as a way of bringing out the self-limitation involved in the creation of a world of open possibilities, it can be held to have some point. But the same end can be achieved by a much more straightforward ascription of temporality and self-limitation to God in creating a world.

At least Pannenberg was trying to grasp the nettle of the relation between time and eternity, a problem that, as we have seen, has dogged traditional and modern eschatology. This can be seen in his very interesting treatment of the meaning of resurrection. Here Pannenberg makes, with great clarity, the essential point that needs to be made against all liberal, existentialist, and political eschatologies: 'It takes a resurrection of the dead to have all human individuals of all times participate in the perfect society of the Kingdom of God.'[21] But he does not see this future participation as standing in simple temporal succession to historical time. The futurity of God's consummated kingdom is the future of all times, past, present, and future, and the whole life of every individual, as indeed the whole of human society and history, will be taken, beyond death, into God's future. This must not be understood, as perhaps it was in Pannenberg's earliest writings,[22] to mean a timeless eternity. That would surely deprive human freedom and decision-making of reality.

[20] Wolfhart Pannenberg, *Basic Questions in Theology*, iii, Eng. trans. (London: SCM Press, 1973), 210.
[21] Cousins (ed.), *Hope and the Future of Man*, 71.
[22] As criticized by Hick in *Death and Eternal Life*, 221–3.

A hint of what Pannenberg meant by talk of God's future can be found in the following quotation from *The Future of Creation*:

> A general resurrection of the dead would obviously be an event which as an event would be out of comparison with any other event. How then can it be imagined to be a member of the same sequence with events of the ordinary kind? If in some way a general resurrection of the dead is to follow other events, then also the temporal sequence itself might be of a different kind than sequences the members of which are all ordinary events. One might think of a deformation of the ordinary form of temporal sequence comparable to the contortion of space according to the theory of relativity.[23]

Pannenberg's eschatology is set out most fully in the third volume of his *Systematic Theology* (German edition 1993). The treatment there is thoroughly trinitarian, with great emphasis on the Church as the anticipation of humanity's being taken into the Kingdom of God. According to Pannenberg, it is the Holy Spirit who enables us to participate in God's eternal life by including us in the filial relationship of the Son to the Father. The Kingdom of God is envisaged as at once the human world being taken into God's eternity and the coming of eternity into time. Pannenberg does not affirm universal salvation, however. 'In certain cases nothing may remain when the fire of the divine glory has purged away all that is incompatible with God's presence.'[24] But, in the end, it is 'the heart-beat of the divine love' that will encompass 'the whole world of creatures'.[25]

A little more will be said in the next section about Pannenberg's view of the historical future. His views will again be compared and contrasted with those of Moltmann. But, whatever the differences between these two theologians, there is no denying the great impetus that their work has given to the construction of an eschatological theology of hope.[26]

---

[23] Cousins (ed.), *Hope and the Future of Man*, 71.

[24] Wolfhart Pannenberg, *Systematic Theology*, iii (Edinburgh: T. & T. Clark, 1998), 620.

[25] Ibid. 646.

[26] Other theologians of hope include Gerhard Sauter in Germany and Carl Braaten in the United States (see his contribution to Cousins (ed.), *Hope and the Future of Man*).

This-Worldly Hope

There was a strong tendency in twentieth-century Protestant, as in twentieth-century Roman Catholic, eschatology to concentrate attention on the bearing of the Christian hope on the earthly historical future. Moltmann's repeated endorsement of liberation theology has already been mentioned. And Latin American liberation theology is by no means only a Roman Catholic phenomenon, as the names of Rubem Alves (b. 1933), Jose Miguez Bonino (b. 1924), and Emilio Castro (b. 1927) will testify. Alves, for example, in his *A Theology of Human Hope*, writes of the history and politics of freedom and of the way in which both Christians and humanists should work together to create a new future. Hope, says Alves, has to be the language of the possible. It inspires work for the realization of real historical possibilities. But, whereas humanism has nothing but human resources to pit against the structures of domination that again and again frustrate people's hopes, Christianity knows that human liberation is the business of a power transcending history and creating possibilities beyond purely human calculation. The historical experience of the biblical communities gives rise to 'a different assessment of what is possible to history, thereby providing a different ground for the hope of human liberation'.[27]

Liberation theology made a great impact on the activities and commitments of the World Council of Churches in the second half of the twentieth century. Indeed, at the Fourth General Assembly of the World Council of Churches at Uppsala in 1968, it was widely felt that the ecumenical movement had become so politicized as to have lost touch with the original Christian gospel, an impression strengthened by the setting-up, in the following year, of the Programme to Combat Racism and the apparent equation of salvation and political liberation at the Bangkok conference on 'Salvation Today' in 1972. The balance was somewhat redressed at the Fifth General Assembly in Nairobi in 1975, where the political implication of the Christian gospel was more clearly seen in their wider spiritual context.

---

[27] Rubem Alves, *A Theology of Human Hope* (Washington: Corpus Books, 1969).

But the Christian social theology of the World Council remains, for the most part, radical, if not revolutionary.

Such radical social theologies represent only one end of the spectrum of Protestant attitudes towards the historical future. Notwithstanding widespread disillusionment with the politics of development, many Protestant theologians continued to adopt a more measured approach to the quest for social justice (such views being comparable to those expressed in the Roman Catholic Church by the official documents of Vatican II). Wolfhart Pannenberg's overall conception of Christian eschatology has already been described. But he has also offered very interesting reflections on the future of human society on earth.[28] From the standpoint of a more systematized theological position and a greater commitment to the ideas of universal history and divine providence than we find in Moltmann's books, Pannenberg recommends a Christian ethic of social and individual transformation rather than a theology of revolution. Not that he rules out the possibility of legitimate revolution in some circumstances. An ethic of social change is set as much against a Lutheran ethic of order as against any form of purely privatized inner religion.[29] Just because the resurrection of Jesus is the anticipation of the end of universal history, Christians must hope and work for the transformation of every aspect of the present. The interest of Pannenberg's essays on this theme lies in the particularity with which he is prepared to see in ecumenism, in the rise of democracy, in the history and overcoming of nationalism, in the peace movement, and even in the European community, provisional forms of unification in freedom that partially reflect the providential, mediated, action of the God of the future.

Jürgen Moltmann, like Pannenberg, sees Christian hope for the ultimate eschatological consummation, through the immanent operation of the divine Spirit, as the basis and resource for this-worldly transformation. In his more recent writing, especially in *The Coming of God*, his commitment to political liberation has included commitment to feminism, ecology, and peace. But the environmental

---

[28] See Wolfhart Pannenberg, *Faith and Reality*, Eng. trans. (London: Search Press, 1975), chs. 8 and 10; *Ethics*, Eng. trans. (Philadelphia: Westminster Press, 1981), chs. 7 and 9.

[29] Pannenberg rightly points out that Jesus's words 'My kingdom is not of this world' refer to the kingdom's provenance, not to its a-political nature.

threat and the nuclear threat remain very real and give continued relevance to the language of apocalyptic. Moltmann's this-worldly eschatology is certainly more dialectical than Pannenberg's.

An Anglican contribution to the theme of hope for the historical future is that of David Edwards (b. 1929) in *A Reason to Hope* (1978).[30] Edwards offers an informed yet optimistic assessment of the potentialities of modern science, technology, politics, and religion for making the world a better place. In each of these four areas, he sees the negative possibilities—those of meaninglessness and tragedy, those of doom and disaster, those of totalitarianism and tyranny, and those of dogmatism and escapism. But against such pessimistic readings of the signs of the times, Edwards, like Pannenberg, suggests a positive interpretation of divine providence working through our increasing knowledge of the world in which we live, through enlightened applications of this knowledge in projects of 'self-liberation' and international cooperation in the use of scarce resources, through participatory democracy and transnational communities such as Europe, and through a greater religious responsiveness and a wider ecumenism.

We may well wonder how far world historical developments since Edwards wrote his book have affected such a relatively optimistic view. Certainly, the collapse of the Soviet Union and east bloc communism and the development of the European Community did, for a time, encourage optimistic expectations for the twenty-first century. But the growing ecological crisis and the signs of a worldwide 'clash of civilizations' have reintroduced a more pessimistic note, to which we shall have to return in the final chapter.

A Dutch Reformed contribution to this whole topic is that of Hendrikus Berkhof (1914–95) in *A Well Founded Hope* (1969) and in *Christian Faith* (1979). On the relation between ultimate and earthly hope Berkhof writes: 'Only the outsider will think that faith in the consummation deprives our earthly life of its importance. The opposite is true: this perspective lends an eternal importance to our earthly life.'[31] But equally, 'because this earthly life is no goal but a

[30] David L. Edwards, *A Reason to Hope* (London: Collins, 1978).

[31] Hendrikus Berkhof, *Christian Faith: An Introduction to the Study of the Faith*, Eng. trans. (Grand Rapids, MI: William B. Eerdmans, 1979), 488.

road, we need not demand and expect everything from it'. From this balanced perspective, the most significant element in Berkhof's treatment is his insistence on the strict parallel between what Christian hope implies for the renewal of the individual and what it implies for the renewal of society and the world.

Traditionally the emphasis was more on the sanctification of the individual by growth in freedom and love. But, just because we are social beings, set in an environment that makes us what we are, Christian faith must also concern itself with the sanctification of the world. As a guiding principle in this connection, Berkhof suggests that 'the renewing work of the Spirit in the world exhibits an analogy to his work in man'.[32] Berkhof is bold enough to expect specific examples of the difference made by the presence of the Christian gospel in those strands of human history where its influence has been most pervasive— namely, Europe and the United States. It is in these strands that the ideas of freedom and social justice have taken firmest root. This leads to a fresh evaluation of the concept of progress. Structural progress in health, education, equality before the law, and greatly increased opportunities and prosperity are undeniable features of modern European and American history, and at least the hope of their extension to the rest of the world exist. But at the same time Berkhof is aware of the limitations that inhibit progress, most notably death and sin. Moreover there is a marked intensification of both sides of this ambivalent modern history. The possibilities for structural transformation are greater than ever before; but so are the possibilities of disaster and destruction. It is at this point that Berkhof stresses the lasting significance of the apocalyptic symbols both of the millennium and of Antichrist. The upshot of this discussion is that neither in the case of the individual nor in the case of the world can we expect sanctification to be completed on earth. The consummation lies beyond death and beyond the end of the world. The relation between sanctification and consummation involves discontinuity as well as continuity.

It is not easy to evaluate the dispute between those, such as Moltmann and the liberation theologians, who emphasize the revolutionary implications of the Christian gospel, and those, such as Pannenberg, Edwards, and Berkhof, who emphasize the more gradual and inevitably ambiguous transformations that divine providence

---

[32] Ibid. 501.

achieves through recalcitrant human material in the history of the world. But few modern theologians, Protestant or Catholic, have been willing to ignore the social and political implications of Christian hope.

Christian Universalism

Returning to the ultimate Christian hope, we now take note of a number of late-twentieth-century advocates, from the English-speaking world, of universalism—the belief that, in the end, all will be saved.

Already, in the 1930s, the Scottish theologian John Baillie (1886–1960), in *The Life Everlasting*, was making the case for universalism. He pointed out that there are three options regarding the ultimate fate of the wicked: (*a*) everlasting exclusion from all blessedness; (*b*) annihilation; and (*c*) universal restoration. On the first option, Baillie stressed the religious and moral difficulty of making distributive and retributive justice the ultimate law of the spiritual universe. That would be to make evil an eternal element in the nature of things. This is intolerable in a religion centred on the supreme good of forgiveness. On the second option, Baillie found himself unable to accept that any created person is unredeemable. That would be 'to set a limit to the power of divine love over the recalcitrant will of created spirit'.[33] Baillie therefore opts for universalism, although he says very little about it, except to insist that it must be of a form 'which does nothing to decrease the urgency of immediate repentance and which makes no promises to the procrastinating sinner'.[34]

Two later theologians who have espoused and defended universalism at length are John Robinson (1919–83) and John Hick. Robinson put the case for universalism in his first book, *In the End, God...*[35] He made the basic point that belief in universal salvation is a consequence of taking absolutely seriously the scope of what God has done

[33] John Baillie, *And the Life Everlasting* (London: Oxford University Press, 1934), 245.
[34] Ibid.
[35] John A. T. Robinson, *In the End, God... A Study of the Christian Doctrine of the Last Things* (London: James Clarke & Co., 1950).

in Christ. This is not a matter of God's overriding human freedom. Rather, God's love is here believed to be so strong and so enduring that, in the end, no one will be able to hold back from free acceptance of that love. Nor does universalist belief, on Robinson's view, deny the seriousness of human choice and decision. From the standpoint of human subjectivity, hell is certainly as real as heaven. Anyone who draws from universalist belief the conclusion that choice and responsibility do not matter is very far from God and, by that very attitude, bringing hell upon themselves. Such a person needs to be transformed, to be won by the love of Christ crucified, into a committed, God-centred, life. Universalist belief simply holds that, in the end, all men and women will be thus transformed and that an objective permanent state of alienation is an ultimate impossibility.

Hick develops similar arguments in *Death and Eternal Life*. He points out that Jesus's existential preaching of the danger of eternal loss is quite compatible, logically speaking, with the theological opinion that, in fact, all will repent and be saved. He also suggests that the divine love and human freedom are not in irreconcilable conflict, if it is in fact our God-given nature 'to seek after God and find him'. The relation between God and a human person is comparable to that of a psychiatrist freeing his patient from inner blockages and inhibitions. Most important of all, Hick develops in this book the inevitable implications of universalist belief—namely, the view that human opportunities are not restricted to this single earthly span, but renewed and extended beyond death in the life of the world to come.

Among more recent advocates of universalism may be mentioned the American philosophical theologians Marilyn McCord Adams (b. 1943) and Thomas Talbott (b. 1941). Adams, in a powerful critique of the notion of everlasting damnation, writes: 'I emphasize a high doctrine of divine resourcefulness (assigning God the power to let creatures "do their damnedest" and still win them all over to heavenly bliss) and a low doctrine of human agency (both ontologically, in terms of the gap between God and creatures, and psychologically, in terms of developmental limitations and impairments).'[36] Talbott, in *The Inescapable Love of God*, argues that belief in everlasting punishment is simply

---

[36] Marilyn McCord Adams, 'The Problem of Hell: A Problem of Evil for Christians', in Eleonore Stump (ed.), *Reasoned Faith* (Ithaca, NY: Cornell University Press, 1993), 325.

inconsistent with belief (*a*) that it is God's redemptive purpose for the world to reconcile all sinners to himself, and (*b*) that it is within God's power to achieve his redemptive purpose for the world.[37]

It has to be said that Christian universalism is a minority view in Protestant theology. Of the theologians considered earlier, Karl Barth and Hendrikus Berkhof, like the Roman Catholic Karl Rahner, would only go so far as to express the hope that it might be true. In Berkhof's own words, 'for God's sake, we hope that hell will be a form of purification.'[38] Only Moltmann was prepared to affirm unqualified belief in the doctrine of universal restoration.

It is worth considering the objections to universalism listed by a sensitive evangelical scholar, Stephen H. Travis (b. 1944), whose two books *Christian Hope and the Future of Man* (1980) and *I Believe in the Second Coming of Jesus* (1982) form valuable contributions to our topic as a whole. Having observed that 'he who has not felt deeply the attraction of universalism can scarcely have been moved by the greatness of God's love,'[39] Travis goes on to make six points against it: it does not take human freedom seriously enough; it does not face up to the depth and radical nature of human wickedness; its implication of a long process of transformation after death is alien to the general thrust of Scripture; it is not the only solution to the problem of adherents of other religions; it does not succeed in separating existential threats of eternal loss from belief about what will actually happen; and its reading of New Testament texts is one sided. The allegedly universalist convictions of Paul are more naturally interpreted as referring to God's saving purpose, which can be realized only through the response of faith. These are weighty objections to belief in universal salvation. They may not be insuperable, but they will have to be pondered in depth before our final conclusion is given in Chapter 11.

[37] Thomas Talbott, *The Inescapable Love of God* (Parkland, FL: Universal Publishers, 1999), 44–5. Talbott's defence of universalism in earlier articles was criticized by William Lane Craig, in 'Talbott's Universalism', *Religious Studies*, 27 (1991), 297–308, and by Jonathan Kvanvig, in *The Problem of Hell* (New York: Oxford University Press, 1993). For Talbott's replies, see Thomas Talbott, 'Damnation and the Power to Sin with Impunity', *Religious Studies*, 37 (2001), 417–34, and in *The Inescapable Love of God*. Talbott's views may most readily be found in his chapter 'Universalism' in Jerry L. Walls (ed.), *The Oxford Handbook of Eschatology* (Oxford: Oxford University Press, 2007), 446–61.

[38] Berkhof, *Christian Faith*, 532.

[39] Stephen Travis, *Christian Hope and the Future of Man* (Nottingham: Inter Varsity Press, 1980), 129–30.

Other Voices

This inevitably selective survey of late-twentieth-century-Protestant work on the Christian hope may be rounded off by brief consideration of a number of writers not so far mentioned, who made significant contributions to the theme.

Eberhard Jüngel (b. 1934) in Germany developed a Barthian approach to death and resurrection. One of the reasons why he wanted to follow Barth in his rejection of life 'after' death was that he saw the importance of death in marking the finiteness and boundedness of human life. In *Death: The Riddle and the Mystery,* he insisted that no credible modern anthropology can treat human beings as if their inevitable death were a thing of little consequence. Following Barth, Jüngel saw resurrection rather as the gathering-up of the whole of one's life before God. In *God as the Mystery of the World,* Jüngel expands this idea in a very interesting, if difficult, footnote:

A Christian eschatology would thus think of *eternal life* as the revelation of life as it is lived with all of the possibilities which surround it, that is, not merely as the eternalizing of the possibility *out* of which our life became possible, but rather as the revelation and implementation of all those possibilities *into* which our life constantly moves without ever having realized them. Then all of the possibilities, the missed ones and the concealed ones, all of which define us, will as such reveal the truth of our life, to each individual as the *subject* of the life he is living.[40]

Jüngel invites us to take this as an expansion of the corresponding remarks in *Death,* which 'apparently were not adequately insured against misunderstanding along the line that the eternalizing of a lived life meant the setting aside of my person as the subject of my life'.[41] Jüngel's attempt to ward off the objection that a Barthian view of resurrection deprives the human subject of a genuine participation in God's future may be welcomed. But our earlier suspicions of Barthian eschatology, now reinforced by the factors

[40] Eberhard Jüngel, *God as the Mystery of the World: On the Foundation of the Theology of the Crucified One in the Dispute between Theism and Atheism,* Eng. trans. (Edinburgh: T. & T. Clark, 1983), 215.

[41] Ibid.

that led us to take seriously the need for further opportunities of growth and repentance beyond the grave, are not likely to be allayed by Jüngel's apparent restriction of those opportunities to the realization of missed possibilities during our earthly life. After all, one becomes the person one is through the realization of some possibilities and *not* others. One may grow and develop through the realization of *new* possibilities, but hardly the renewal of those already passed by.

It seems that those most influenced by Bultmann have moved further from their master's viewpoint than those most influenced by Barth. If we turn now to two scholars in the former category, Gerhard Ebeling (1912–2001) in Germany and Schubert Ogden (b. 1928) in the United States, we find that neither has remained content with a purely existentialist interpretation of biblical eschatology. Both identify the object of eschatological assertions as the fulfilment of creation and the human world in relation to God. But, whereas Ebeling, in the third volume of his *Dogmatik des Christlichen Glaubens* (Dogmatics of the Christian Faith) (1979) speaks of a real future fulfilment of creation by the triune God in a new creation beyond death, Ogden resorts to the kind of eschatology and doctrine of God that we found in process theology. In fact, this enables him to stay closer to Bultmann's existentialist interpretation. According to Ogden, to speak of resurrection is certainly to speak of a new self-understanding, but it is also to speak of an act of God, a God who loves (and judges) his creation for what it is, and embraces it eternally in his love. But Ogden's allegiance at this point to something like the 'divine memory' theory of process theology is clear from his explicit denial that his view entails our survival of death as subjects of further experience. In the final chapter of his *The Reality of God* (1967), where Ogden deals with these issues, we find him sharply criticizing John Robinson's espousal of universalism, precisely on the grounds that Robinson has not consistently demythologized the eschatological myths of the New Testament, but has illicitly retained a theory of an objective final state of the cosmic process. But, if our criticisms above of the tendency in process theology to rest content with the divine memory have any force, then we must affirm, with Robinson and against Ogden, that Christianity is concerned with the eventual consummation of the creative process and that that is what the biblical myths are about. The device of combining a Bultmannian existentialist interpretation with a 'process' doctrine of God does nothing to save Ogden from the implausibilities of both positions regarding the ultimate future of creation.

Another theologian who finds himself disposed to embrace something like a 'process' view of eternal life is John Macquarrie (1919–2007), who, in his *Christian Hope*, defends the idea that the past (that is, our bounded temporal lives on earth) is taken up, healed, and renewed in the experience of God, 'as he brings his creation and his own striving in the creation to a new consummation'.[42] Macquarrie makes interesting use of relativity theory in his defence of the idea of a living, dynamic relation between God and the past of creation, but it may be doubted whether he succeeds in giving any real content to the belief that such a relation involves a genuine participation by us in God's eternal life (since then it would not be just an embracing of the past). Macquarrie himself admits that his view 'is built on a consideration of the temporality of the self'[43]—by which he means the temporal boundedness of the self between birth and death. Again we may suspect that a secular anthropology is being allowed to prescribe the limits of what can be said in Christian theology.

A much more soundly based theological treatment of the issue is by Stephen Sykes (b. 1939) in an essay entitled 'Life after Death: The Christian Doctrine of Heaven'.[44] Sykes defends the use of the phrase 'life after death' against both secular anthropologies and theological revisionism, and makes it quite clear that considerations of theodicy constitute an important reason for its retention. Very few of the mass of humankind throughout history have had the opportunity of finding fulfilment in relation to God in the course of their earthly life. The Christian doctrines of resurrection and judgement cannot, therefore, be understood in terms of the validation (or condemnation) of people's earthly life alone. They contain a promise of victory and fulfilment that makes sense only on the supposition of life after death. Claims that it is more 'realistic' to concede the finality of death

---

[42] John Macquarrie, *Christian Hope* (Oxford: Mowbrays, 1978), 119.

[43] Ibid. 117.

[44] In Richard W. A. McKinney (ed.), *Creation Christ and Culture: Studies in Honour of T. F. Torrance* (Edinburgh: T. & T. Clark, 1976), 250–71. It should be noted that Sykes interprets Moltmann's position much less sympathetically than I have done above.

have no place in Christianity, which is centrally concerned with the breaking of the grip of death.

Mention may be made of another English theologian, Austin Farrer (1904–68), whose chapter on 'Heaven and Hell' in his *Saving Belief* repays repeated reading. Having argued that a serious Christian belief in God and in Christ entails belief in the raising of the dead to the life of heaven, Farrer points out that it is not enough simply to say that heaven is the presence of God. If God raises the dead, he brings about a new creation, and heaven must be thought of as 'a created sphere where God bestows his presence by his action'.[45] Farrer deftly deals with the problem of the relation between the new creation and this world by appealing to the theory of relativity—in a much more intelligible way than with Macquarrie. Another space, spatially unrelated to the present universe, is quite conceivable. For 'unless the beings or energies of which heaven is composed are of a sort to interact physically with the energies in our physical world, heaven can be as dimensional as it likes, without ever getting pulled into our spatial field'.[46] These remarks may be compared with our previous speculations on the new, non-material, environment of the resurrection world (see p. 174 above).

The topic of the Parousia has not been as central in recent eschatology as it was in traditional Christian belief, and it is interesting to observe how even conservative scholars, concerned to defend the doctrine, have inevitably treated it, not as the return of Christ to this world, but as the final manifestation of Christ at the end of the world. Thus Stephen Travis writes: 'the Parousia will . . . be an event marking the climax of our present historical order but will itself be beyond history in that it will introduce a new order discontinuous with the present course of history.'[47] Similarly, according to Anthony Thiselton, 'history is moving towards the goal of the great and final "coming" when that which is ambiguous and fragmentary will be done away'.[48] Christian eschatology does indeed see the ultimate

---

[45] Austin Farrer, *Saving Belief: A Discussion of Essentials* (London: Hodder & Stoughton, 1964), 144.
[46] Ibid.
[47] Travis, *Christian Hope and the Future of Man*, 91. See also Stephen Travis, *I Believe in the Second Coming of Jesus* (London: Hodder & Stoughton, 1982), 106.
[48] Anthony Thiselton, 'The Parousia in Modern Theology: Some Questions and Comments', in *The Tyndale Bulletin* (1976), 27–53.

future as unambiguously centred on the risen Christ, the incarnate Son of God, in whom God eternally reveals his love. But these authors are surely right to treat the language of 'coming on the clouds of heaven' as symbolic of that future, transcendent, consummation, and specifically not as referring to a literal return into the present order of things.

11

A Christian Eschatology for the Twenty-First Century

Introduction

Reflection on the very varied and conflicting ideas that have been put forward in the history of Christian eschatology will lead us to suppose that we are dealing here with an area of doctrine much less securely fixed or mapped out in its details than any other. We may hope to reach fairly broad agreement on the overall dimensions of the Christian hope, but there is bound to remain diversity of opinion over the more specific problems concerning the 'last things' that have perplexed Christian minds down the centuries. In this concluding chapter, then, while some main features of the Christian eschatology proposed will be defended without reservation as belonging to the essence of Christianity, the more detailed and speculative points will be offered tentatively, claiming no more authority than their rational and religious plausibility in the light of all the relevant factors— theological, ethical, and scientific.

Among the former category—those matters belonging essentially to Christian faith and hope—is the conviction that God's creation is moving towards an eternal consummation in which all men and women from all ages will participate. Such a conviction is only possible for a religion that takes God seriously both as omnipotent creator and as the God of love. For it is conviction of God's creative power that leads us to suppose that he can raise the dead, and it is conviction of God's nature—his goodness and his love—that leads us to suppose that he will raise the dead. Christians believe, of course, that God's power and love are already revealed and effective in the creation of the world and in the redemption of humanity, so that it is present experience of both creatureliness and salvation that forms the existential basis on which a Christian eschatology may be constructed.

But, if it is the revealed and experienced nature of God that makes the Christian mind discern the promise of an eternal destiny and a fulfilment of the creative process beyond death, it is precisely the fact of death and the facts of evil and suffering in the world that raise doubts in many people's minds about the existence of an omnipotent God of love at all. The issue of theodicy (of justifying the ways of God in face of the facts of evil) affects the Christian hope in two ways. In the first place, it is considerations of theodicy that add particular sharpness and poignancy to the argument from the love of God to personal immortality. For it is not just the fact that the Christian mind cannot entertain the idea of personal relations between human beings and the God of love being extinguished for ever by death; it is also the fact that so many human beings have led stunted, thwarted, and prematurely curtailed lives in the midst of largely unrealized potentialities. But the problem of evil is not solved by the postulation of an eternal destiny for all. We find ourselves also asking why the world is as it is in the first place. Only if we can see the point of a creative process that entails so much suffering on the way can we remain convinced of God's power and love, and thus go on to accept the argument from divine love to immortality. So the second way in which considerations of theodicy affect the topic of Christian hope lies in the demand for an intelligible explanation of why the world as we know it is as it is.

The Relation between the Historical Future and the Ultimate Future

Our first task, however, is to try to achieve a proper balance between an understanding of Christian hope for the historical future and an understanding of Christian hope for the ultimate future beyond death. At first the immediate effect of Christian hope was located in the sphere of individual life and the Church community, nourished by the Christian sacraments,[1] rather than in the sphere of social transformation and a just world. The early Christians had little or no hope for society on earth apart from the millennial rule of Christ and the saints, subsequent to the Parousia. At most, the providence of God would ensure conditions in which the gospel of salvation would be preached.

After the conversion of Constantine we begin to find, within the horizon of the Christian hope of heaven, very varied forms of this-worldly hope as well. As a broad generalization one can say that, for a long time, sober realism about the wickedness of men and women, especially in respect of conflict and the use of power, prevailed over more or less utopian views of a Christian empire or a spiritually perfected Christian world. The earthly city or the kingdom of the world might be sustained by divine ordinance and subject to criticism and reform in the light of God's revealed will; but the mainstream churches, before and after the Reformation, continued to set people's sights primarily on the world above. The Reformers may have seen eternity brought to bear more vividly and immediately upon the present life of Christian men and women in the world, but few attempts were made, except by sectarian enthusiasts, to translate the liberating Christian gospel into socio-political reality.

The eighteenth and nineteenth centuries saw great changes here. Although belief in the immortality of the soul remained a common presupposition, the weight of most people's concern, including that of broad sections of the churches, shifted and now came to rest on hope for the education of the human race and the gradual realization of an ethical Kingdom of God on earth.

Only in the modern period has something of a balance between this-worldly and other-worldly hope been found. On the one hand, the dimension and perspective of eternity were rediscovered and recognized to constitute a source of both criticism and inspiration for provisional realizations and anticipations here on earth of the ultimate future heavenly kingdom. On the other hand, few would now deny the social and political demands that Christian faith, hope,

---

[1] See Geoffrey Wainwright, *Eucharist and Eschatology* (London: Epworth Press, 1971).

and love make regarding the future of the human world. There is still a great deal of disagreement over the revolutionary or reformist nature of these implications, but commitment to the sanctification of the world, as well as commitment to the sanctification of the individual, is clearly seen to follow from recognition of the ultimate end and ultimate dynamic of the creative process in the midst of which we find ourselves. Just as the hope of heaven inspires and enables the acquisition and growth of Christian character and commitment at the level of an individual Christian's earthly life, so does it inspire and enable the transformation of human society into a more just and more caring world community. Moreover, it is not simply a matter of holding to the strict parallel or analogy between the individual and social aspects of this-worldly hope. The two aspects are inseparable. Just because individuals can find their ultimate fulfilment only in relation to each other and to God, there can be no purely individual sanctification and thus no hope for either a better future on earth or a perfected future in heaven that does not embrace the whole human fellowship. The history of Christian eschatology is the history of the extension of this recognition from the small community of believers to the community of all human beings.

One can understand the criticism, so prevalent since the Enlightenment, that hope of heaven deflects attention from urgent and immediate tasks and represents an illusory consolation, inhibiting radical protest against unjust and alienating conditions here on earth. But, properly understood, the dynamics of the ultimate Christian hope should have quite the opposite effect. Precisely because the history of the world is seen as moving, under God, towards a perfect, just, and loving consummation in the end, and precisely because God is seen as identifying himself with the poor and the unloved and as beginning the healing and transforming process here and now, Christians are to discern the divine Spirit at work wherever the task of making a more just and humane world is being undertaken. Moreover, as members of the Church, the Body of Christ here on earth, they are aware of, and in touch with, the divine resources for such a humanizing of the world. They know that the construction of a just and living world community is a task in accord with the ultimate nature of things and they know that the spiritual resources for a realistic and unflinching commitment to this task are available to men and women of faith.

Christian hope for the historical future is realistic hope, however, because it acquires, from the perspective of eternity, a critical and uninflated character. It does not embrace unrealistic, short-lived, enthusiasms; it does not identify God's Kingdom with some particular utopian scheme; it does not ride roughshod over people as they are. Above all, it recognizes human sinfulness and the seriousness of the problems facing our attempts to build a better world. It recognizes the provisional nature of all social and political achievements and the continuing need to allow the power of God's future to transcend and refashion every present form of human community. The realism of Christian hope also consists in its recognition of the inevitable limitations of this-worldly hope that stem from the unavoidable facts of suffering, evil, and death. Although much suffering and evil can be prevented or overcome by human action here on earth, there remain much unavoidable tragedy and pain and, especially, the universal presence of the death of human beings. Hope for this world, therefore, requires the ultimate Christian hope if it is to maintain confidence, as well as realism and patience, in the face of otherwise overwhelming odds.

The Creative Process and the Problem of Evil

No overall evaluation of the created universe can afford to restrict its scope to the word as it is at present. To speak of God's 'good' creation is to speak of the whole creative process including its future consummation. Here modern science has helped Christian theology to see the world as in process and to see creation as the gradual formation of the conditions in which personal beings can evolve and emerge into the spheres of rationality, spirit, and love. Christian theology goes beyond modern science, of course, in seeing all this as but one stage in a creative process destined for eternity and for the consummation of a communion of persons in relation to God and indwelt by God beyond all death, perishability, and loss.

But the question immediately arises why God creates persons in this way—that is to say, gradually and indirectly in and through a material universe, whose fundamental energies and forces may have the remarkable property of being able so to interact and combine as to produce persons in the course of cosmic evolution, but that also produce very great suffering and evil—for animals as well as for persons—and not least the ever-present fact of death. Put crudely, the question is this: if persons are made to be raised into eternity, why does God not create heaven directly, without going through the agonizing phase of gradual, indirect, creation, in and through a physical universe that is cause of so much pain?

The answer seems to be that it is logically impossible, even for omnipotence, to create heaven directly. There is a stronger and a weaker form of this answer. The weaker argument would seek to show that it is logically impossible to have the specific values of human personal and communal life without the law-governed physical environment out of which that life and those values are fashioned. And, since it is the very same system of interacting energies and forces that is both productive of those values (for example, physical beauty, tenderness, sensitivity, the possibility of long-term planning, the overcoming of problems, the arts, sport, courage, sympathy, ecstasy, and human love) and also responsible for the clashes, accidents, and malfunctions that constitute so much of the problem of evil, then one cannot wish away the latter without wishing away the former as well. Moreover, a physical system of organic life in which such human values are rooted is necessarily a self-reproducing system, where individual lives are bounded by birth and death. Once fashioned this way and established in being, a human person finds himself or herself existing in the world of the spirit—the world of rationality, interpersonal relation and love, including religious experience and spirituality. As such, he or she becomes destined for eternity. Now to suppose that God can and will resurrect or immortalize human persons is to suppose that some at least of the aforementioned values are not essentially corporeal or temporary in their nature. In a later section, we shall discuss which values are immortalizable and what happens to the others. The present point is simply that specifically human values must first be established in being in their earthly context, before their bearers can, as it were, become candidates for eternity. The material creation is a necessary stage, therefore, in the whole creative process. The stronger argument would seek to show that it is logically impossible to have any created personal beings at all, without their being rooted and grounded in some such world as this. On this view the material creation is not only a necessary stage in the establishment of specifically human values, but a necessary condition of creaturely personal being as such. This would be a much more difficult case to make out. Fortunately, it is not necessary for present purposes to try to decide the issue between the weaker and the stronger forms of this answer to the problem of evil.[2] For, in either case, a regular, law-governed physical universe, with inevitable concomitant possibilities of damage and hurt, is necessary for the initial production of values that may then come to be immortalized.

Death and Life after Death

It was pointed out in the preceding section that a self-reproducing person-making system would necessarily involve the boundedness of lives by birth and death. The repeated reproduction of new persons requires the eventual disappearance of previous generations and a limited, mortal, life span for each individual. It is a corollary of this fact that, in the world to come, where persons are immortalized, the creation ceases to be self-reproducing. There are no new persons in heaven. Indeed this fact reinforces our previous argument that an earthly self-reproducing stage is a necessary stage in the production of persons to be immortalized in the end.

A further undeniable fact is that all the values of human life, at least at first in the productive and reproductive phase of the creative process, are rooted in these conditions of mortality and related to the boundedness of human life. This is true of the acquisition of value through education and experience, and it is true of the limited, temporary, nature of our experience and enjoyment of value within the horizon of our inevitable death. A serious anthropology, in its characterization of what it is to be human, must reckon with this boundedness of human life. Moreover, it should be pointed out that

[2] On the problem of evil, see further Austin Farrer, *Love Almighty and Ills Unlimited: An Essay on Providence and Evil* (London: Collins, 1962); John Hick, *Evil and the God of Love* (London: Macmillan, 1966; 2nd edn., 1977); Alvin Plantinga, *God, Freedom and Evil* (London: George Allen & Unwin, 1975); Brian Hebblethwaite, *Evil, Suffering and Religion* (London: Sheldon Press, 1976; rev. edn., London: SPCK, 2000).

the fact that our lives on earth are lived within the horizon of inevitable death is not a purely negative fact. It gives much of the colour, poignancy, and character to the actual values that we enjoy as human beings. Secular anthropologists will be liable to assert that all human values are essentially limited and temporary just because of the universal fact of death, and that it is illusory to think of their transposition into a different, immortal, key. Much recent Christian eschatology (one thinks of Tillich, Rahner, Hartshorne, Jüngel, and Macquarrie) has tended to share this sense of the essential boundedness of the self, and it is one of the reasons why they have questioned the idea of life *after* death. But Christian theology has no business to be following secular anthropology here. For one thing, some of the values that, on any view, can come to characterize a human life themselves suggest intimations of immortality. This is true of reason, love of beauty, ecstasy, and love. It is obviously true of specifically religious values, such as mystical experience and the worship and love of God. But the main reason why Christian theology cannot follow secular anthropology in its conviction of the essential boundedness of the self is its primary conviction of the reality and nature of God. As argued at the beginning of this chapter, to take God seriously is to discern the promise of a future consummation of the creative process, beyond death, in which all persons will participate.

The other main reason why some contemporary theologians have questioned the idea of life *after* death is a more apparently respectable theological reason—namely, the conviction that God's eternity must be conceived in non-temporal terms and that therefore to be taken into God's eternal life is to be taken into a dimension where there can be no talk of 'before' and 'after'. However, increasing recognition that it is both unnecessary and unintelligible to locate God wholly outside time, and that a living, purposive, and active God of love must be thought of, at least analogously, in temporal terms, has deprived this second reason for questioning life after death of any theological force.

If neither anthropology nor theology requires us to reject the idea of life *after* death, we can rest content with the religious reasons that have led Christianity—and other theistic religions—to see this earthly life as but a stage in the creative process and to look to God for fulfilment and a new life beyond the grave and beyond the conditions of mortality. This future destiny must, if we are to preserve the plain meaning of words, be characterized as life after death.

The conception of an endless life after death is not, of course, without its problems. But we tend to be bedevilled by a certain poverty of imagination here. The philosopher Bernard Williams (1929–2003) makes apparently telling use of the play *The Makropoulos Case* (turned into a splendid opera by Janácek), in which, unknown to everybody else, the heroine has lived on and on through one relationship after another for 342 years, in order to bring out the utterly boring quality of the idea of unending life.[3] But such a model of eternal life is hopelessly unimaginative and pedestrian. The attempt must be made to raise the level of the discussion of life after death by indicating how certain values of human life, rooted though they are in our bounded, temporary, earthly life, might be thought to be capable of being both renewed and transformed in the conditions of eternity.

It is not easy to steer a middle path between lack of imagination, on the one hand, and unintelligibility, on the other. But it seems clear that a living gracious personal relation cannot possibly be characterized in terms of the past, present, and future of our earthly life being experienced together from the non-temporal standpoint of God. Moreover, if there are good reasons for postulating further stages and opportunities of growth and development for creatures beyond the grave, then time is clearly of the essence of the life to come. But even the final consummations of all things, when God will be all in all, cannot be thought of in wholly non-temporal terms. That state of ultimate perfection must itself involve an endlessly dynamic movement of experience, ecstasy, exploration, and activity (although one hopes for some rest as well!).

Temporary Values and their Relation to Eternity

If we are to think of our lives being taken into another dimension of God's time, renewed, purified, and transformed into the imperishable conditions of eternity, we must look much more closely at the

---

[3] See Bernard Williams, *Problems of the Self* (Cambridge: Cambridge University Press, 1973), ch. 6.

question of which aspects of creaturely life are capable of being transposed into such different, imperishable, modes of being.

Some good things depend wholly on perishable corporeal substance for being what they are, while others seem less inevitably tied to their material base. A rose, for example, is inherently fragile and perishable, whereas a philosophical idea is not. It is possible to think of our ideas, feelings, imaginings, memories, characters, and interpersonal relations being transposed into another, non-material, medium, whereas it is not possible to think of material objects being so transposable. Of course, the *idea* of a rose, or *memories* of material objects may be translated into eternity, but not the rose, the animal, the mountain, the cathedral, themselves.

It is not temporality as such that entails perishability. It is only the past of material things that crumbles and is lost for ever except to memory. We can appreciate this by considering relatively permanent things. Mount Everest, for example, endures through time but loses very little of its nature vis-à-vis the past. Of course mountains *are* perishable, and one day Mount Everest, like the rest of the planet, will be swallowed up in the death of the sun and its planetary system. It too will then, like the rose, be lost for ever except to memory. Genuinely imperishable things retain their full nature and value eternally. To think of God in temporal terms is to think of him as having a past, a present, and a future. But, being imperishable, God does not lose his past, though for him too it *is* past and not present. Of course God's relation to his own past is not the same as his relation to the past of perishable things. Once creatures have perished, they can be retained only in memory. Now being retained in memory is something quite different from being in living relation to some presently actual being. This is why we cannot suppose that being held in the divine memory, however vividly, is an adequate way of understanding our eternal life. Only if creatures, by an act of new creation, are made imperishable can *they* participate in God's eternal life. This is why we must distinguish between those creaturely values that can be made imperishable and those that cannot. The latter may indeed be retained very vividly in the divine memory (though one imagines that the divine memory is selective—only some perishable things are *worth* remembering), and we may well suppose that those creatures who are made imperishable may be permitted to share the divine memories as well as to retain their own—moreover to share and retain such memories with the vividness, where appropriate, of dreams. But creaturely persons themselves must be thought of as presently actual beings, given a new, imperishable, mode of existence and a new, imperishable, environment.

The question may be asked what makes a perishable creature a candidate for translation into such conditions of eternity. We can hardly suppose, as has been suggested, that all sentient beings will be immortalized. Animal life is surely an inherently temporary value. However beautiful and full of exuberance and vigour, it is too much rooted in perishable corporeal substance to be thought of as potentially resurrectable in a non-material, imperishable, form. With animals, the creative process has not yet given birth or gained access to the world of creaturely spirit. At most the excellencies of animal life will be retained in memory. But with rational, personal, spiritual beings, the creative process reaches a new stage. We may suppose that the capacity to enter into personal relations, not only with one's fellow human beings but also with one's God, is the mark of a creature destined for eternity. All the arguments from God's love to immortality come into force at the point where that love can be reciprocated and not before.

However, the distinction between what is temporary, because inherently perishable, and what is immortalizable, because already reaching out into spirit and eternity, is blurred just because it is bodily creatures who achieve this level of spirituality. Human beings inhabit both worlds. What in other, non-spiritual, creatures remains inherently perishable, and therefore temporary, in human beings can be transmuted into spiritual, and therefore immortalizable, reality. A particularly instructive example is that of sexual love. In 1982, Pope John Paul II caused some astonishment in the media by saying that there will be no sex in heaven, but that men and women will remain sexually differentiated. This only reveals the media's ignorance of the teaching of Thomas Aquinas, who says precisely this in the *Summa Contra Gentiles*.[4] The reason for this teaching is not far to seek. Sexual love as such is an inherently temporary value. It is bound up with perishable bodily existence and belongs, as argued above, to the economy of the first stage in the creative process, where new persons are made in and through a self-reproducing physical system. But, as is

---

[4] Book Four, chapters 83 and 88.

well known, sexual love can also become the vehicle of ecstasy and spiritual union in human beings in a way impossible for animals. The language of sexual love indeed becomes the language of mysticism, and furnishes the most powerful metaphors for the love of humans for God and the love of God for us.[5] Far from meaning that mysticism is to be reduced to sexuality, this suggests rather that sexuality in human beings can come to be seen as an image and shadow of mystical union. Sexual love is not in itself immortalizable, but it points beyond itself to possibilities of ecstasy and union that are indeed among the highest spiritual capacities and values and therefore quintessential candidates for being made imperishable in the resurrection world. One presumes that there such ecstasy and spiritual union lose not only their physical base but also their relatively exclusive quality, as reflection on the gospel story of Jesus's dispute with the Sadducees over the woman who had seven husbands should suggest. Moreover, although Aquinas and perhaps John Paul II may be faulted for unintelligibility when they speak of sexual organs being retained yet transformed into the imperishable conditions of eternity, it can certainly be argued that masculinity and femininity represent differentiated personal and spiritual characteristics that will continue to qualify our natures in the resurrection world. After all, we have learned to acknowledge the feminine as well as the masculine in God, without ascribing sexual organs to God. As Genesis puts it: 'God created humankind in his image, in the image of God he created them; male and female he created them.'[6]

The way in which the physical may be the image of the eternal and yet become transcended by it was glimpsed long ago by Plato in the *Symposium*. Enjoyment of physical beauty is a starting point for the ascent to contemplation of—indeed to union with—Beauty itself. Christian theology parts company with Plato only in affirming the personal (and temporal, though imperishable) nature of the absolute reality into relation with which creatures are drawn in the course of their journey from nature to spirit. Physical ecstasy and union are not to be set in opposition to spiritual union. They may be inherently temporary and destined to be left behind, but they point to what

---

[5] See, in the Old Testament, *The Song of Songs*. All this shows how great a mistake it is to drive a wedge between *Agape* and *Eros*.

[6] Gen. 1: 27.

transcends them—namely, the mystical union and communion of the redeemed in God.

Resurrection

Already, in Chapter 10, we saw some grounds for retaining the idea of immortality within the broader doctrine of resurrection. For, if it is the very same person who first comes to be in a perishable mode of existence in a perishable physical environment who is then translated into an imperishable mode of existence in an imperishable non-material environment, then we must postulate some element of continuity across this great divide of death and resurrection. The physical body itself, if it is in fact left behind and replaced by a new non-material means of individuation, cannot fulfil that role. Continuity must rather be ensured by means of the person who has come into existence, admittedly in and through a particular physical organism, but who already transcends that material base in virtue of his or her rational, spiritual, capacities. It is the spiritual being, the person, who is raised to new life in the resurrection world.

But we certainly need to speak of resurrection as well as of immortality; for it is implausible to think of God's act of 'new creation' solely in terms of his holding in being a disembodied spirit in a society of pure spirits, perhaps related only telepathically. The Christian doctrine of creation and of the consummation of creation in a new heaven and a new earth suggests rather a new imperishable environment for risen persons and a new imperishable mode of individuation, relation, and action in that new world for all participants in eternal life.

Something should be said here in explanation of our preference for understanding 'the resurrection of the body' to mean the resurrection of the person rather than the transformation of the body itself into something permanent and incorruptible. It is really a question of intelligibility in the light of modern scientific understanding of matter. A physical body is a particular, complex, configuration of atoms and molecules in continual exchange with an ever-changing physical environment. Although the particles or quanta of energy and the forces that constitute the basic stuff of the world out of which all material objects are made do not themselves appear to be perishable, nevertheless all organized matter is inherently perishable, and it is not clear what could possibly be meant by saying that *matter* will be raised and transformed into something incorruptible in heaven. For this reason it was suggested above that inherently corporeal values, such as sex and Gothic architecture, are unavoidably temporary in nature, and cannot be raised into eternity and immortalized, but only retained in memory. The spiritual values that appear here in bodily clothing must therefore, in heaven, be rehoused in a non-material medium and environment. This can be *called* a spiritual 'body'; but it is the person not the physical body that is raised. If we keep the 'body' terminology, it is a new non-material body that he or she is given in resurrection.

In this view, the material creation is a temporary phase and destined to be left behind, presumably annihilated (perhaps after the 'heat-death' of the universe), when its function in the whole creative process is complete and the last new creaturely person has been taken up and transformed into the conditions of eternity. The material creation, then, should be compared to the chrysalis, not to the caterpillar, vis-à-vis the future butterfly. We may recall that even Teilhard de Chardin, who was most concerned to stress the continuities in the creative process up to point Omega, wrote of 'the passage, by translation or *dematerialisation*, to another sphere...' (emphasis added; see p. 152 above).

One of the problems that dogged traditional Christian eschatology was that of the relation between the fate of the soul at death and the general resurrection at the end of history. The considerations advanced here will lead us to forgo the idea of a period of waiting before a general resurrection at the end.[7] It seems much more plausible to suppose that God raises persons when they die to the life of the world to come. The transition to the new world and the new dimensions of eternity takes place immediately. Of course, there remains a temporal gap between such a resurrection and the final consummation of all things. For one thing, the history of the world goes on and new generations continue to be born and to die. For another thing, there must be time for the love of God to work upon the risen soul, perhaps

---

[7] This idea is still defended by N. T. Wright. See his *The Resurrection of the Son of God* (London: SPCK, 2003).

even to win it, purify it, and enhance it, time for the risen person to repent, to grow and change, and to mature. More will be said about this intermediate phase between death and the final consummation in the section on 'pareschatology' below.

There is no need, then, to think in terms of a postponed general resurrection at the end. The idea may retain some value as a symbol; for all will be raised, and there will be a final consummation. But resurrection itself is best hoped for immediately as we commend our own lives or those of others into God's hands at death.

Judgement

Similar considerations operate when we turn to that other vexed problem of traditional eschatology—namely, the relation between the particular judgement at death and the Last Judgement prior to the final consummation. Even in New Testament times, we find the idea that men and women are judged already by their own reaction to the incarnate Word that had come into their midst. There is no serious suggestion that such judgement here on earth is final and irrevocable at any time prior to death. The possibility and hope of repentance, forgiveness, and renewal are always there. According to tradition, it is only at death that the set of someone's will is discerned as irrevocably bent on either heaven or hell. Given the importance of death in traditional eschatology, it is not surprising to discover that the idea of the particular judgement at death came to prevail in popular piety over that of the Last Judgement. But, if we question this idea of the finality of death and allow for further opportunities of repentance and growth beyond the grave, it follows that the judgement brought upon oneself by one's reaction to the love of God encountered after death is no more permanent and final than the judgement experienced throughout an earthly life. Only in the end, in the final consummation, does the creature's relation to God acquire a permanent, unchangeable, character.

Let us recall the reasons why the religious mind has come to revolt against the traditional conception of the finality of death. It is once again chiefly a question of theodicy. The majority of human beings, in the span of their earthly lives, do not receive a fair chance to hear the Word of eternal life or to realize their spiritual potential in terms of growth in the knowledge and the love of God. This is as true of lives conditioned by particular social constraints as of those cut short or otherwise afflicted. Reflection on the love of God revealed in the story of Jesus Christ leads us to postulate further opportunities beyond the grave.

What then of the Last Judgement? The picture of a great Assize, like that of the General Resurrection, remains a powerful symbol. It symbolizes the fact that all created persons will in the end be brought to see themselves as God sees them, and that God's perfect love and justice will in the end prevail. But it may be suggested that there is greater religious plausibility in applying this picture continuously to the whole period, not only from death but also from the present moment, right up to the final consummation.

It must be admitted that greater ambiguity attaches to the picture of the Last Judgement than there does to that of the general resurrection. This is because the Christian tradition, particularly in medieval times, but also in the nineteenth century, tended to interpret divine judgement in harsh, juridical terms and in the language of rewards and punishments alone. This accords ill with the gospel of divine forgiveness. But, of course, the point of Christian insistence on judgement lies not in an abstract sense of justice or desert, nor in a legalistic demand for appropriate distribution of rewards and punishments, but in the sense that fellowship with others and with God can find fulfilment only in the context of complete self-knowledge and absolute truth. This means that the life of heaven is logically impossible for one caught in the snares of self-deception or inauthentic life. Men and women have to face up to what they are and to what they have done, if ever they are to be able to accept forgiveness and be reconciled with one another and with God. This is why the absolutely searching and penetrating love of God can seem such a terrible thing to those who have made their lives a lie or who are turned in on themselves and alienated from their own true good. Such persons must not only be forgiven; they must accept forgiveness and be radically transformed before the very possibility of entering the communion of saints in heaven can arise. It is the merit of the doctrine of purgatory to have recognized this need for change, purification, and growth even in those not set against the will of God. But clearly the doctrine must be extended to cover all humankind, if there are indeed to be further opportunities, beyond the boundaries of earthly life, for creatures to respond to the love of God revealed in Jesus Christ.

On such an understanding of judgement, we shall do well to play down the picture of God or Christ as Judge. A range of alternative models—the healer, the therapist, the patient lover, the counsellor—all seem more appropriate for bringing out the primary interest of divine judgemen—namely, the restoration of human creatures to integrity and the winning of their love in return, despite what they have done or made of themselves in the past. The measure of the seriousness of God's love is that the task of forgiveness and enabling hinted at in the above-mentioned models led Christ to his Cross, and the measure of the difficulty of achieving it is the agony of self-knowledge in those brought by the Cross to see themselves as they really are, to say nothing of the continuing perversity of many.

Hell and Universal Salvation

But can such perversity last for ever? The strength of the case for universalism—for the belief, that is, in the eventual salvation of all men and women—has been allowed to make itself felt at various points in this book. But also the objections to universalism have been noted. The Christian mind appears to be pulled in two directions on this difficult problem. On the one hand, contemplation of the love of God, revealed and enacted in the whole Christ event, leads us to suppose that God's love will in the end prevail, and that everyone will eventually be forgiven, transformed, and drawn into that love's embrace. On the other hand, contemplation of the wickedness and perversity of human beings leads us to suppose that, unless God acts by force—and thus fails to respect the free person that the creature has become—human freedom may always have the last word, and people may persist in their rebellion for ever. The strength of the universalist's case lies in the fact that Christian theology ought surely to be able to let contemplation of God's love have the last word rather than contemplation of human freedom. Yet realism about human freedom and perversity is not easy to suppress.

It does, from any point of view, seem very hard indeed to see how Christian theology can go on affirming the objective reality of a state or sphere of everlasting loss and self-inflicted alienation for some of God's personal creatures within the final, consummated state of the whole creative process. Such permanent evil makes no religious or moral sense. If creatures can rebel against the divine ground of their being to such an extent as to render themselves absolutely unredeemable, then there seems no point in God's keeping them in being for ever in such an unending state of deprivation. It is much more plausible to suppose that the language of damnation and everlasting loss is symbolic language, designed to bring out the awesome possibility that some, by their action and their attitudes, can forfeit their eternal destiny and render themselves incapable of being drawn into the life and love of God. But, if such a terrible possibility is in fact realized, it must mean that the lost bring about their own annihilation and disappear from being rather than find themselves held in a state of everlasting damnation. The sheer pointlessness of such a state being allowed to continue for ever shows clearly that conditional immortality is more religiously plausible than everlasting punishment.

One would like to be able to hope or believe that even the possibility of eternal loss in the sense of annihilation is never in fact realized. To suppose that there comes a time when the God of love, who went to the lengths of the Cross of Christ to win our love in return, has to write off a created person as absolutely unredeemable is a hard supposition for a Christian to make. Once we free ourselves from the old idea that opportunities to repent and respond to God's love are restricted to a single life span on earth, we may be the readier to suppose that God's patient, self-sacrificial love will in the end prevail over even the most recalcitrant sinner. In other words, the notion of conditional immortality makes greater sense in conjunction with the old idea of the finality of death. In the context of an extended 'purgatorial' phase of experience and growth beyond death, it makes greater sense at least to hope that universalism may be true.

All the same, the objections to universalism must be given due consideration. It will be recalled that six points against universalism were made by Stephen Travis (see p. 192 above). The first was that it does not take human freedom seriously enough. This is a weighty, but hardly a decisive, objection. For the whole point in postulating an extended purgatorial phase between death and the final consummation is to allow for God's love to work, by grace alone, upon free creatures and to win their free response. A much weightier objection is the second—namely, that universalism does not face up to the depth and radical nature of human wickedness. Indeed we must retain a sense of moral realism here. The depths of human evil as experienced on earth are so great that it may seem meaningless to suppose that a Hitler or an Eichmann can eventually be brought to face up to the enormity of his past deeds and allow himself to be forgiven, purified, and reconciled with himself, with his victims, and with his Maker. Nevertheless, this natural human reaction may itself betray a lack of spiritual imagination. Remarkable conversions and personality changes do occur even on earth; and in the new, imperishable, conditions of the life to come, freed from the constraints of the physical organism that perhaps have contributed to the warping of personality, and confronted unambiguously by the healing love of God in Christ, even the most perverse creature may prove incapable of holding out for ever against the mind and heart of the creator. The third objection was that universalism's implication of a long process of transformation after death is alien to the general thrust of Scripture. But there are different ways of assessing the general thrust of Scripture. It could be argued that it is precisely the revealed love of God in the whole Christ-event to which Scripture bears witness that has led many Christian minds in the direction of universalism, and that such a sense of the love of God is a better measure of the general thrust of Scripture than a series of alleged proof texts, mostly drawn from the details of parabolic imagery. The fourth objection, that universalism is not the only solution to the problem of adherents of other religions, will be considered in the next section, where it will be suggested that, although it may not be the only solution, it has some claim to the best.

Travis's last two objections revert to the question of the interpretation of Scripture. On the one hand, he expresses the view that universalism does not succeed in separating existential threats of eternal loss from belief about what will actually happen. On the other hand, he argues that allegedly universalist texts are more naturally interpreted as referring to God's saving purpose, which can be realized only through the response of faith. To these objections, one can reply only that perhaps the general thrust of Scripture, in the sense of what it reveals about the self-sacrificial love of God, *constrains* the Christian mind to read threats of loss existentially rather than objectively, and also to hope that the free response of faith will indeed be forthcoming in the end from all.[8]

'Pareschatology': The Intermediate State

The word 'pareschatology' has been introduced to refer to discussions of the 'next to last' things—namely, the intermediate state beyond death and prior to the final consummation. It takes up traditional concern with purgatory and expands that notion to include the whole next phase of the creative process. We have already mentioned a number of reasons why it has been widely felt that such an expanded conception of purgatory is needed. In the light of the revealed nature of God, considerations of theodicy and of moral and religious plausibility encourage us to envisage further opportunities beyond the grave for men and women, denied such opportunities on earth, to respond to God's love and realize their potential as creatures destined for eternity. We have seen this sense that there must be more to the creative process than a series of single decisive life spans coming to expression in other world religions as well.

Evangelical Christianity has tended to resist such pressures, even where the more restricted Roman Catholic doctrine of purgatory is concerned, largely because it seems to conflict with the priority of God's grace and with justification by faith alone. But the doctrine of purgatory is not in conflict with the doctrine of justification. It is

---

[8] It should be noted that Christian universalism would presumably imply either that fallen angels too will eventually be redeemed, or else that all references, in Scripture or tradition, to the devil, demons, etc. are better understood as pictorial ways of representing the temptations and the radical evil, both individual and collective, that undoubtedly afflict the human world.

rather an aspect of sanctification, a process recognized as far from instantaneous, even by the most committed believers in justification by faith. It is quite compatible with conviction that salvation is God's work alone to hold that it takes effect gradually through experience and growth in spirituality both this side of the grave and beyond it. Moral realism dissuades us from supposing that instantaneous transformation from imperfection to perfection takes place at death any more than it does at conversion during one's earthly life. Moreover, it is not unreasonable to extend the scope of these considerations from the further sanctification of Christians beyond the grave to the enlightenment of 'anonymous' Christians of other faiths or none, and to the eventual winning of those still alienated from God at death.

The bearing of pareschatology on the problem of Christian hope for adherents of other religions deserves to be spelled out a little. The main problem for a Christian theology of religion has been that of doing justice both to the spirituality and faith manifest in all the great religions and also to the uniqueness and finality of Christ as summed up in the Christian doctrines of Incarnation and Redemption. Roman Catholic theology—notably that of Karl Rahner (see pp. 163–7 above)—has had to resort to the idea of 'anonymous Christians'—those whose life and faith reflect the spirit of Christ unbeknown to themselves. But this idea hardly helps anyone perplexed by the fate of the many millions in whom the spirit of Christ is not reflected at all. To postulate further salvific encounters with God in Christ beyond the grave is to envisage time and space for non-Christians to come to recognize the human face of God uniquely in the risen Christ and to find in him the universal focus of divine–human relations, after which, in their different ways, the religions of the world have been feeling. It is curious that John Hick, who develops pareschatology further than any other Christian theologian,[9] does not use it to solve the problem of the finality of Christ vis-à-vis other religions, but prefers to demythologize the doctrine of the Incarnation and to treat Jesus Christ as but one channel of divine–human encounter among others.[10] This solution would be more plausible if Hick had felt bound to accept the finality of death.

[9] See John Hick, *Death and Eternal Life* (London: Collins, 1976), sect. IV.
[10] See John Hick, *God has Many Names: Britain's New Religious Pluralism* (London: Macmillan, 1980), ch. 5.

The next phase of the creative process will lack two features that account for the slow progress towards unification with God in Christ that characterizes human history on earth. One is the material basis of our present human life, which, necessary though it is in the formation and reproduction of persons, nevertheless at many points inhibits growth into the knowledge of God. The other is the fact that beyond death there is no reproduction and therefore no new persons beginning life's journey afresh. Only those fashioned on the earth can and will go on, through resurrection and purification, to enter the kingdom of heaven. The feature that made Schleiermacher pessimistic about the eventual consummation of the Church on earth (see p. 106 above) will not, in the next phase of creation, keep slowing down the momentum of sanctification as it does during this earthly phase.

The question may arise whether we are to think of the next stage beyond death—that is, according to this account, the first stage of the resurrection life—in unitary terms as a single environment into which the dead are raised and gradually purified, or whether we are to think of it, as John Hick suggests,[11] in disparate terms as a phased series of 'worlds' in which persons experience further stages of spiritual development. Christian theology must surely think in unitary terms here. If the aim of creation is unification and if the risen Christ has the central focusing role in respect of divine–human encounters that the Christian faith ascribes to him, then the process must be seen as a single process in which all are gradually drawn together into a single communion of inter-related persons. It seems best, then, to think in terms of a single, multi-faceted, spiritual environment for further growth.

Acceptance of the case made here for some such extended 'purgatorial' environment will naturally reinforce the case for prayer for the dead as an integral part of the Church's liturgy and private devotion alike. The fact that such prayer is recognized as appropriate not only by Roman Catholics but also, increasingly, by representatives of the evangelical tradition may be illustrated by the booklet *Prayer and the Departed* by Christopher Cocksworth.[12]

---

[11] Hick, *Death and Eternal Life*, ch. 20.
[12] Christopher Cocksworth, *Prayer and the Departed* (Cambridge: Grove Books, 1997).

The Parousia

Something must now be said about the doctrine of the Parousia that has played, from earliest times, so central and yet so misleading a role in Christian eschatology. We have to remember that the idea of a transcendent messianic figure on the clouds of heaven belongs to the symbolism of pre-Christian apocalyptic. That was taken over by the early Christians to express their confidence that their ultimate future lay with the risen Christ, whose appearance in glory would mark the end of the age. This apocalyptic symbolism seems to have been modified in two opposite directions. The more literalist minds came to envisage a return of Christ to earth in glory—an event that would be preceded by the messianic woes and the 'signs of the times', and would itself mark the end of the age. Occasionally we find, as in Revelation 20, the idea of a millennial rule on earth subsequent to the Parousia, an idea that, as we have seen, came to be maintained only in more or less sectarian forms of Christianity. Still more extreme was the much later idea of a secret second coming, analogous to the Incarnation itself. Nothing could be further removed from the 'coming of Christ in glory' as envisaged even in Christian apocalyptic.[13] The other way in which this symbolism was modified was in the direction of a purely spiritual interpretation. Christ would come, and indeed does come, again and again, in the Spirit, wherever groups of Christians meet in his name and wherever the Eucharist is celebrated. Neither modification successfully captures the heart of the Parousia doctrine. For the meaning of the Parousia is to be found in the conviction that in the end it will be the risen Christ who will manifestly reign in glory over a transformed creation and who will be for ever the divine–human focus of all people's knowledge and love of God through all eternity.

It has to be admitted, therefore, that the idea of a 'return' or even a 'coming-again' (as we find this in the creeds) requires some demythologizing before it can be accepted as a central Christian truth. Theologically, it has to be insisted that the Parousia will take place

---

[13] Morris West's espousal of the idea of a secret second coming in his *The Clowns of God* (1981) mars an otherwise religiously powerful novel.

beyond the horizon of death and resurrection; for it is in God's eternity that Christ will be manifest and will appear as the head of all creation. That is the ultimate truth to which all symbolism of Christ's 'coming on the clouds of heaven' refers.[14]

If the arguments for an extended further phase of growth, development, and transformation beyond death in the resurrection world itself are allowed to prevail, then it is inevitable that a further 'postponement' of the Parousia will have to be envisaged. Certainly we may suppose that the risen Christ will make himself known to those in 'purgatory' in less ambiguous ways than he necessarily does to Christians still in the midst of their earthly pilgrimage. Moreover, the risen Christ will be quite unambiguously 'present' to those already sanctified and taken into the life of heaven. But the final, universal, manifestation of the risen Christ at the head of all creation would have to be located at the end of the 'pareschaton' rather than at the end of the world. For it belongs to the consummation of all things.

Heaven and the Consummation of All Things

It has already been suggested that heaven must be understood not simply as the presence of God, but as the created sphere in which God is fully present and active and in which all men and women will find their ultimate and unending fulfilment in relation to God and to each other.

It is possible for human beings to enjoy a foretaste of heaven while still on earth. We have already referred to the ecstasy of love, to the contemplation of beauty and to mystical experience, worship, and communion, as examples of this. The fellowship of Christians, but also human fellowship more generally, can also be thought of as pointing beyond themselves to the life of heaven. But, although

---

[14] It is in some ways a pity that the third clause of the central acclamation of the modern versions of the Eucharist is expressed still in apocalyptic symbolism. Instead of 'Christ has died, Christ is risen, Christ will come again', it would have been better, as was proposed in the course of the revision, to phrase the acclamation, 'Christ has died, Christ is risen, in Christ shall all be made alive'—an equally biblical, but more theologically direct, form.

while still on earth we are caught up into the world of the spirit, the objective sphere and environment of heaven will not be attained until we have passed through death and been raised to the imperishable conditions of eternity. The sphere of heaven is the resurrection world beyond death, where mortal men and women put on immortality.

If our previous speculations about pareschatology have any force, it will be apparent that, while the objective sphere of heaven exists already with the resurrection of the dead into the resurrection world, and while those already sanctified are now with Christ in God in enjoyment of the life of heaven, their destiny is not yet completely fulfilled, since many millions of their fellow men and women are still on the way, whether here on earth (where many are yet to be born) or in the purgatorial stage beyond death. There the resurrection world presumably has yet to be experienced *as* heaven by those whose eyes are not yet fully opened. Only when *all* the redeemed from every age, not only after death but after the end of the world and after the pareschaton, are fully united with each other and with God is the unending life of heaven finally realized. For we are all members of the human family, and even the saints in heaven lack the fullness of communion for which they were made until all are drawn into the consummated state, where God is all in all.

The speculative mind may ask when heaven began. Was it with the death of the first human being—the first creature able to respond to the love of God being at once taken up into a new resurrection world? It seems, if so, that that would be a resurrection world without the risen Christ. An alternative Christian view might be that the resurrection world was established in being only with the resurrection of Christ, who, having (in the biblical imagery) harrowed hell, brought with him from the sleep of death those who had died before his time. A third possibility, that all men and women sleep in death until a general resurrection at the end of the world, is hardly compatible with Christian belief in the living presence and activity of the risen Christ, and has therefore been discounted here. It seems most plausible to suggest that, just as the history of the world finds its central pivot in relation to God with the Incarnation, which happened at a specific place and time, so the history of the resurrection world is focused on the risen Christ, notwithstanding his being raised at a particular time. This would mean that God's relation to those who died and were raised before Christ would be different from what it was after the resurrection of Christ, but that should cause no problems for those who see the whole creative process, including the resurrection world, as passing through various stages, and still incomplete until the final consummation.

Returning to the question of the nature of heaven in its consummated state, we need first to remind ourselves of the fact that it is simply not given to humankind, in this life, to know in any detail what God has prepared for his personal creatures. Anything we say about the final consummation of all things can only be a matter of broad generalization, supplemented by extrapolation from present experience of God and of Christ and of the glories of creation.

Among the broad generalizations that can be made about the consummated state of heaven is that, if God is really to be all in all, the whole creative process must be thought of as being brought to a stage where there is no evil, deprivation, grief, or pain, and no falling-away from perfection whatsoever. It was this consideration that made us reject categorically the idea of an everlasting, objective, hell. If it puzzles us to think of a state of perfection from which free creatures will never fall away, we may recall Origen's recognition that 'perfect love, unambiguously experienced, will restrain every creature from falling' (see p. 46 above).

A second generalization that can be made is that, just as we should abandon attempts to think of God in non-temporal terms, so should the end-state of the creative process be conceived dynamically and as temporally extended to infinity. It is sufficient to quote the English philosopher, A. E. Taylor, on this:

Even a heavenly life... would still be a forward-looking life... The blessed would always have new discoveries awaiting them, more to learn than they had already found out of the unspeakable riches of God. And in the same way, if we are to think morally of Heaven, we should, I suggest, think of it as a land where charity *grows*, where each citizen learns to glow more and more with an understanding love, not only of the common king, but of his fellow citizens.[15]

[15] A. E. Taylor, *The Faith of a Moralist*, i (London: Macmillan,1930), 420–1.

The final state of the blessed—the state for which men and women were made—is traditionally summed up in three powerful symbolic phrases, the first bringing out the individual, and the other two the social, aspects of the consummation: the beatific vision, the communion of saints, and the Kingdom of God.

The notion of the beatific vision or the vision of God is an extrapolation from contemplative, mystical, experience and from the sense of wonder that can, even in this life, capture the human soul and lift it to the heights of ecstasy. In this connection we may think also of the perfected creature being able to see and understand, perhaps with the aid of the divine memory, all the secrets and wonders of creation. In this sense, we shall, perhaps, see all things in God—not all at once, but in an endless journey of exploration. But the vision of God cannot be isolated from the communion of saints and the Kingdom of God; for, if God is love, the object of our contemplation is the pattern and inspiration of all interpersonal relationship and communion. We may well suppose that, in the perfected consummation, individual life and experience are not lost but transcended in corporate experience and interpersonal solidarity. It has already been suggested that this unification and communion of persons with one another and with God is anticipated, in present experience, in the love and fellowship that enhance our earthly life with ecstasy and deep joy. It is entirely proper, in this connection, to look forward to the time when relationships broken by death may be renewed and deepened in another mode of being. It is, of course, unrealistic to suppose that a finite creature will be equally related, in fellowship and acquaintance, to all other finite creatures in the Kingdom of God, but there will be no barriers between persons, and the communion will be complete only when it is known that all the sons and daughters of God are present and perfected and participating in the life of heaven.

The reason why the notions of the beatific vision and the communion of saints are inseparable in the Christian doctrine of heaven is that the God in whom we shall find our true being and destiny is the trinitarian relational God of love given, love received, and love shared still more. We are not to picture the consummated resurrection world as standing over against the God who made it in a single dipolar relation of creation to creator. We have already stressed the central role of the glorified Christ in focusing both God's presence and activity within his created world and also the perfected creation's response to God through all eternity. This same God will also be immanent within the perfected creation, as God is now, by the Holy Spirit. At all its stages, and most unambiguously so in its consummation, the creative process is and will be caught up into the inner relations of love given, received, and shared within the blessed Trinity. Just because we cannot think of God as an isolated individual but must think rather of an inherently relational divinity, we are prepared to speak likewise of the transcending of individuality in the society of the redeemed.

It is fitting, in conclusion, to return to the intimations of heaven already given in present experience. Apart from the ecstasy of love itself, it is perhaps the poets, artists, and musicians who afford us our most penetrating and evocative glimpses of heaven. One thinks of Abbot Suger gazing at the gems on the altar cross and at the glowing stained glass in the new Gothic ambulatory at St Denis in 1144 AD and feeling, in his own words, transported 'to some strange region of the universe between the slime of earth and the purity of heaven'. One thinks of Dante contemplating the Empyrean, with Beatrice enthroned among the petals of the snow-white rose. One still thinks of the antiquated but utterly beautiful idea of the music of the spheres, caught by Shakespeare in the magical words of Lorenzo in *The Merchant of Venice*:

> Sit, Jessica: look how the floor of heaven
> Is thick inlaid with patines of bright gold:
> There's not the smallest orb which thou beholdst
> But in his motion like an angel sings
> Still quiring to the young-eyed cherubin;
> Such harmony is in immortal souls.

I think, too, of winter evenings in Cambridge, when I have stood motionless at the back of King's College Chapel, listening to the soaring voices of the choir in some exquisite anthem and watching the glow of candlelight on the Rubens altarpiece in the distance and on the incomparable fan-vaulting above. The anthem might indeed be Edmund Spenser's poem set to peerless music by Sir William Harris:

> Faire is the Heaven, where happy souls have place
> In full enjoyment of felicitie;
> Whence they doe still behold the glorious face

Of the divine Eternal Majestie.
Yet farre more faire be those bright Cherubims,
Which all with golden wings are overdight,
And those eternal burning Seraphims
Which from their faces dart out fiery light.
Yet fairer than they both and much more bright
Be the Angels and Archangels, which attend
On God's own person without rest or end.
These then, in faire each other farre excelling
As to the Highest they approach more neare;
Yet is that Highest farre beyond all telling
Fairer than all the rest which there appeare,
Though all their beauties joyn'd together were.
How then can mortal tongue hope to express
The image of such endless perfectnesse?

Bibliography

General

Baukham, Richard, 'Eschatology', in Adrian Hastings, Alistair Mason, and Hugh Pyper (eds.), *The Oxford Companion to Christian Thought* (Oxford: Oxford University Press, 2000), 206–9.

Brandon, S. G. F., *Man and his Destiny in the Great Religions* (Manchester: Manchester University Press, 1962).

—— *The Judgment of the Dead: An Historical and Comparative Study of the Idea of a Post-Mortem Judgment in the Major Religions* (London: Weidenfeld & Nicolson, 1967).

Braaten, Carl E., and Jenson, Robert W. (eds.), *The Last Things: Biblical and Theological Perspectives on Eschatology* (Grand Rapids, MI: Eerdmans, 2002).

Charles, R. H., *A Critical History of the Doctrine of a Future Life in Judaism and in Christianity* (otherwise entitled *Eschatology, Hebrew, Jewish and Christian*) (2nd edn.; London: A & C Black, 1913).

Rahner, Karl, 'Eschatology', in *Sacramentum Mundi*, ii (London: Burns & Oates, 1968), 242–6.

Schwarz, Hans, *Eschatology* (Grand Rapids, MI: Eerdmans, 2000).

Toner, Patrick, 'Eschatology', in *The Catholic Encyclopedia* (New York: Robert Appleton Company, 1909).

Walls, Jerry L. (ed.), *The Oxford Handbook of Eschatology* (Oxford: Oxford University Press, 2007).

Biblical

Old Testament

Barr, James, *The Garden of Eden and the Hope of Immortality* (London: SCM Press, 1992).

Bright, John, *Covenant and Promise* (Westminster: John Knox Press, 1976).

Clements, Ronald E., *Old Testament Theology* (London: Marshall, Morgan & Scott, 1978), ch. 6.

Gowan, Donald E., *Eschatology in the Old Testament* (Philadelphia, PA: Fortress Press, 1986).

Johnston, Philip S., *Shades of Sheol: Death and Afterlife in the Old Testament* (Downers Grove, IL: Inter-Varsity Press, 2002).

Madigan, Kevin J., and Levenson, Jon D., *Resurrection: The Power of God for Christians and Jews* (New Haven: Yale University Press, 2008).

Mowinckel, S., *He that Cometh*, Eng. trans. (Oxford: Basil Blackwell, 1956).

Preuss, Horst Dietrich, *Old Testament Theology*, ii (Edinburgh: T. & T. Clark, 1996), ch. 14.

Rad, Gerhard von, *Old Testament Theology*, Eng. trans. (2 vols.; London: SCM Press, 1976).

—— *Wisdom in Israel*, Eng. trans. (London: SCM Press, 1972).

Vos, Geerhardus, and Denison, James T., *The Eschatology of the Old Testament* (Phillipsberg, NJ: Presbyterian & Reformed Publishing Co., 2001).

Vriezen, Theodoor Christiaan, *An Outline of Old Testament Theology*, Eng. trans. (2nd edn.; Oxford: Blackwell, 1970).

Westermann, Claus, *Prophetic Oracles of Salvation in the Old Testament*, Eng. trans. (Westminster: John Knox Press, 1991).

Zimmerli, Walther, *Man and his Hope in the Old Testament* (London: SCM Press, 1971).

Jewish Background

Gillman, Neil, *The Death of Death: Resurrection and Immortality in Jewish Thought* (Woodstock, VT: Jewish Lights, *c.* 1997).

Hengel, Martin, *Judaism and Hellenism*, Eng. trans. (2 vols.; London: SCM Press, 1974).

Lohse, Eduard, *The New Testament Environment*, Eng. trans. (London: Abingdon Press, 1976).

Nickelsburg, G. W. E., *Resurrection, Immortality and Eternal Life in Inter-testamental Judaism* (Cambridge, MA: Harvard University Press, 1973).

Rowland, Christopher C., *The Open Heaven: A Study of Apocalyptic in Judaism and Early Christianity* (London: SPCK, 1982).

Schürer, Emil, *The History of the Jewish People in the Age of Jesus Christ*, ii (rev. edn.; Edinburgh: T. & T. Clark Ltd. 1979).

New Testament

Beasley-Murray, George R., *Jesus and the Future*, London: Macmillan, 1954.

Cullmann, Oscar, *Immortality of the Soul or Resurrection of the Dead*, Eng. trans. (London: Macmillan, 1958).

Davies, W. D., and Daube, D., *The Background of the New Testament and its Eschatology* (Cambridge: Cambridge University Press, 1958).

Dodd, C. H., *The Parables of the Kingdom* (London: James Nisbet, 1935; Fontana edn., London and Glasgow: Collins, 1961).

—— *The Founder of Christianity* (London: Collins, 1971).

Dunn, James D. G., *Unity and Diversity in the New Testament. An Inquiry into the Character of Earliest Christianity* (London: SCM Press, 1977).

—— *The Theology of Paul the Apostle* (Edinburgh: T. & T. Clark, 1998).

Fee, Gordon D., *Paul, the Spirit, and the People of God* (Peabody, MA: Hendrickson, 1996).

Hooke, S. H., *The Resurrection of Christ* (London: Darton, Longman and Todd, 1967).

Jeremias, Joachim, *New Testament Theology,* Eng trans. (London: SCM Press, 1971).

Käsemann, Ernst, *New Testament Questions of Today,* Eng. trans. (London: SCM Press, 1969).

Kümmel, Werner G., *The Theology of the New Testament,* Eng. trans. (London: SCM Press, 1973).

Lincoln, Andrew T., *Paradise Now and Not Yet: Studies in the Role of the Heavenly Dimension in Paul's Thought with Special Reference to his Eschatology* (Cambridge: Cambridge University Press, 1981).

Meier, John P., *A Marginal Jew: Rethinking the Historical Jesus,* ii (New York: Doubleday, 1996).

Otto, Rudolf, *The Kingdom of God and the Son of Man,* Eng. trans. (London: Lutterworth Press, 1938).

Perrin, Norman, *The Kingdom of God in the Teaching of Jesus* (London: SCM Press, 1963).

Riches, John K., *Jesus and the Transformation of Judaism* (London: Darton, Longman & Todd, 1980).

Robinson, John A. T., *Jesus and his Coming* (London: SCM Press, 1957).

Strawson, William, *Jesus and the Future Life* (London: Epworth Press, 1959).

Wright, N. T., *The Resurrection of the Son of God* (London: SPCK, 2003).

Historical

Early Church

Bynum, Caroline Walker, *The Resurrection of the Body in Western Christianity 200–1336* (New York: Columbia University Press, 1995).

Daley, Brian Edward, *The Hope of the Early Church: A Handbook of Patristic Eschatology* (Cambridge: Cambridge University Press, 1991).

Kelly, J. N. D., *Early Christian Doctrines* (London: Adam & Charles Black, 1958).

230 | BIBLIOGRAPHY

Middle Ages

Boase, T. S. R., *Death in the Middle Ages: Mortality, Judgement and Remembrance* (London: Thames and Hudson, 1972).

Bynum, Caroline Walker, *The Resurrection of the Body in Western Christianity 200–1336* (New York: Columbia University Press, 1995).

Cohn, Norman, *The Pursuit of the Millennium* (Oxford: Oxford University Press, 1957).

Dante Alighieri, *The Divine Comedy 3: Paradiso*, trans. and ed. Robin Kirkpatrick (London: Penguin Books, 2007).

McGinn, Bernard, *Visions of the End: Apocalyptic Traditions in the Middle Ages* (New York: Columbia University Press, 1979).

Reformation

MacCulloch, Diarmaid, *Reformation: Europe's House Divided 1490–1700* (London: Allen Lane (Penguin Books), 2003).

Schlink, Edmund, *Theology of the Lutheran Confessions*, Eng. trans. (Philadelphia: Muhlenberg Press, 1961).

Toon, Peter (ed.), *Puritans, the Millennium and the Future of Israel* (Cambridge: Cambridge University Press, 1970).

Torrance, Thomas F., *Kingdom and Church. A Study in the Theology of the Reformation* (Edinburgh: Oliver & Boyd, 1956).

Post-Enlightenment

Martin, J. P., *The Last Judgement in Protestant Theology from Orthodoxy to Ritschl* (Edinburgh: Oliver & Boyd, 1963).

Rowell, Geoffrey, *Hell and the Victorians: A Study of the Nineteenth-Century Theological Controversies Concerning Eternal Punishment and the Future Life* (Oxford: Clarendon Press, 1974).

Walker, D. P., *The Decline of Hell: Seventeenth-Century Discussions of Eternal Torment* (London: Routledge & Kegan Paul, 1964).

Wheeler, Michael, *Death and the Future Life in Victorian Literature and Theology* (Cambridge: Cambridge University Press, 1990).

Systematic Theology

Alberione, James, *The Last Things* (Boston: St Paul's Editions, 1964).

Alves, Rubem, *A Theology of Human Hope* (Washington: Corpus Books, 1969).

Baillie, John, *And the Life Everlasting* (London: Oxford University Press, 1934).

Balthasar, Hans Urs von, *Theo-Drama: Theological Dramatic Theory*, v. *The Last Act*, Eng. trans. (San Francisco: Ignatius Press, 1998).

Barth, Karl, *The Resurrection of the Dead*, Eng. trans. (London: Hodder & Stoughton, 1933).

Baukham, Richard (ed.), *God Will Be All in All: The Eschatology of Jürgen Moltmann* (Edinburgh: T. & T. Clark, 1999).

—— and Hart, T. A., *Hope against Hope: Christian Eschatology in Contemporary Context* (London: Darton, Longman & Todd, 1999).

Berdyaev, Nicolas, *The Beginning and the End*, Eng. trans. (London: Geoffrey Bles, 1952).

—— *The Destiny of Man*, Eng. trans. (London: Geoffrey Bles, 1937).

Berkhof, Hendrikus, *Christian Faith: An Introduction to the Study of the Faith*, Eng. trans. (Grand Rapids, MI: Eerdmans, 1979).

Blanchard, John, *Whatever Happened to Hell?* (Darlington: Evangelical Press, 1993).

Bowker, John, *The Meanings of Death* (Cambridge: Cambridge University Press, 1991).

Braaten, C. E., *The Future of God: The Revolutionary Dynamics of Hope* (New York: Harper & Row, 1969).

Brunner, Emil, *Eternal Hope*, Eng. trans. (London: Lutterworth Press, 1954).

—— *The Christian Doctrine of the Church, Faith, and the Consummation: Dogmatics*, iii, Eng. trans. (London: Lutterworth Press, 1962).

Bultmann, Rudolf, *History and Eschatology*, Eng. trans. (Edinburgh: Edinburgh University Press, 1957).

Carnley, Peter, *The Structure of Resurrection Belief* (Oxford: Clarendon Press, 1987).

Cousins, Ewart H. (ed.), *Hope and the Future of Man* (Philadelphia: Fortress Press, 1972).

Edwards, David, *A Reason to Hope* (London: Collins, 1978).

Glasson, T. F., *His Appearing and his Kingdom: The Christian Hope in the Light of its History* (London: Epworth Press, 1953).

Gleason, Robert W., *The World to Come* (New York: Sheed & Ward, 1958).

Guardini, Romano, *The Last Things* (Notre Dame, IN: University of Notre Dame Press, 1965).

Healy, Nicholas, *The Eschatology of Hans Urs von Balthasar: Eschatology as Communion* (Oxford: Oxford University Press, 2005).

Herzog, Frederick (ed.), *The Future of Hope: Theology as Eschatology* (New York: Herder and Herder, 1970).

Hodgson, Leonard, *For Faith and Freedom*, ii (Oxford: Basil Blackwell, 1957).

Jüngel, Eberhard, *Death*, Eng. trans. (Edinburgh: Saint Andrew Press, 1975).

Körtner, Ulrich H. J., *The End of the World: A Theological Interpretation*, Eng. trans. (Westminster: John Knox Press, 1995).

Küng, Hans, *Eternal Life?*, Eng. trans. (London: Collins, 1984).

Ludlow, Morwenna, *Universal Salvation: Eschatology in the Thought of Gregory of Nyssa and Karl Rahner* (Oxford: Oxford University Press, 2000).

McDowell, John, *Hope in Barth's Eschatology: Interrogations and Transformations beyond Tragedy* (Aldershot: Ashgate, 2000).

Macquarrie, John, *Christian Hope* (London: Mowbrays, 1978).

Moltmann, Jürgen, *Theology of Hope: On the Ground and the Implications for a Christian Eschatology*, Eng. trans. (London: SCM Press, 1967; new edn. with preface by Richard Bauckham, 2002).

—— *The Future of Creation*, Eng. trans. (London: SCM Press, 1979).

—— *The Coming of God: Christian Eschatology*, Eng. trans. (London: SCM Press, 1996).

Niebuhr, Reinhold, *The Nature and Destiny of Man: A Christian Interpretation*, ii (London: Nisbet & Co., 1942).

Niebuhr, Richard R., *Resurrection and Historical Reason: A Study in Theological Method* (New York: Charles Scribner's, 1957).

Oakes, Edward T., and Moss, David, *The Cambridge Companion to Hans Urs von Balthasar* (Cambridge: Cambridge University Press, 2004).

Pannenberg, Wolfhart, *Systematic Theology*, iii, Eng. trans. (Edinburgh: T. & T. Clark, 1998).

Pieper, Josef, *The End of Time: A Meditation on the Philosophy of History* (New York: Pantheon, 1954).

Quick, O. C., *Doctrines of the Creed* (Welwyn: Nisbet, 1938).

Rahner, Karl, *Foundations of Christian Faith: An Introduction to the Idea of Christianity*, Eng. trans. (London: Darton, Longman & Todd, 1978).

Ratzinger, Joseph, *Eschatology: Death and Eternal Life*, Eng. trans. (Washington: Catholic University of America Press, 1988).

Robinson, John A. T., *In the End, God* (London: James Clarke, 1950).

Schleiermacher, Friedrich D. E., *The Christian Faith*, Eng. trans., ed. H. R. MacIntosh and J. S. Stewart (Edinburgh: T. & T. Clark, 1928).

Schmauss, Michael, *Dogma 6: Justification and the Last Things* (Kansas City and London: Sheed & Ward, 1977).

Simon, Ulrich, *The End is Not Yet: A Study of Christian Eschatology* (Welwyn: Nisbet, 1964).

—— *Heaven in Christian Tradition* (London: Rockliff, 1958).

Tillich, Paul, *Systematic Theology*, iii (London: SCM Press, 1964).

Torrance, Thomas F., *Space, Time and Resurrection* (Edinburgh: Handsel Press, 1976).

Travis, Stephen, *Christian Hope and the Future of Man* (Nottingham: Inter-Varsity Press, 1978).

—— *I Believe in the Second Coming of Jesus* (London: Hodder & Stoughton, 1982).

Wainwright, Geoffrey, *Eucharist and Eschatology* (London: Epworth Press, 1971).

White, Vernon, *Life beyond Death: Threads of Hope in Faith, Life and Therapy* (London: Darton, Longman and Todd, 2006).

Philosophical

Badham, Paul, *Christian Beliefs about Life after Death* (London: Macmillan, 1976).

Haught, John, *God after Darwin: A Theology of Evolution* (Oxford: Westview Press, 2000).

—— *Deeper than Darwin: The Prospects for Religion in the Age of Evolution* (Oxford: Westview Press, 2003).

Hick, John H., *Death and Eternal Life* (London: Collins, 1976).

Lash, Nicholas, *A Matter of Hope: A Theologian's Reflections on the Thought of Karl Marx* (London: Darton, Longman and Todd, 1981).

Lewis, H. D., *The Self and Immortality* (London: Macmillan, 1973).

—— *Persons and Life after Death* (London: Macmillan, 1978).

Lucas, John, *The Future: An Essay on God, Temporality and Truth* (Oxford: Basil Blackwell, 1989).

Penelhum, Terence, *Survival and Disembodied Existence* (London: Routledge & Kegan Paul, 1970).

Phillips, D. Z., *Death and Immortality* (London: Macmillan, 1970).

Pittenger, Norman, *After Death Life in God* (London: SCM Press, 1980).

Polkinghorne, John, *God of Hope and the End of the World* (London: SPCK, 2002).

Price, H. H., *Essays in the Philosophy of Religion* (Oxford: Clarendon Press, 1972).

Ramsey, Ian T., *Freedom and Immortality* (London: SCM Press, 1960).

Taylor, A. E., *The Faith of a Moralist*, i (London: Macmillan & Co., 1930).

Teilhard de Chardin, Pierre, *The Future of Man*, Eng. trans. (London: Collins, 1964; Fontana edn., 1969).

Ward, Keith, *The Big Questions in Science and Religion* (West Conshohocke, PA: Templeton Foundation Press, 2008).

Index of Biblical Passages

Index of Names and Topics